Critical Muslim 44

History

Critical Muslim is published quarterly by C. Hurst & Co. (Publishers) Ltd. on behalf of and in conjunction with Critical Muslim Ltd. and the Muslim Institute, London.

All editorial correspondence to Muslim Institute, Canopi, 7-14 Great Dover Street, London, SE1 4YR
E-mail: editorial@criticalmuslim.com

C. Hurst & Co (Publishers) Ltd., New Wing, Somerset House, Strand, London, WC2R 1LA

ISBN: 9781787388192 ISSN: 2048-8475

To subscribe or place an order by credit/debit card or cheque (pounds sterling only) please contact Kathleen May at the Hurst address above or e-mail kathleen@hurstpub.co.uk

Tel: 020 7255 2201

A one-year subscription, inclusive of postage (four issues), costs £50 (UK), £65 (Europe) and £75 (rest of the world), this includes full access to the *Critical Muslim* series and archive online. Digital only subscription is £3.30 per month.

A Cataloguing-in-Publication data record for this book is available from the British Library

Critical Muslim

Subscribe to Critical Muslim

Now in its eleventh year in print, *Critical Muslim* is also available online. Users can access the site for just £3.30 per month – or for those with a print subscription it is included as part of the package. In return, you'll get access to everything in the series (including our entire archive), and a clean, accessible reading experience for desktop computers and handheld devices – entirely free of advertising.

Full subscription

The print edition of *Critical Muslim* is published quarterly in January, April, July and October. As a subscriber to the print edition, you'll receive new issues directly to your door, as well as full access to our digital archive.

United Kingdom £50/year
Europe £65/year
Rest of the World £75/year

Digital Only

Immediate online access to *Critical Muslim*

Browse the full *Critical Muslim* archive

Cancel any time

£3.30 per month

www.criticalmuslim.io

CM44

AUTUMN 2022

CONTENTS

HISTORY

ARTS AND LETTERS

REVIEWS

ET CETERA

HISTORY

INTRODUCTION:
I, HISTORIAN

Iftikhar H. Malik

'Until African lions have their historians, tales of the hunt shall always glorify hunters.' I came across this quotation by the Nigerian novelist and poet, Chinua Achebe, during my postgraduate years at Michigan State University. It is a critique of Eurocentricity in historical scholarship, a traditionally narrow and thinly defined discipline – High History, which ignored the huddled masses as if they never had any voice or initiative. But during the 1970s, when I was working on my doctorate, this approach to history began to be questioned. Scholars, artists, and activists began to question the invisibility of vast swathes of humankind's history and other areas of humanities, and a new genre called Third World Studies gradually began to evolve. The Third World was also sometimes called the Afro-Asian world; it symbolised progressive and liberationist aspects in what was later called the 'South'. Worldwide protests on campuses and the rapid decolonisation of Africa in the preceding decades provided the vibrant context where iconic Western figures and dictums, in the words of Achebe, began to 'fall apart'. It is under these circumstances that I set out to become a historian. By the time I began to plan my retirement after a half-century of teaching and research, 'decolonisation' had occupied the centre stage in academic discourses, though its journey stays ambivalent, and often vulnerable to a hasty dismissal.

During my undergraduate days, history was largely written from a European perspective. History was important to Europe, as Ebrahim Moosa points out, 'in the sense that the story of the European discovery of the new "man" had to be told, shared with others, and on many occasions foisted on others with European expansion. This new dimension created a more self-conscious individual and society which was widely touted in education and contributed to European ascendancy.' Even anti-colonial/

postcolonial history, Abdelaziz El Amrani tells us, 'relied on the Eurocentric secular nature of historical interpretive devices, and accordingly they failed to address the fact that historical events are driven by a certain particular religious heritage'. Indeed, the vital role played by religious groups in dethroning colonialism, and the consciousness shaped by Muslim nationalists, was totally written out. The 'European ascendancy' itself was being challenged by the Soviet Union, leading to the 'Cold War'. The Soviet Union was in turn reeling from the atrocities of Joseph Stalin. As Anna Gunin notes, Stalin had committed historicide: 'deliberate erasure of a people's collective memory'. The Soviet authorities persecuted 'entire social classes', and sent dissenters to a 'concentration-camp network known as the Gulag' or had them executed by firing squads. Families were deliberately separated, and the names of the children changed to prevent the family members from finding each other.

Given this background, I defined myself at the beginning of my career, not so much as a chronicler or a historian-in-making. Instead, I saw myself as a transformer, full of ebullience and optimism. History heralded the idea of progress. But two or three terms further down the academic rigmarole, a kind of scepticism began to creep in. The world appeared multi-polar, pluralistic, full of histories, and not unilinear as I had naively assumed. Few years further down the same path, our discourses in graduate seminars began to show the inadequacy of human outreach while confronted with the powerful nations and their multinational corporations ruthlessly seeking a major chunk of flesh of the less powerful and marginalised.

Several decades later after teaching in Pakistan, Britain, Africa, and the Continent while spending long hours in seminars and libraries, a new realism began to set in. Now, instead of seeing the human career simplistically as black or white, scholars zeroed in on a multi-layered and expansive grey which, like the cosmic black hole, appeared both seductive and unfathomable. The greatest challenge to historical scholarship came with postmodernism in the 1990s and it seemed then as if my discipline would lose its primacy by turning into a hollow narrative. Yet, history resiliently survived this monstrous onslaught which, as Richard Evans put it in his 1997 volume *In Defence of History*, was itself grounded in modernity and did not prescribe any substantive alternatives. It was also during that very decade when 'the end of history' was a major talking point thanks to the neoliberal ideologue, Francis Fukuyama. But even his neoconservative colleagues were not too sure of what lay ahead though they, enthused by a unipolar world, zealously suggested redesigning the Middle East, often echoing their evangelist colleagues who were raising their heads from a host of woodworks. Their simplistic but no less dangerous views on human history were further augmented by Samuel Huntington whose grounding in the prophesying subject of political science led him to interpret otherwise complex human relationships within the limited premise of clashes and schisms. Huntington, as Robert Irwin notes, was influenced by the historian Bernard Lewis, who first used the phrase 'clash of civilizations'. 'Huntington's *The Clash of Civilizations and the Remaking of the World Order* was published in 1996,' writes Irwin, 'and attracted a great deal of controversy. It argued that future grand conflicts would not be between nation states, but between cultures that were shaped partly by religious history. It suggested that the Islamic bloc, which was experiencing a massive population growth and consequent pressure from the demands of young people, would eventually seek an alliance with China and its Sinified allies. Whereas Huntington believed that such clashes were inevitable, Lewis, in line with his belief that it was possible that Muslim territories should adopt Western values, denied the inevitability of any clash. *The Clash of Civilizations* possibly owed more to Arnold Toynbee's grandiose and long discredited twelve-volume, *A Study of History* (1934–1961).'

These ideologised groups needed a new outrageous enemy and political Islam, thanks to a few Muslim hotheads, provided them with an opportunity to zero in on 'the bloody frontiers of Islam', as if a state of 'siege' fermented a grievous 'crisis' among Muslims, whose indifference towards modernity and science had now been internalised to the extent of causing horrendous civilisational fissures. Naturally, 9/11 invigorated a neo-Orientalism in its wake with a vast array of opinion makers – from V. S. Naipaul to Bernard Henri-Levy, Paul Berman to Christopher Hitchens – vehemently advocating invasions of Muslim lands amidst a fanatical sense of higher mission and an indefatigable faith in American weaponry. My historical research took shape amidst all these varying, contested and no less impactful global developments.

Much of the work of a historian takes place in archives and libraries. Historians, as Joshua S. Lupo indicates, use 'letters, speeches, meeting notes, reports – to reconstruct an account of the past that is compelling to those reading about it in the present. Such an account would be persuasive or unpersuasive based on the quantity and quality of the evidence presented in defence of its thesis'. The history of faiths, however, follows a different model. The history of religions is the history of an idea: religion itself. This in itself is not unusual. But 'what makes the history of religions distinct is that its primary term and concept, religion, floats above material history without ever really coming down to earth'. Thus, Lupo argues, 'to write a history of religions then is not to write a human history, ultimately, but the history of something which in essence is outside of history. It is to describe a manifestation of the divine without ever presuming to have captured the divine itself.'

El Amrani, however, follows the conventional model. He excavates early twentieth century Salafi magazines, 'such as *al-Fath, al-Manar, Majalla al-Salafiyya,* and *al-Haq*' to develop a post-secular approach to history and explores the role of Islam in Moroccan anti-colonial resistance. The early Salafis 'advocated the return to the simple principles of Islam and hence had a profound impact upon the Moroccan nationalists particularly in Fez, Tangier, Rabat, Sale, and Tetouan'. Leela Prasad's journey begins with the discovery of '*Old Deccan Days* in a secluded aisle of a university library in the American Midwest': 'attracted by a thumb-sized image of a golden Ganesha donning a British crown on a maroon cover, I had serendipitously pulled out a yellowed book from the stacks. I leafed through the first pages. A hand-drawn picture captioned "Government House" startled me. At the bottom of the page, it said, "Anna Liberata de Souza died at Government House, Gunish Khind, near Poona, after a short illness, on 14th August, 1887".' Thus began the quest for 'Finding Anna'.

My own research, which initially focussed on modern South Asia, was conducted in the archives at Columbia University, New York Public Library, the Library of Congress, and the University of Pennsylvania. Research at the special collections at the University of California in Berkeley enabled me to undertake detailed reconstruction of South Asian political activism on the West Coast where some early Sikh, Hindu and Muslim immigrants had settled. They established the Ghadr Party with its multilingual magazine, *Ghadr Ki Awaaz,* and steered a first-ever political activism of diasporic nature. It was exactly at this time in 1914 that the tragic incident of 'Komagata Maru' happened off the Canadian Pacific Coast. More than four hundred Indian immigrants, who had spent their life savings to board this Japanese ship to reach British Columbia, were refused entry. After months of tense bureaucratic haggling at the behest of the British authorities they were sent back to India. Some of them died on the way; the survivors were arraigned on their arrival in Calcutta on sedition charges. Similarly, Punjabi Ghadrites were tried in San Francisco in 1916-7 with the British sleuths sitting through the trials. The seventy-seven volumes of the Trial kept in San Bruno Archives proved a shocking and tortuous research. I often walked by the Ghadr memorial in San Francisco's Center Street and thought of those Punjabi farmers and former soldiers who felt so strongly for a sovereign Hindustan, over and above communal and ethnic concerns. The Ghadr Party was, in fact, established in Portland, Oregon, in 1907, exactly half a century after the Rebellion of 1857 which was still remembered as Ghadr in common parlance. Some of these farmers had been soldiers brought to Britain to participate in Queen Victoria's jubilee celebrations and on the way back wanted to see other regions held by the British Empire. A group of them decided to move into the states of Washington and Oregon as lumberjacks with a few getting politicised.

I came across contemporary Indian intellectuals such as Maulvi Barkatullah, Har Dayal, Sohan Singh Bhakna and Lajpat Rai who undertook some political work across the United States. I followed their careers from the files on the Pacific Coast but mostly at Columbia's Butler and the New York Public Library. Lajpat Rai brought out a New York-based monthly, *Young India,* whereas Har Dayal briefly taught at Stanford before moving to Philadelphia. Bhakna remained one of the major brains behind the Ghadr and is one of the very few intellectuals that some well-informed South Asians may still remember. Within California, the descendants of the early Sikh agriculturalists view people like Bhakna and other Ghadrites as expatriate revolutionary Indians who suffered for South Asian causes. The Muslim activist, Maulvi Barkatullah Bhopali, was a roving soul who for a while taught in Japan and visited Russia, possibly Afghanistan as well, during the War years and then moved to California. Often, he would be leading prayers but there are several unanswered questions about his activities including his associations with the Khilafat movement or the Azad Hind Provisional Government in Kabul which for a time included some leading Deobandi ulama. Some of them were handed over to the British Government that exiled them to distant places like Malta and Andaman whereas others disappeared altogether though a few younger Muslim students from Lahore and other institutions ended up in Turkey fighting the Allies and the Greeks and saved fellow Turks from total marginalisation. Some served with the Turkish troops when Mustafa Kemal declared his republic and were deeply respected for their services to fellow Turks.

At the University of Pennsylvania, I went through the correspondence between Mrs Ruttie Jinnah (1900–1929) and Kanji Dwarkadas (b.1892), since they shared a close friendship during the time when Jinnah's wife was ill. Ruttie was the daughter of Jinnah's close friend and an affluent Bombay-based Parsi and it was during Jinnah's vacationing at their resort in north-eastern India that Ruttie and the senior lawyer fell in love, though there was some notable age difference between Bombay's most eligible bachelor-barrister and the talented daughter of a Bombay industrialist. In 1929, Jinnah nursed an ailing Ruttie in Paris; was deeply aggrieved over her early death; never remarried and devoted his life single-mindedly for the welfare of the Indian Muslims, eventually gaining Pakistan in Muslim majority areas. Yet he never felt alienated from Bombay, Aligarh or Delhi. Some of these lonely men and women were deciding on the fate of millions around them and that is where I felt Mahatma Gandhi, Pundit Nehru, Jinnah, Subhas Bose, B. R. Ambedkar and the rest marking their place in history. Still, I wouldn't reduce historical events to a few individuals, as for example, A. J. P. Taylor, who once claimed to simplify entire recent history to Napoleon, Bismarck and Lenin. (No wonder, Sir Syed's contemporary and a fellow reader in the British Museum's reading room, Thomas Carlyle too felt the same way and chose to confine historical developments to a few heroes and villains.) My teaching and research at Oxford would frequently usher me into the labyrinthine rows of the Bodleian system along with a few other collegiate libraries. On occasion, I found myself lodged at the Oriental Institute, History Faculty, and the long-gone Indian Institute with occasional visits to India Office Records and Library that was located in an old building south of the river

Thames. Simultaneously, given a growing accent on political Islam amidst furore over the Rushdie affair and ethnic cleansing in Bosnia, I began wrestling with two parallel strands—South Asian studies and Muslims in Europe with the result that I was able to publish three volumes in St Antony's-Palgrave Series and one with Pluto, followed by another on Balkan Muslims.

Another very significant development that took many by surprise was the growing number of voices representing female Muslim academics, journalists, commentators, artists and fiction writers. Certainly, Leila Ahmed, Fatima Mernissi and amina wadud were the pioneers of what now was being defined as Muslim feminism. However, by now feminism itself had gone through three waves. And as Sunera Thobani argues, the concepts and politics of each wave 'developed from the experience and perspectives of middle-class white women and universalised their fears, anxieties, and interests as the general condition of gendered humanity. The power relations of race, colonialism, and imperialism (historical and contemporary) were thus jettisoned from these feminist conceptual frameworks'. Thobani suggests that western feminist practices 'extended the Islamophobic ideology and imperialist ambitions of western nation-states through the war on terror', 'set up Muslim women, men, and sexual/gender minorities for particular kinds of violence and disciplinary projects', and projected Islam as 'irrational and fanatical'. However, the Islamophobic trajectory of western feminism has not stopped a whole new generation of highly articulate and confident women, born or brought up in the diaspora, coming to the fore – a historical phenomenon that is daily flourishing.

Academically, I am sceptical about single-factor focus on the state and its high politics in disciplinary areas such as political science and international relations exactly the way we historians, for a long time, reduced history to the narratives of rulers and conquerors, until we woke up to our deficiencies. Enlightened past historians such as Ibn Khaldun, or more recently Arnold Toynbee and Edward Thompson, have broadened our remit to civilisations and masses yet more rigour and grassroots work were required all along and only happened belatedly. Edward Said's *Orientalism* might have caused one of the greatest stirs in scholarly pursuits besides the evolution of critical theory but I was always worried that it might deter many western scholars from researching Muslims besides dangerously providing Muslims an easy alibi to transfer their own culpability to an ill-defined West – categorised monolithically as a frigid and persistently hostile trajectory. I began to brood over the idea of civil society, which could include both modern and traditional clusters limiting the vetoing forces of state and society. India, for a time, appeared to feature a vocal civil society but then the quick rise of the Bharatiya Janata Party (BJP) and other Hindutva forces only exposed the inner dissensions and even fragility within the civic ethos. My own travels to Muslim states such as Turkey, Iran, Morocco, Egypt, Pakistan, Bangladesh, Bosnia, Uzbekistan, and the UAE exposed me to varying degrees of imbalances with the state often holding unilateral powers even if otherwise slow and adrift on delivery. In several cases, clerical groups operate as power brokers, sometimes in cahoots with the official authorities, or through some other props mainly to claim their larger share of flesh. Both the state and clergy, quite routinely and more so behind the scenes, engineer mutual collaboration to contain civic forces and political opposition by decrying them as 'liberals' and 'maghrib zadda' – western stooges - denying them their authenticity, space, and agency. This hand-in-glove interdependence between the statist and religious authorities acutely persists at the expense of civil societies of Muslim nations. No wonder we end up with groups like Boko Haram, ISIS, Al-Qaeda and the Taliban whose weaponisation of religion is starkly at odds with the vocal and reformative groups including women. This strangulating plight certainly allows critics to see Muslim problems as a problematique of Islam, needing urgent reformation and renaissance. Looking at India may reveal that such a nutcracker situation is not just Muslim-specific per se but might be bedevilling a wide variety of states including those where democratic political systems have worked longer and economic growth has been steady.

Perhaps, it is equally fair to take our societies to task instead of only incriminating the state and clergy, since people at large, as observed in Muslim societies, are generally irreverent to public space and other civic obligations that a citizenry must perform before it starts demanding its rights. This task was taken up by the Indonesian *alim* and philosopher, Abdul Malik Karim Amrullah, known popularly as Hamka (1908-1981). As Khairudin Aljunied explains, Hamka accused Muslims of two varieties of ignorances: 'thin ignorance (*jahil tipis*)' or 'simple ignorance' and 'thick and layered ignorance (*jahil tebal dan berlapis*)'. The first, common amongst the masses, could be overcome: 'those with thin ignorance usually have pure souls and sincere hearts. They were open to reminders when they erred. They showed an acute willingness to listen, to learn, and to engage in reasoned discussions because they were aware of their weaknesses.' The second type was more dangerous. Those suffering from this compound ignorance suffer from hubris, are 'totally averse to any forms of knowledge, advice, and reminders', 'unwilling to change', and 'predisposed to becoming *fasik* (one who violates religious laws and norms)'.

However, there is no denying the fact that ordinary people, ignorant or otherwise, have been on the receiving end or were made totally invisible from history altogether, and it is only in recent times that their accounts and achievements have attained centre stage. Perhaps Las Casas, the Spanish writer, priest and former clerk to Columbus, is the pioneer who documented the miseries and disappearances of the natives following the arrival of Conquistadores by leaving us the earliest primary source on how millions were reduced into thousands thanks to the brutality of new arrivals and the epidemics they brought with them. In more recent times, Primo Levi cautioned us against an insidious normative when 'we tend to simplify history', through his account of the obscene corruption that happened in concentration camps. Levi's *The Grey Zone* is undoubtedly a good example of how history would read when told by the victims in their own words. The narratives by former slaves persistently remind us of what the life of a slave was in the Northern Hemisphere. *Narratives of Frederick Douglass,* Solomon Northup's *Twelve Years a Slave,* Booker T. Washington's *Up from Slavery* and Gretchen Gerzina's *Black England* based on accounts by the slaves are landmarks in such an impactful genre. Similar accounts by women, workers, peasants, and indigenous communities formed the mainstay of Howard Zinn's *A People's History of the United States,* itself a trendsetter in historiography. Historians like Zinn, Eric Hobsbawm and Victor Kiernan belonged to the leftist tradition and, like the Indian Subaltern historians, redirected historical pursuits towards largely ignored 'majorities' at a time when staying silent rather than critiquing colonialism was the norm. Similarly, African Studies and Peasant Studies owe much to the laudable efforts by historians such as Barrington Moore and Taj Hashmi, whereas a parallel tradition focuses on gender which has certainly brought forth an impressive cadre of Muslim women sociologists and historians.

Sometimes, historians have to venture out of archives and libraries into the world outside. My travels across Central Asia have enriched my thoughts, both personally and academically. The memories of well-meaning souls whose struggles vacillated between basic survival to macro challenges such as the preservation of sublime heritage have taught me much as a historian. Worried about the gnawing threats from unbridged urbanisation, a superficial scientism and often unplanned infrastructures, such voices are toiling to make officials and the laity concerned about the vulnerability of heritage sites at a time when authorities prioritise only selective monuments for tourist injections. Certainly, Tamerlane's tomb, Registan, and Shah-e-Zinda are places of exceptional architectural munificence. As is the city of Granada, where, as Medina Tenour Whiteman writes, Nasrid rulers developed 'the Alhambra palaces, adding poetry to the walls, patios with pools, gates and towers, and fostering a court full of scholars'. The 'gardens throughout the emirate meant that even the poor ate well, and provided silk, sugar, and dried fruit for export'. But so do the inner, twisting lanes of old Fez and old Lahore or longstanding madrasas in Bukhara, or Takht-i-Baburi in the Salt Range.

In my journey on the Silk Road, I was inspired by the now deserted site where Al-Biruni learnt Sanskrit and wrote his masterpiece—*Kitabul Hind*. I felt reconnected with Rumi at Shams Tabrizi's modest tomb though it reminded me of a similar tomb in Multan with the same name. I hobnobbed with younger Iranians in cafes that overlooked the splendid Maidan, Masjid-i-Shah, Shah Abbas's royal abode, Lutfullah Mosque and the nearby gardens where some of the rarest Safavid miniatures reveal parleys between the Persian rulers and their neighbouring kings. Teaching in Bath—the world heritage city—had not prepared me for another world heritage city, Khiva, where traditional norms, architectural edifices and septuagenarian craftsmen took me back by centuries to the glorious past of Khwarazm. While delivering a lecture at the University of Urgench, the City of Zoroaster, my brain was trying to assimilate the features of my younger audience who belonged to Turkmen, Tajik, Kirghiz, Uzbek, Persian, Afghan and Tatar ethnicities and were equally proud of their Transoxiana heritage that once was the heartland of the Aryans and Jews before other multiple layers of history engulfed them, including a recent configuration under Stalin. But now as I could see across this civilisational artery, it was not Stalin or Lenin whose statues held their ground in the main square. They were replaced by those of Jalalud Din Khwarazm Shah, the only Central Asian monarch who had defeated the Mongols. But he had to run towards India while being chased by Chengiz Khan. It was at Attock that Jalalud Din made his stead cross the Indus, leaving a vengeful but laudatory Chengiz Khan behind. He was one of thirty-five kings and princes who had sought asylum with Sultan Altutmish in Delhi – himself a former slave and now a king who kept the Mongols away from Hindustan.

I guess as a historian, these encounters with archives and heritage sites replenished my instinct and nourished my keen desire to introduce younger Muslims everywhere to the bounties and frailties of their prodigious inheritance. We need, as Moosa says, 'not only a sensibility of history from below, but also an experiential philosophy of life of which history is only a reflection'. By dealing with 'the past immutable fact', Muslims have created 'a sense of history that leaves the future open, for humans will not achieve except that for which they strive (this is according to a piece of Qur'anic wisdom). It is that striving that is critical to making history.'

I like to think that my life as a historian has been an attempt at 'striving'. In the process, I found myself ensconced in a vast realm of heritage that appeared both limitless and precarious and I rushed to record its manifestations in a personal way before it was too late for all of us.

HISTORICAL BEINGS

Ebrahim Moosa

History's importance to human society cannot be underestimated. Although we can track social organisation to a time when people painted on the walls of Altamira between 10,000 and 20,000 years ago, professional historians think of history as a story of the past 5,000 years. Whether this latter claim still holds true might be subject to debate. But our debt to some loose account of history is obvious. Sacred scriptures invoke historical narratives and myths recalling memories going back millennia to serve us with moral and other edificatory lessons. Great empires demonstrated their success, as history teaches us, through mind-boggling architectural feats, inventions and the production of art, music, and literary classics that leave us breathless just wondering about the talents, abilities, and endurance of the human race and our ability to transform our environment.

We used to think that changing our environment by making it habitable was a good thing, but now we realise that our tampering is sending our planet on an irreversible course and increasingly unable to self-repair as it once did. Now we must help the planet to repair if we are interested in its and our survival. Yet, countless women and men left their traces on earth, for the benefit of posterity, or so we would like to think. Non-literate and literate societies left us legacies. We deem what we can glean from the traces left by our pre-hominid and hominid ancestors as pre-history. But when legions of palaeontologists, archaeologists, anthropologists, as well as palaeobotanists, and experts in palaeomedicine serve us with accounts of our ancestors literally from the ruins of history in *National Geographic* magazines and documentaries, we recognise ourselves or parts of ourselves in those accounts. We wonder why it is called 'prehistory' because we can relate to their history, or we see glimpses of ourselves in those accounts.

Why History?

Why is history so important in the modern world? From 1350 onwards, first Europe and then gradually different parts of the world experienced the impact of modernity with all its benefits and distractions. As this modern momentum created different kinds of global changes from the age of discovery and imperialism, a change in the conception of religion occurred, especially religion and politics in Europe thanks to the Reformation. Gradually a different kind of self and personhood became the standard, at least in Europe, because that history and story is well-researched and much clearer to us. What happened in China, Africa, or in Muslim domains in Central Asia, Africa, South and East Asia, and the Middle East and North Africa to the idea of the individual is less clear, but we do have some glimpses and insights. But we do not have a thick archive to speak confidently of the trends and timelines.

History became important in Europe in the sense that the story of the European discovery of the new 'man' had to be told, shared with others, and on many occasions foisted on others with European expansion. This new dimension created a more self-conscious individual and society which was widely touted in education and contributed to European ascendancy. With it came the more self-conscious deployment of reason and the need to marginalise irrationality. History is also the preoccupation of the winners and conquerors of history.

In an earlier period of human history, Muslims and other communities wrote their own histories in a different key with different goals in mind. The famous Ibn Jarir al-Tabari (839–923) from Tabaristan in present-day Iraq wrote the monumental *History of Prophets and Kings*. Why? He saw the glory of Islam rise with his very eyes and wished to document this success of prophecy and kingship and everything that flowed in between these two elements for posterity to admire and learn. Muslim civilisation's good fortune was that it quickly entered the era of writing and documentation from its oral beginnings. This is thanks to the rapid spread of its intellectual centres to societies that already enjoyed writing and literacy like Egypt, Iraq, and Persia.

Around about the same time that Europe experienced its Renaissance which is marked as the beginning of the modern age, a north African scholar and statesman, 'Abd al-Rahman Ibn Khaldun (1332–1406), decided to document *The Book of Warnings or Moral Lessons and the Collection of Beginnings and Historical Information*, of which the lengthy *Introduction (Muqaddima)* has brought him great repute. Scholars have spent much ink about the genre and type of accounts of history that Ibn Khaldun gave. But the *Muqaddima* and his longer multi-volume treatise, *The Book of Warnings*, remain largely unstudied as a historical treatise or a source for the intellectual history of Islam in the fourteenth century and what preceded it.

Someone like Ibn Khaldun can give us a sense of his self-consciousness and that of other elites in his time. An indication of this awareness is the way he writes about himself and others. And through this he wishes to share with us how at least he viewed the world. The perspective of how someone records and documents the world at a particular time is history. The motives for writing, whether deeply subjective or objective, prompted by ideological biases or for purposes of salvation, do not detract from the craft of writing.

In his eloquent testimony about the purpose of history, Ibn Khaldun writes: 'the inner meaning of history involves speculation and verifying the truth, subtle causal analyses of the origins of things and deep knowledge about the conditions under which events occurred and their reasons. For this reason, history is rooted in philosophy and thus deserves to be counted among the disciplines of philosophy *(hikma)*'. Ibn Khaldun here fully recognises the utility of history as a process of verifying the truth. But he is also empirical in his approach. Always seeking after origins of claims was the habit in Islamic accounts of recording opinions and knowledge, just as he deemed the context of events to be as important as the events. This is a form of history that is driven by a desire for empirical certainty about the past. But Ibn Khaldun insists in a very deliberate way that the understanding of history is related to philosophy. Although Ibn Khaldun is critical of philosophy, especially the use of philosophy in theology to help resolve questions of faith and to grasp the meaning of the divine, it is undeniable that he counted philosophy to be indispensable to history. We might even be bold enough to say that he was advancing a philosophy of history, even though this approach has fallen in disfavour in late modernity. Philosophers of history like Giambattista Vico (1668–1744) and Friedrich Hegel (1770–1831) are bold enough to state in which direction history is going, most often the trajectory on which their own cultures or civilisation are on. Ibn Khaldun too thought that things are going in the direction of his culture and civilisation, even though he could be brutally critical of aspects of his civilisation. His major theory was to show under what conditions do dynasties and political institutions endure and what causes them to become buried under the remnants of time.

Given the rigorous scrutiny to which we subject our sources today to accurately retrieve past accounts, the certainty that people like Herodotus (484–425 BC) and Ibn Khaldun enjoyed about the facts of history is possibly something of the past since we are infinitely more sceptical of things. We are uncertain as to whether we can identify origins. Yet, one might ask, what work does origins do for us and what purposes do they serve? Does knowing the origins of something confer greater authority and conviction on it? Are origins a mirage? Is it important to know exactly how the past looked like?

If the discussion of origins signals the beginning of a conversation in the history of ideas, they fulfil a valuable function. Often the search for origins is directed at finding a master story to prove all others wrong, as Orientalism and certain forms of orthodoxy, Islamic as well as others, do. Those obsessed with origins often do so with the goal of proving other ideas that emerged from those origins to be wrong and their version of the origins to be right. Once they found the right idea in the past, they are forced to take a sledgehammer to every other different version of origins. They first deem the 'wrong' origins as inauthentic, false, or a history that should not have been. Little do they realise that there could have been very different accounts of the origins from the get-go. Hurriedly, every version of history, other than theirs, is wrong. Political Islam in its various guises quickly dismisses the Islamic empires – Umayyad, Abbasid, Ottoman, Mamluk, Safavid – as illegitimate monarchies that distorted Islam. Idealism thus becomes a fantasy projected on to the past to eradicate reality. To many Islamists only the pious caliphate was authentic and legitimate. Yet they are the first to claim the achievements of these inauthentic political orders as the products of a 'great Islamic civilisation'.

Take the pyramids as an example. We see, witness, and admire these ancient relics. But do we know why the ancient Egyptians resorted to such architectural feats for the purpose of burial places for their nobility? Surely, it had to do with their religion and their journey into the afterlife. Ancient histories told us that much. But were the Egyptians trying to tell us something more about themselves, their societies, and times? These are the questions modern historians probe. Why? Because most moderns, not all, are often more preoccupied with the question of whether the past provides a road map for the future. Or we might later realise that we have insufficiently explored ancient history, that they too had their eyes on a future. The difference is that theirs was an eschatological or cosmic future, ours is a material future given our dilemmas. These great architectural feats serve a purpose for people of thinking. And yet, those driven by unthinking ideologies are the enemies of history. Some of them even voiced their desire to literally take the sledgehammer to the pyramids, in the same way the Taliban took dynamite to the ancient statue of the Buddha in Bamiyan, Afghanistan to demonstrate their craven 'authentic' Islamic credentials.

History in Muslim Traditions

What kind of trajectory of time and change does the Muslim tradition offer? To answer this question, I turn first to the period immediately prior to the advent of Islam which Muslim historiography strangely labelled as the Jahili (ignorant) period. This era was renowned for its poetry, and the Arabs took pride in it as their choicest repository of wisdom. It was a repository in the sense, writes the renowned Palestinian-Lebanese historian, Tarif Khalidi, that the Jahili period 'supplied much of the wisdom and the practical moral standards handed down from one generation to the next'. Proverbial wisdom involved a heroic conception of life where the 'unforeseen change from prosperity to wretchedness, the fleeting character of life and friendships, the exhilaration of love and wine, pride in lordly generosity or even-handed revenge' featured in human life.

With the advent of Islam, some of this wisdom was translated into Islamic categories. The Islamic vision of history added a sense of space and time to these categories. Space and time were ideally inhabited by those who acknowledge God's lordship and majestic power in creating the world for the use of humans. Human responsibility involved being a witness of

God on earth and undertaking the task of stewardship. Time, however, is less of a chronology of events in the Qur'an and more of a continuum in which past, present, and future are collapsed. Adam, Abraham, Moses, and Muhammad are 'eternally present' says Khalidi, and all of history is present to God in terms of divine omniscience. Humans are invited to see the parables in the scriptures and in the handiwork of God in nature. Truth is captured in knowledge and humans are obliged to seek knowledge from the cradle to the grave. By the fifteenth century the writing of history in Islamicate societies had already 'transitioned' to new conceptions of history. The earliest phase was a transition from prophetic wisdom to history; from 'providential to communal history', from 'the overwhelming and monumental Qur'anic time', writes Khalidi, 'to the sequential listing, dating and recording of individual actions performed by members of a community that was beginning to realise the merit of its progress in time... and the coming into being of a time scheme which strove to historicise early Islam and to use it to establish hierarchies of moral or social seniority or prestige'. History, in my view, can best be described as a series of responses to contingencies and explanations of the conditions in the world. Sometimes these contingencies are expressed in distinctive genres and topics. In some eras history is preoccupied with the exploits of prophets and kings. At other times it meticulously documents the lives of influential scholars and pious figures as servants of knowledge and learning. History also often seeks to understand what moral lesson every epoch provides, and thus what improvements might be made as we move into the future.

Two brief illustrations exemplify how history is conceived in modern Muslim experiences and it shows the difference I wish to further probe in terms of the subtle difference as to whether history is about 'improvement' or whether it is about 'change' and 'progress.'

In his book, *The Road to Mecca*, Muhammad Asad, the Austrian journalist-scholar, documents his six years of travel on camel-back in Arabia after his conversion to Islam in 1926. He talks movingly about his very close friend Zayd with whom he travelled the length and breadth of Arabia. Asad also had a close relationship with King Ibn Saud, the founder of modern Saudi Arabia. Zayd however was a member of the Al Rashid, a rival kinship group to the Al Saud clan. In the early years of the twentieth century, the Al Rashid lost out in influence and power to the Al Saud in terms of control of the Arabian Peninsula. At one point in the book, Asad and Zayd reach a city called Hail. Zayd had not been to the city for many years because the city was now in the control of the Al Saud whom he mildly resented.

'How does it feel Zayd, to be back in the town of thy youth after all these years?' Asad asked his companion. Zayd had always refused to enter Hail whenever he had the occasion to visit. 'I am not sure my uncle,' he replies slowly. 'Eleven years since I was here last. Thou knowest my heart would not allow me to come here earlier.' After citing a passage from the Qur'an about God being the one who gives and takes sovereignty and political power, Zayd adds:

> No doubt God gave sovereignty to the House of Ibn Rashid, but they did not know how to use it rightly...they were reckless in their pride. So God took away their rule and handed it back to Ibn Saud. I think I should not grieve any longer—for is it not written in the Book, 'Sometimes you love a thing, and it may be worst for you—and sometimes you hate a thing, and it may be the best for you?'

Muhammad Asad's comment that follows this exchange is illuminating and wise:

> There is a sweet resignation in Zayd's voice, a resignation implying no more than the acceptance of something that has already happened and cannot therefore be undone. It is this acquiescence of the Muslim spirit to the immutability of the past—the recognition that whatever has happened had to happen in this particular way and could have happened in no other—that is so often mistaken by Westerners for a 'fatalism' inherent in an Islamic outlook. But a Muslim's acquiescence to fate relates to the past and not to the future: it is not a refusal to act, to hope and to improve, but a refusal to consider past reality as anything but an act of God.

In this example there is not only a sensibility of history from below, but also an experiential philosophy of life of which history is only a reflection. Important to note in this insight is how Muslims have dealt with the past as an immutable fact. It is a sense of history that leaves the future open, for humans will not achieve except that for which they strive (this is according to a piece of Qur'anic wisdom). It is that striving that is critical to making history.

If the past is rendered immutable it does not preclude one to act, to hope, or to improve, as Asad put it. Nor is it a future that is preordained, as in the secularised version of progress. In a century or more we have learned that a certain kind and form of progress can come at a cost to humans and nature, reminding us all the more of the importance of Asad's insight. If the end of history is already set, then there are no contingencies – whether they are ecological or planetary disaster – which might require us to reset or reconfigure our aims.

Fazlur Rahman, the Pakistani émigré scholar to the US and professor of Islamic thought at the University of Chicago, who influenced my thinking early in my career, expressed his conception of history in his *Islamic Methodology in History* in the following words: 'Islam is the first actual movement known to history, that has taken society seriously and history meaningfully because it perceived that the betterment of this world was not a hopeless task nor just *pis aller* [a last resort or expedient] but a task in which God and man are involved together.'

While history and society feature as crucial elements in Rahman's writings in the 1960s, his task at the time was to depict Islam as a civilisational force as well as a faith tradition for individuals. The idea of history also served a greater purpose in Rahman's thought. His various studies led him to conclude that an understanding of history allowed one to reshape the normative questions in Islamic thought. For Rahman the story of the advent of Islam, its scripture, norms, and symbols, the actual forces of Arabian culture, were all constructively manipulated for a moral cause. 'If history is the proper field for Divine activity,' Rahman wrote, 'historical forces must, by definition, be employed for the moral end as judiciously as possible.' In other words, early Islam revealed the proper end of human action, but it was up to humans to progress towards that end.

Rahman is, of course, a Muslim modernist. He proudly wore that label and thus had a different viewpoint from Asad. Muslim philosophy of history, or more accurately philosophies of history, are somewhat compelled to discern the providential element in history. In the hands of earlier historians, the past was dissected as an act of God. For modernist Muslim thinkers like Rahman, however, there was a greater emphasis on historicism, similar to that of his earlier counterparts in Egypt, notably Taha Husayn (1889–1973). On this view, it was necessary to inscribe moral ends as the end (telos) of history. We see here that the secular idea of progress did indeed impact certain trends in Muslim thinking for it too has a telos. And on the face of it, few can quibble with these moral ends. Historicism and historiography come in different forms. One form of historiography is what the historian David S. Landes calls 'optative'. Derived from grammar, the optative mood expresses a wish and a desire. So, optative historiography is that history 'might', 'must', or 'should' have gone in xyz directions, but alas, did not do so. This is not history but a wish list, but this sentiment often subtly shadows historical writings like a doppelganger, a twin. This is very common in some Muslim historiographical writings, if only Muslim politics was the humbled and rustic version of the model of Medina and not that of Damascus or Baghdad the optative historians would say. They ponder little whether such less complex political systems could have even survived the rigours of history.

The question for those who see ends in history is this: Whose morals are the aim? How do you know which morals are the right ones to hold? And should the moral ends necessarily be hitched to the wagon of history? Even when Rahman does rethink his position, he cannot extricate himself from the modern moral circle. '"Progress" we all want,' Rahman the philosopher-theologian clarifies, 'not despite Islam, nor besides Islam but because of Islam for we all believe that Islam, as it was launched as a movement on earth in seventh-century Arabia, represented pure progress-moral and material,' Here I have hopefully more than telegraphed two modern Muslim modes of thinking with competing accounts of the meaning and end of history. For Asad, the present and the future we create can be an improvement upon the past, but there is no end or guarantee of this. For Rahman, however, history has a moral purpose that ties the past and future together in the march of progress.

Thinking Historically

'Thinking,' wrote Ibn Khaldun, is what makes the human being distinct from other animals, in addition to the feature of sociality, the ability to cohabit with other people; the enabling capacity humans do possess to co-operate with each other in social settings and organisations. An insightful analysis, from the fourteenth century North African thinker, who binds thinking to the complex idea of human nature. Yet, Ibn

Khaldun sometimes offers sobering surprises, especially for moderns who are preoccupied with scripturalist, fundamentalist, and instrumentalising approaches to religion.

How we conjure and describe our thinking process is intimately related to how we imagine distant figures and events: in other words, the instrument determines the nature of the picture to use a simple analogy. In today's parlance we call these to be epistemic virtues which provide for a deeper reflection as to how the experience of the self – through a range of scientific practices – are moulded by image-making, image-reading, and procedures of knowledge-making, at large. We acknowledge and acquiesce to the teachings of ancient prophets and comply to their prescribed teachings based on how each person imagines the search of afterworldly salvation, Ibn Khaldun says. The very act of thinking (*fikr*), Ibn Khaldun suggests, is often historical thinking. The way we relate to others in the past, present, and future. In other words, historical thinking is part of self-knowing and meaning-making. The British philosopher of history, Robert G. Collingwood, later said something similar. In *Speculum Mentis*: he writes 'We try to understand ourselves and our world only in order that we may learn how to live. The end of our self-knowledge is not the contemplation by enlightened intellects of their own mysterious nature, but the freer and more effectual self-revelation of that nature in a vigorous practical life.'

More noteworthy is how frequently Ibn Khaldun referred to the well-being of social units. He shows an awareness of what makes organised habitations such as cities and towns function better compared to minimally organised habitations such as rural areas and desert locations. His notion of society is one that is supportive of human flourishing. One must take seriously Ibn Khaldun's frequent references to the social sphere or what we would today call, 'society', as something constructed by people. The importance of society for human flourishing remains one of the abiding lessons he provided. And here is one of the implications of his teachings about society: if people were crucial in making the rules of how social organisation and society functioned, then they were also capable of changing and modifying the rules of society. To my mind this is a vital insight gained from the work of Ibn Khaldun.

All matters regarding the regulation and smooth function of society requires attention and reflection. 'A human being thinks constantly about all these things,' he points out, 'not remiss to think for even the duration of the blinking of the eye.' Ibn Khaldun is charmed by the speed of thinking and artfully writes: 'in fact, the speed of thinking is faster than a glance'. Connecting thinking to our senses means humans share in common with animals aspects such as sensory perception, movement, nutrition, and the need for shelter among other animal needs. Even though Ibn Khaldun is exhilarated by the capacity and speed of humans to think, it is the combined animal and cognitive dimensions of humans which he singled out as the unique features of humans. His observations about the speed of human thinking are merely incidental to his major point about the mind's ability to process many things at once. It is not sufficient to accumulate facts and information as an historian he implies, but it is more important to make sense of all the knowledge that history had laid at our door.

All this serves as a prelude for Ibn Khaldun to say something more profound about human nature and thinking in the understanding of history. 'For the very purpose of thinking,' Ibn Khaldun points out, 'namely, the inherent nature of the human being – in fact even animal being [of humans] – is predisposed to be summoned by nature. One such predisposition is that thinking is always eager to acquire elusive perceptions. It follows then that one either consults those who previously acquired knowledge, or those who possessed more knowledge [than oneself] or, those who were endowed with greater perception [than oneself]. Or perhaps one acquires this knowledge from past prophets who transmitted such learning to someone who met such a prophet.' Human biology, natural capacities, and human nature are all garments to embody culture and religion. Here he claims that it is in our nature to pursue the trait of human curiosity, the search for afterworldly salvation, the acquisition of knowledge, and to gain a sense of one's place in history. All this Ibn Khaldun affirms, constitute the tapestry of our human nature.

In short, Ibn Khaldun implies, we are historical beings. How? Well, thinking historically does not only link people across time. Rather, in his view thinking produces some of the resources from which we extrapolate historical data and knowledge: knowledge of multiple sciences and disciplines fuse with varieties of technologies and crafts to form the sources of history. History teaches us, Ibn Khaldun would say, why every moment in time has both commonalities and differences with the preceding era and so too will future epochs have continuities and discontinuities with their succeeding periods.

Such a realisation reinforces the nature of temporality as well as the complexity of time, bringing into view something else: experience. Experience becomes the basis of our claim as to how and why our age differs from the past and by implication the future. History notifies us how people identified the good and the bad in societies of the past. Sometimes these histories are contained in the accounts of prophecies, scriptures, philosophies, cultic practices, and rituals.

Experiences, the late German historian Reinhart Koselleck tells us, determine the language of the historian. Nevertheless, in one way or another, the authority of history is invoked to validate an idea or practice from the past or to reject it. As Tarif Khalidi shows, even in trying to resolve weighty matters of religion, such as say whether governance should be based on some revelatory or theocratic model (sharia model) or whether doctrines of common-sense governance based on interests and political wisdom, we now know many past thinkers turned 'to history' for resolution. If ethics is about proper reasoning and philosophy is about how to differentiate right from wrong, then there are several reasons why history becomes important: it is a repository of human experience in its multiple imaginations and contexts. Within human experience we observe the moral formations of different societies and recognise how each culture and society encountered the ethical challenges of their time.

Few people understood the relationship of the past with the present as well as Ibn Khaldun did. On the surface of things, many people think history is merely information about past events, details of dynasties, and the successes and failures of people, he says. Besides entertainment value, he clarifies, history helps us 'understand human affairs' and 'how changing conditions affected' human affairs. Most interesting is how Ibn Khaldun injects an element of contingency in history and what modern philosophers call 'historicism'. Simply put, historicism means, says Georg Iggers 'that the human mind knows no other reality than history: history is made by human beings and therefore reflects human intentions, that is, meaning... Historicism is thus closely bound up with a certain form of epistemological idealism.' History is not only the purveyor of ideas and thoughts, Georg Iggers explains, but it amounts to giving us an account of the experiences of people and the meaning those experiences held for them. History itself is invested in a philosophical enterprise to realise certain ideals in human society such as to be good servants of a deity or fulfil some moral purpose in life.

Is History About Progress?

Often people think the arrow of history leads to progress. This idea has come under some pressure in the postcolonial era. People living in the global South realised that the process of modernisation that came to them under the banner of civilisation, modernity, and progress, was indeed clothed in something else: Western imperialism and colonialism. In its wake, the practice of modernity altered their history. How? Modern Western education kept the idea of history tethered to a Western universal history fed by its triumphalism and progress. All other histories and experiences were either downgraded as local events with no greater consequence for humanity. For indigenous and colonised people, tradition and religion both served as shields against a raging modernity. In the process tradition and religion were both altered by the new world and cosmos that unfolded in the surrounding environment and in the hearts and minds of the colonised. Despite their best intentions to retrieve it, the pasts of the colonised will remain very distant foreign places. Only dedicated labour can excavate the histories of the people of Asia, the Middle East, Africa, and that of the indigenous peoples of the Americas and Australasia. The pathbreaking book, *The Dawn of Everything* by David Graeber and David Wengrow, who are deemed as anarchists, shows that some of those experiences of neglected pasts can be retrieved in order to counter the accounts of human existence that for the past 400 years were almost exclusively constructed by Western experiences. There is reason for optimism but no need for premature celebration. What the human past will look like in the next 500 years might, in itself, hold many possibilities for the future viability of our embattled planet.

The colonial experience and resistance to colonisation has taught us that progress is not inevitable, but that it is possible. In other words, human agency is still central to the enterprise of history. History, sure, is often the history of the victors. But in the modern world, the oppressed and dispossessed can also narrate history based on their experiences if they were given the opportunity to do so. We might more accurately begin to talk about multiple histories. Feminists have already reminded us that men have entirely told the story of humanity primarily from their experiences as (his)story. Now it is time to devote time, energy, and resources to excavate (her)story from the debris and archives of history to give a fuller and accurate account to women's contribution to the making of the world. The same applies to indigenous peoples and other marginalised groups around the world who are making similar demands for greater visibility and recognition for their contribution to the long duration of human history. The possibility that 'progress' in history could mean a fuller and richer account of the human drama on earth would indeed be a salutary notion of progress.

The conundrum is not only the possibility of progress or humans trying to advance instead of surrendering to the inevitability of a certain vector of progress. Two things complicate the venture of history for not only the 'rest' but for all: first, the nature of historical development and second, the impending planetary crisis. The grave and pessimistic predictions about the future of our planetary system could make our preoccupation with history to be analogous to fiddling while Rome is burning. I do not hold this view. There might even be a chance that we learn from history if it serves as a mirror in how we might deal with the planetary crisis.

Collingwood in his *The Idea of History* explains that societies that undertake historical changes rarely conceive of their alterations as 'progressive' including the very people who undertake the change. Often, they make these changes in obedience to a blind impulse to destroy what they do not comprehend by deeming certain practices and objects to be 'bad' and to be replaced by something 'better'. We are no longer sure whether hunter-gatherers and agriculturalists were at war with each other since Graeber and Wengrow tell us a different story. But for a long time, we held the view that these two groups were in mortal pursuit of each other. In more recent history we know that monotheistic faiths were eager to displace polytheistic faiths, because the latter were bad or the incarnation of evil and as idols of falsehood they challenged the authority of the unseen God. And urbanised and mechanised communities and societies deemed themselves above those who lacked such amenities.

Collingwood finds a helpful way to nuance what we could mean by progress: 'but progress is not the replacement of the bad by the good, but of the good by the better. In order to conceive a change as a progress, then, the person who has made it must think of what he has abolished as good, and good in certain definite ways.' He might be more than hinting at the fact that change is a form of improvement and advancement in pursuit of the good. This is a benign form of progress that might be synonymous to improvement. Collingwood also imagines that the person undertaking the change or advocating the change must have some idea of the old life she is leaving behind, namely, one has to possess historical knowledge while actually living in the present that she is creating. In other words, he says, all actors in human history are scripting some kind of history in their very acts of creating, making, and changing.

What he conceives of as 'historical knowledge' is a sensibility that, he believes, the contemporary actor who brings about change ought to possess. In his words: 'for historical knowledge is simply re-enactment of past experiences in the mind of the present thinker'. Collingwood has been criticised for this highly idealistic proposal of re-enacting past experiences in the mind. But I think his suggestion does have merit. He wants one to think and reflect and ask whether the change to be made and the progress to be initiated are really warranted. 'Only thus,' he writes, 'can the two ways of life be held together in the same mind for a comparison of their merits, so that a person choosing one and rejecting the other can know what he gained and what he has lost, and decide that he has chosen the better. In short, the revolutionary can only regard his revolution as progress in so far as he is also an historian, genuinely re-enacting in his own historical thought the life he nevertheless rejects.'

Now it is precisely the idea of progress in history that has come under scrutiny by critics in the wake of the dark night of colonisation and the practices of Western modernity. Some thinkers prefer improvement, instead of progress, like Muhammad Asad, while others like Fazlur Rahman are fairly content with progress provided it is progress by certain Islamic normative standards. But the question of progress in history has deeper implications. The critique of modernity resulting in anti-structuralist and postmodern French theory together with greater attention to the environment in development studies and the rise of postnormal studies by

Ziauddin Sardar as well as the rise of decolonial studies are all invitations to reconsider the epistemological inheritance of especially the Enlightenment. It is not an invitation to throw the baby out with the bathwater, I hope, and to start the knowledge process afresh. However, the knowledge enterprise is largely dependent on our self-understanding bequeathed to us by history.

Is History Creative Destruction?

Globalisation over the past 300 years has made each culture and civilisation interdependent on others where some are more independent and powerful than others. The technology-driven economic productivity from 1750 onwards gave European nations the edge on a global scale. But it also brought about dramatic changes in better medicine, nutrition, reducing maternal and infant mortality, and preventing famines that are human-induced. The interdependence of vast swaths of humanity over several centuries is now an indispensable reality that make delinking from the world system a pipedream and potentially a hazardous and irresponsible adventure with self-destructive consequences for societies who might contemplate such a position. Capitalist economies scaled up what Joel Mokyr called 'macro-inventions' in the form of radical new ideas that suddenly altered production possibilities all by themselves, as Kenneth Pomeranz explains in the *Great Divergence*. The Industrial Revolution (1750-1830) literally altered the face of parts of the world. And the second industrial revolution from 1870 with America at its centre spreads the products of the industrial revolution far and wide, as Brad De Long writes in *Slouching Towards Utopia*. Of course, all of this did come at a price of rapid and now accelerating planetary disaster, we recognise in hindsight.

Progress is indispensable to capitalistic economic growth. In 1942, the Austrian emigre economist to the United States Joseph Schumpeter (1883–1950) wrote in *Capitalism, Socialism and Democracy*: 'in dealing with capitalism we are dealing with an evolutionary process...Capitalism, then, is by nature a form or method of economic change and not only never is but never can be stationary. And this evolutionary character of the capitalist process is not merely due to the fact that economic life goes on in a social and natural environment... The fundamental impulse that sets and keeps the capitalist engine in motion comes from the new consumers' goods, and new methods of production or transportation, the new markets, the new forms of industrial organisation that capitalist enterprises creates.' Not only did he find the evolutionary metaphor helpful, but Schumpeter latched on to a biological term, what he called 'industrial mutation'. This drive and constant alteration 'incessantly revolutionises the economic structure from within, incessantly destroying the old one, incessantly creating the new one.' Changes to the productive processes and apparatuses of a typical farm ranging from crop rotations, ploughing the land, fattening the herds, to the mechanised processes of farming today that connects to railroads constitute in Schumpeter's words 'a history of revolutions'. Each is the product of some technological and scientific revolution. The same applies to the production of iron and steel, the power production plants from the waterwheel to the coal and nuclear-driven power plants and the radical innovations in transportation from the mail-coach to the aeroplane. This was before the advent of cyber technology which brought about another revolution in communication and information sharing.

Schumpeter calls this process and its various transformations 'Creative Destruction' as the essential fact about capitalism. 'It is what capitalism consists in,' he wrote, 'and what every capitalist concern has got to live in.' In other words, the nature of capital is constantly changing. He views capitalism as natural as evolution and mutation in nature. One could ask whether this mutation and evolution is sustainable given the finite resources of the earth and growing populations, but any attempt to answer this now will detract from my point.

Accelerated capitalist market-driven growth, affluence and subsistence have made progress and creative destruction necessary components of our psychological, spiritual, and self-understanding as human beings. It is not progress that drives capitalist growth but rather capitalism that makes modern progress possible.

Over the longue durée, human societies underwent change, improvement, transformation, and even made progress. But the rhythm of 'progress', I hazard to say, prior to global capitalist expansion, was of a very different order, intensity, and calibration. We have to be open to the idea that progress and change could have had many permutations, and that our most recent experience with change had many radical and revolutionary changes, as Schumpeter and scores of economic historians of the modern period tell us. Hence, our concept of history has undergone radical change with history increasingly being introspective. But it would be a mistake to assume that history and progress in the distant past were identical, just as it would be erroneous for moderns to assume that only they experience self-conscious change.

Concluding Dilemmas

Our understanding of history is at a crossroads, precisely because we are in an ambivalent and agonistic relationship in our experience of knowing, knowledge, and the history of knowing. Two examples will shed light on my point. The great English historian, Edward Hallett Carr, in his well-known book *What is History?* grapples with the questions at hand. One such question is how does one form historical judgments? Historical judgments are not made on the basis of an abstract standard of the desirable, and then deployed to condemn the past, Carr wrote. Objectivity in history is a moving standard depending on the accumulation of evidence that would either make judgment easier or more challenging. He was sure of one thing: 'objectivity in history does not and cannot rest on some fixed and immovable standard of judgment existing here and now, but only on a standard which is laid up in the future and is evolved as the course of history advances.' For Carr, history in its essence is change and movement and he adds 'if you do not cavil at the old-fashioned word—progress.' Our construction of history has much to do with a notion that we assume we are going somewhere. Therefore, says Carr, 'our view of history reflects our view of society.' Would it then be any surprise why societies caught in the rhythms of capitalist growth and creative destruction would cultivate any other view than the fact that history is about progress and that it is a moving process?

History for Carr begins when humans begin to think of time not in terms of natural processes but a series of events in which humans are, and this for him is crucial, to be 'consciously involved and which they can consciously influence'. History is the long struggle of humans to break with nature with the awakening of consciousness. 'Man now seeks to understand, and to act on,' Carr writes, 'not only his environment but himself...' It thus is no wonder that the modern period is the most historically minded period of history because humans are self-conscious to an unprecedented degree and therefore are deeply conscious of history as a result. Moderns have remade themselves as different from their ancestors and therefore cultivated for themselves a different image with consciousness at the centre. Historian and ideologue Karl Marx too placed the emphasis on conscious revolutionary action in order to change history.

Yet there is a sober counterpoint to Carr, albeit from thinkers who do take some risks in their accounts at first blush. Our requirement of a certain recognised self-understanding of humans as conscious actors in history might be the product of modern hubris. It might also be an unfortunate turn in order to treat modern humans as exceptional and radically different from our very earliest forbears when we might not be so different. Graeber and Wengrow challenge this settled understanding of history and human beginnings. If history begins by asking about the question of human inequality, then we are forced to explain it with a myth about the fall of humanity, and talk of the sinful and violent nature of humans. A tradition like Islam and several other faith and cultural traditions do not subscribe to the idea of a flaw in humanity at creation as Christianity does. Hence, history will be viewed differently given a different story of human beginnings. Any move away from such boorish human behaviour would thus be 'progress' and 'civilisation'. The myth itself becomes a self-fulfilling prophecy, in other words, generating its own questions and answers. History then is more oracle-like at its imaginary level, I conclude from the insights offered by Graeber and Wengrow. The tragic story of history also boosts the 'progress of Western civilisation' narrative, Graeber and Wengrow argue. Except that the Western claim has one great gap in it: if Western civilisation was that good and desirable, why did it not spread by its own accord? Why did Europeans spend the last 500 years 'aiming guns at people's heads in order to force them to adopt it', they ask.

Recall that Carr made consciousness a condition for the conception of history. In other words, history is coterminous with the dawn of human consciousness. All the major Western thinkers were reluctant to think that people in early epochs had consciousness. In their critical disagreement

Graeber and Wengrow write: 'Yet most modern thinkers have clearly found it bizarre to attribute self-conscious social projects or historical designs to people of earlier epochs. Generally, such "non-modern" folk were considered too simple-minded (not having achieved "social complexity"); or to be living in a kind of mystical dreamworld; or at best, were thought to be simply adapting themselves to their environment at an appropriate level of technology.'

Graeber and Wengrow argue that most 'big histories' place a strong focus on technology and associate the human past primary with materials like stone, bronze, and iron and their tools and weapons. Their research shows that it is easy to overstate the importance of tools and technologies among our early forbears. Technologies always create revolutionary bursts as Schumpeter's rhetoric remind us. Capitalist innovation is all about the revolution in invention, or the invention of invention. Yet the authors of *The Dawn of Everything* show that Neolithic societies led by women accumulated significant discoveries over the centuries. The making of bread with microorganisms we call yeast were the gifts of prehistoric inventions. Similarly in agriculture and a range of inventions they gave us much, including ceramics. The very term prehistoric signifies that hitherto historians and anthropologists assumed those humans to have achieved such ends without a sense of self-awareness, which now is hard to believe.

History, we are forced to acknowledge, is entangled in the self-perception of the hegemonic Western civilisation and its knowledge disciplines. It will require a herculean task to critically examine some of its ideological commitments and challenge it in order to gain a more unbiased and fuller picture of our species.

THE HISTORY OF HISTORY OF RELIGIONS

Joshua S. Lupo

Early twentieth-century scholars of religion, especially in Europe and the United States, cultivated a curious understanding of 'history' when they named their field 'the history of religions'. Innocent observers outside the West might have understood this field to be history in the 'normal' sense of a chronology of past events. Outsiders on occasion might have also thought of this as the comparative study of religion, which it partially was, but this qualification made the approach no less bewildering.

In reality, debates in 'the history of religions' were concerned with the 'essence' of religion, which now appears to be a relic of a bygone past. And yet, while the names and theoretical approaches associated with this branch of religious studies are no longer in vogue, the underlying concerns they raised about the study of religion remain unresolved. For example, the category of 'religion' continues to be important for demarcating departments of religion as separate from departments of theology and from other humanistic and social scientific-focused departments, such as sociology and anthropology. While scholars no longer seek the essence of religion, they nonetheless operate on the assumption that the study of something called 'religion' is a field of research worth preserving in the modern university.

Philosophical concerns sustain the debate about religion. Since the heyday of history of religions, other academic fashions like deconstruction, genealogy, affect theory, and new materialism, have emerged. But the conundrums surrounding issues of contingency, theology, and the role of philosophy, which the history of religions field sought to address, remain unsettled.

A brief history of 'the history of religions' field deserves attention in order to help scholars evaluate the genealogical study of religion, which explores relations of power, knowledge, and the body in the practice of religion. It also questions narratives centred on the primacy of origins and of unchanging truths. Yet there are scholars who take this approach express a longing for a pre-modern religious world, a world that the history of religions also sought to bring to life. We should be wary of the tendency that calls for a return to a more authentic way of being that is in the past. It is necessary to challenge this call for a 'return' because it results in an uncritical appropriation of the past that often aligns itself with politically reactionary causes. Such causes often harm rather than buttress the flourishing of those who live on the margins.

The History of Religions

The field of 'history of religions' arose in the nineteenth century in Europe and spread to the US during the latter part of the century. During the twentieth century 'the history of religions' became the common way that scholars who were not theologians identified their field of study. Unlike those who sought to defend or attack religion from an apologetic perspective as theologians often did, scholars working from within this field sought to understand different religious traditions on their own terms. This did not mean that they did so without theological motivations. Many hoped, for example, that the result of their study would be the demonstration of the ultimate supremacy of Christian beliefs. But it did mean that those theological motivations were considered after having gathered the necessary facts about another tradition. In other words, these studies were less polemical in their descriptive accounts of non-Christian religious traditions, even if their interpretations of these descriptions were sometimes skewed.

Importantly, these thinkers also approached religion from a comparative perspective. Early influential scholars like C. P. Tiele (1830–1902) of the Netherlands, Max Müller (1823–1900) of Germany, and P. D. Chantepie de la Saussaye (1848–1920) also of the Netherlands, were interested in the similarities and differences between religious traditions, while never doubting that something called 'religion' ultimately unified them. There were multiple normative approaches that made up the early history of religions. One thread followed the evolutionary approaches to religion influenced by the work of the philosopher Herbert Spencer which explored the evolution of man from more 'primitive', that is, non-western forms of religion, to 'advanced', 'Western' forms. Another thread includes phenomenological approaches, which sought to identify the inner essence of religious expression and then categorise and give labels to those varied expressions such as 'worship', 'ritual', 'cosmology'. These categorisations also included hierarchical arrangements of traditions like Buddhism, Hinduism, Islam, and so forth. Often Christianity was listed at the top of the civilisational ladder.

In addition to emphasising the importance of comparison, the early approaches to the history of religions also stressed the importance of providing data to substantiate one's claims. History was one such data set. In addition, scholars included ethnographic, psychological, and textual studies as part of their data set. But the history conducted by those who claimed to be 'historians of religion' does not match up to what we now imagine to be the kind of history produced in departments of history in the modern university. The approach of this brand of historians of religion was not to take up an event, say the Reformation, and attempt to make sense of the decisions of political and religious leaders that plunged Europe into strife. In such proper histories, one typically draws on empirical evidence – letters, speeches, meeting notes, reports – to reconstruct an account of the past that is compelling to those reading about it in the present. Such an account would be persuasive or unpersuasive based on the quantity and quality of the evidence presented in defence of its thesis. One might write the history of an individual, a nation, or a group for a specified period of time under the rubric of history proper.

The history of religions differs from this model. It seeks not to unearth the practical motives of people of the past based on the evidence available in the present. Rather, the history of religions is the history of an idea: religion itself. Histories of ideas, of course, are not uncommon. Histories of concepts like 'kingship', 'politics', and 'debt' have also been written. Yet, what makes the history of religions distinct is that its primary term and concept, religion, floats above material history without ever really coming down to earth. Politics, for example, is conditioned on the communal lives of human beings. While we cannot trace to a particular moment in time as to when politics began, we can at least show that it is a human enterprise that arises in response to the unique problems that face our species. For religion, on the historian of religion's account, it would seem that a similar option is not available. This is, in part, because of an explicit presupposition that guided much of early study of religion, namely that religion transcends our knowledge and experience of the world. To write a history of religions then is not to write a human history, ultimately, but the history of something which in essence is outside of history. It is to describe a manifestation of the divine without ever presuming to have captured the divine itself.

To return to the reformation, a historian of religion would see the theologian Martin Luther's break with the Catholic Church not as a decision that was driven by a variety of causes, such as political, institutional, or social change. Rather, for historians of religion, Luther's break would be seen as the manifestation of the reformation spirit, which is common to all religions. Gerardus van der Leeuw, for example, created a typology called 'The Reformer' under which he included not only Luther, but also Zarathustra, the Buddha, Jesus, and Muhammad. Van der Leeuw describes how a religious typology manifests itself in different times and places throughout the world in this section of his magnum opus, *Religion in Essence and Manifestation*. This type of history would not be recognisable as such today, but it is what passes as an early iteration of a 'history of religion'.

The Essence of Religion

For van der Leeuw, as for others, it was an assumption that 'the holy' or 'divine' was present in religions around the world that led them to believe that even those who would not have translated their traditions and practices with the term 'religion,' nonetheless had one. Hinduism, for example, we know now was an abstraction of various indigenous traditions which was instituted by British colonists in conjunction with Indian leaders to manage colonised subjects. Yet, under the assumption that non-Muslim Indians had to have something like 'religion,' Hinduism was introduced as a religion just like Christianity, Judaism, and Islam. Religion, to use van der Leeuw's language, is something whose essence is manifested in various settings across the world, even by those who lack a name for it. To write a history of religion, then, is to write a history of those manifestations. Here we find ourselves far astray from the modern discipline of history. Where this form of history, if done rightly, deals in the contingencies of politics, economics, social life, and so forth, the history of religions deals in truths unburdened by chance and change.

Unearthing this truth was the purview of the field of phenomenology of religion, a subset of and sometimes synonym for the history of religions. Scholars associated with this field, such as Rudolf Otto (1869–1937), Gerardus van der Leeuw (1890–1950), and Mircea Eliade (1907–1986), sought out common features of the world's religions that would allow for a comparative study of religion. These scholars were careful to record examples of the various manifestations of the universal form of religion in their studies. But these examples were merely the physical manifestation through which the deeper reality of religion becomes manifest. The example of the reformer in van der Leeuw's account exemplifies this approach. To penetrate the reality of religion, these scholars adopted a set of procedures. They for instance 'bracketed' (*epoché*) their assumptions about the world in order to accurately 'see' the essence (*eidos*) of religion. Several names for this unchanging essence were coined. These names included the 'holy', the 'sacred' or 'ultimate reality'. These thinkers borrowed several key terms from the distinct school of philosophy associated with the philosopher Edmund Husserl (1859–1938). Husserl is famed as a philosophical phenomenologist. He too was interested in the essence of objects that humans observed in the world. But his concerns were often more mundane. He was interested, for example, in discerning the essence of the idea 'table' or 'red' more often than more complex terms like religion. While many drew from Husserl's thought, it is important to note that their engagement did not extend far below the surface of his thought.

A deep anxiety also animated the work of those who identified with the phenomenology of religion. This anxiety stemmed from the concern that people in the modern world were losing contact with the essence of religion. When they lost that essence, they became alienated from the sacred in the world. For the Romanian scholar Mircea Eliade, the most famous historian and phenomenologist of religion, this anxiety was expressed clearly in how he approached the idea of history itself. For

Eliade, history, or more precisely, historicism—the idea that history was ultimately a set of contingencies and happenstances—was a terror from which modern man needed to awaken. A modern human being could only become truly free, Eliade contended, if he drew on the sources of 'archaic,' or 'religious' man. This human being, for Eliade, was always 'man' who experiences past, present, and future in cycles of birth, life, death, and rebirth, rather than in a barrage of contingencies from which no ultimate meaning could be discerned. He famously wrote in *The Myth of the Eternal Return*: 'by virtue of this view, tens of millions of men were able, for century after century, to endure great historical pressures without despairing, without committing suicide or falling into that spiritual aridity that always brings with it a relativistic or nihilistic view of history'. The 'history' that Eliade ascribes to 'archaic man' is of course not history as we know it today. This 'history' is rather a 'mythic history': as a myth its importance is the meaning it gives to human lives. This mythic history is present in the lives of men and women as they go about living and making meaning in their everyday lives. In a passage from *The Sacred and Profane* Eliade describes this model of history in an example that he borrows from Chinese religion:

> From the seventeenth century, arranging gardens in pottery bowls became the fashion among Chinese scholars. The bowls were filled with water, out of which rose a few stones bearing dwarf trees, flowers, and often miniature models of houses, pagodas, bridges, and human figures; they were called 'Miniature Mountains' in Annamese and 'Artificial Mountains' in Sino-Annamese. These names themselves suggest a cosmic signification.... But these miniature gardens, which became objects of aesthetes, had a long history, or even a prehistory, which reveals a profound religious feeling for the world. Their ancestors were bowls whose perfumed water represented the sea and covered the mountain. The cosmic structure of these objects is obvious. The mystical element was also present, for the mountain in the midst of the sea symbolized the Isles of the Blessed, a sort of Paradise in which the Taoist Immortals lived. So that we have here a world apart, a world in miniature which the scholar set up in his house in order to partake in its concentrated mystical forces, in order, through meditation, to re-establish harmony with the world.

What we can see here is that Eliade is beginning in the present, articulating the meaning of the ritual in relation to a myth that we would only describe as history if we were to stretch the term beyond recognition. Ironically, the most famous historian of religion himself was opposed to history, at least as we understand that term in the modern academy.

There is a similar anti-historicism in Rudolf Otto's emphasis on the irrational as the grounds of religious experience. For Otto, 'every religion which, so far from being a mere faith in traditional authority, springs from personal assurance and inward convincement (i.e., from an inward first-hand cognition of its truth)—as Christianity does in unique degree—must presuppose principles in the mind enabling it to be independently recognised as true. But these principles must be *a priori* ones, not to be derived from 'experience' or 'history'. In Otto's account, the essence of religion is in the inward experience of it, which appears outside of history. The latter is merely the manifestation of it in one instance. Again, history is the occasion for the manifestation of the sacred or holy. As such, contingent developments which might explain the phenomenon through other means—social, economic, political, among others—are from the beginning ruled out.

Essentialisations of the type that pervade Eliade's and Otto's visions of religion and in much of what has gone under the name 'history of religions', advance a particular ideological position, although they rarely acknowledge this. The insidiousness of the ideology, however, makes its lack of acknowledgement even more suspect. Historians of religion are not alone in putting forward an essentialisation to advance a particular normative view of the world. One might think, for example, of the way that the 'history' of Christianity might be constructed differently by a Catholic or Protestant theologian, or the history of Islam by a Sunni or Shia scholar. For these different groups, there is a version of the tradition that is said to be the standard or normative definition of tradition. This definition is then read back or inserted into the history of the tradition in order to buttress the standing of that particular group. Differences in theological opinions become heresies and the accepted accounts are deemed as orthodoxy. While potentially harmful in some instances, given the identification of those pursuing these constructions, such accounts are unsurprising. Yet, where one can see these constructions to be in service of promoting a specific identification with a tradition, one should ask: what ideological purpose does the concept of religion serve for those writing from the perspective of historians and phenomenologists of religion? One way to approach this question would be to pay less attention to the intentions of those who have written such histories and more to the wider historical and social context in which they were written. Tomoko Masuzawa's *The Intervention of World Religions*, published in 2005, moves in this direction by tracing the development of 'world religions' as an ideology that was part and parcel to the enterprise of colonisation. But we might also engage in an immanent critique of these works – that is, a criticism that engages with a thinker or tradition on his or her own terms – and in doing so reveal other important matters related to the early goals of history of religions.

These histories of religions express a discomfort with modernity. This is perhaps latent in the work of early historians of religion, but reaches its zenith in Eliade, we can see that the 'history' of religions is meant to preserve a pre-modern way of being in the world. It wishes to safeguard the 'other' of modernity: the archaic, the communal, and the ancient craftsman over and against the modern, the autonomous individual, and the consumer. As Eliade and other historians of religion make clear, the modern world is one that should be looked on with suspicion as it deprives people of a meaningful way in which to make sense of their lives.

History and Genealogy

While this turn to the 'other' of modernity, such as the archaic and the sacred, might seem naïve, it is significant that it finds resonance with more contemporary forms of traditionalism. Specifically on the rise in the modern academy are thinkers who follow the Scottish-American philosopher Alasdair MacIntyre's critique of liberalism and his argument for a return to the Catholic Aristotelianism of Thomas Aquinas, the latter of which preserves the sacred and archaic as part of tradition. For MacIntyre, a return to virtue ethics marks a decisive break with the emotivism, utilitarianism, and consequentialism of modern liberal politics and culture. Its focus on the necessity of character development through the formation of virtues is intended to provide an alternative that will cure society of these ills. MacIntyre's argument is no doubt more rigorous in its analysis of what the development of an alternative to modern liberal society might look like when compared to what historians of religion have to offer. Yet, he nonetheless shares with them a wish that things be different than they are in the present, and that the place to search for something different is in the past, whether that past be real or imagined.

MacIntyre's influence has been felt not only in the realm of Christian theology (amongst thinkers like John Milbank, Stanley Hauerwas, and William Cavanaugh), but also in the field of anthropology amongst thinkers focused especially on Islam, such as Talal Asad and Saba Mahmood. These genealogical approaches to religion are, like those in history of religions, suspicious of the claims of modernity, especially in its political mode of liberalism. Under the influence of French intellectual Michel Foucault's genealogical approach, these thinkers seek to show the contingencies of the development of liberal societies and the role of power in making them what they are today. Such approaches challenge the self-image of liberalism as being natural and based on universal principles, human rights, and equality before the law. In showing how liberal societies have often gone against these very principles in the name of preserving power, these critics demonstrate the hypocrisy lurking behind liberalism. Genealogists thus push back against the narrative of modernity as having improved the lives of people. But whereas historians of religion relegated their anti-modernism to the more abstract realm of ideas, modern anthropologists like Asad do so by juxtaposing Islamic discursive traditions to those of the secular modern West. For Asad, the West has misunderstood Islam because of the way it holds up ideals like liberalism, autonomy, secularism, and free market capitalism. This is not to say that for Asad, Islam is pure of such influences. This would be impossible in a globalised world, and Asad is also careful not to treat Islam writ large as a homogenous tradition. Yet, it is curious to note that in his article 'The Idea of an Anthropology of Islam', Asad affirms MacIntyre's notion of tradition as one that he adopts with no caveats. Mahmood likewise cites MacIntyre as a source for her thinking on tradition, although with more qualifications. Scholars have debated the degree to which thinkers like Asad and Mahmood are normatively invested in these alternatives to the modern West and the degree to which they are merely describing an alternative that appeared before them in their fieldwork. I would contend that their willingness to cite theologians and ethicists who are invested in normative interpretations of the idea of tradition suggest the former is the case.

What is worthy of note here is that in what are often taken to be less naïve 'studies of religion' or 'religious studies' approaches in the present we find nostalgic longings for a pre-modern world. What this means is that we are not as far away from the 'history of religions' approach in the present as we might imagine. This does not mean these two approaches are identical. In fact, other than this nostalgic orientation toward the past and the suspicion of liberalism they share few epistemological, ontological, or metaphysical concerns in common. What history of religions perhaps brings into relief, partly because it is not clouded in the trendier theoretical terms of today, is that the instinct to embrace the pre-modern and/or the anti-modern are deeply embedded in the study of religion. While this longing is obviously present in the 'radical orthodoxy' of a thinker like the English theologian John Milbank, it is no doubt also present in the work of Mahmood and Asad, two thinkers associated with the more 'rigorous' side of current theoretical debates in the study of religion. The danger in both these visions is that in holding up a normative view of the world as a descriptive view they obscure other angles of vision which might shed a different light on the object of study. In doing so, they preserve an idea of tradition as an ahistorical alternative to modernity.

Does this mean we should reject approaches like Mahmood's and Asad's? Absolutely not. Their work has been vital in expanding the theoretical vocabulary by which we investigate the ideological underpinnings of liberalism, secularism, and modernity. But it should perhaps make us more wary of whether such work can be pursued in an ideologically neutral manner. Once we take account of this ideology, we are then able to think more about how our methods might need modification. This might mean, for example, taking an account of the normative underpinnings of how we imagine tradition and making clear what the limits are of that theoretical approach, and where we might need to engage in self-criticism. In closing, I would like to suggest that history remains one of the tools by which we can promote such self-reflexivity.

History as Corrective

One of the imperatives of the discipline of history is to 'correct' the record when ideological blinders have obscured the full reality of a past event or a person under study. To show how this works, we might reflect on the landmark study of W.E.B. Du Bois, *Black Reconstruction in America,* which was first published in 1935. Reconstruction is shorthand for the turbulent period of US history between 1865–1877 when an attempt was made to reintegrate the breakaway southern states and around four million freed blacks into the United States after the bloody civil war. At the time when he wrote the story of reconstruction in the American south, much of the history had been told through the lens of white historians. Given the explicit racism of their day, it is unsurprising that the failures of reconstruction were pinned on newly freed black slaves. It was the contention of white historians that these slaves were intellectually incapable of governing, and that this incapacity led to the failure of their policies to create functioning state governments throughout the south. These historians, some of whom were professors at prestigious Ivy League universities, had ideologically constructed the history of the reconstruction era to fit to their own worldview, rather than the facts as they occurred. Du Bois writes, 'what we have got to know, so far as possible, are things that *actually happened* in the world. Then with that much clear and open to every reader, the philosopher and the prophet has a chance to interpret these facts; and until we distinguish between these two functions of the chronicler of human action, we are going to render it easy for a muddled world out of sheer ignorance to make the same mistake ten times over.' In his expansive volume, Du Bois engages in the tedious work of sifting through newspapers, notes from congressional sessions, letters, and bureaucratic records, to chronicle just how erroneous the story of reconstruction was as told by the white historians. In doing so, he changed the course of our understanding of the period following the civil war and asked the country once again to confront its racist past and present. He showed the power of history to reframe our understanding of society and ourselves.

Given the theoretical concerns with access to the past as 'it actually happened', as Du Bois told it, many today would view his statement as naïve. For it goes against the genealogical approach that looks for how power and knowledge unfold in contingent circumstances rather than for the causes of events. Yet Du Bois' counter history serves as a cautionary tale to what potentially happens when we relinquish that desire—namely that we come to accept ideological positions with relation to the past as inscrutable. Without necessarily saying that we have unfiltered access to the past from the present, we can say that there are better and worse ways of recounting the past and that Du Bois, while not accessing what 'really happened' during reconstruction, was able to provide a more compelling account than what had come before by being inclusive of a larger tapestry of actors and sources. History of religions no doubt failed to provide a compelling account of the development of religion over time due to its very narrow and European and Christian-centric views of the religions of the world. But genealogical approaches also have their own limitations. This is due to the lack of acknowledgement on the part of genealogical historians of their own normative ideology. In our current moment, the latter is often covered over by the reverence of scholars in the humanities for theory. Adopting a fallibilistic approach to not only our knowledge of the past but also the theoretical approaches we employ to interpret it is a vital scholarly virtue if we are not to repeat the errors of history. It is easy to employ the latest theoretical developments with an uncritical eye to ensure we do not fall behind the advances in scholarship. Yet, it is also imperative that we remember that no theoretical approach is sacred, that every theory has a history.

PAST FUTURES OF ISLAM

Robert Irwin

'We have been disappointed. The Syrian army is as fanatical as the hordes of
the Mahdi. The Senussi have taken a hand in the game. The Persian Moslems
are threatening trouble. There is a dry wind blowing through the East, and
the parched grasses wait the spark...Whence comes that wind, think you?'

John Buchan, *Greenmantle* (1916)

In the 1970s, I lectured on medieval European history at the University of
St Andrews in Scotland.

The shadowy and superficially unpromising history of European
countries (in an age before either 'Europe' or 'countries' really existed)
was implicitly a story which would inevitably foreshadow the triumph of
the West. Indeed, *The Triumph of the West* had been the title of a book my
former Oxford tutor, John Roberts, published in 1985 to accompany a
thirteen-part documentary television series and it celebrated the triumph
of Western imperialism, technology, and commerce. For why, as one
viewer asked, did no Arab dhows or Chinese junks ever dock at
Southampton?

The prosopographical historian of Hanoverian MPs, Sir Lewis Namier,
argued that 'one would expect people to remember the past and to
imagine the future. But in fact, when discoursing or writing about history,
they imagine it in terms of their own experience, and when trying to
gauge the future, they cite supposed analogies from the past.' He
paradoxically concluded that 'historians imagine the past and remember
the future'. (In quite another context a superficially similar paradox was
put forward by the crime novelist Ellery Queen: 'the detective is a prophet
looking backwards'.) Namier's version of the historical vision is one that
has been widely shared by modern historians and we shall come back to it.

But first we should mention the proposition set out by both early Muslim and Christian eschatologists that the historical past and future coexisted in, as it were, a single pre-existing, divinely ordained document or *nunc stans* and that therefore the development of the future could be known in some detail. Thus, the fourteenth-century Damascan historian Ibn Kathir produced a chronicle entitled *al-Bidaya wa'l-nihaya* (The Beginning and the End) which as its title suggested, began with the Creation and ceased with the End of Time. Ibn Kathir had managed to preconstruct the final sequence of events, in which the Mahdi, Dajjal (the Deceitful Messiah), and Jesus will be the protagonists. Prior to the appearance of these millennial figures there would be a widespread corruption of morals, linked perhaps to the fact that women will come to outnumber men by fifty to one. Ibn Kathir's version of the Last Days was created by conflating a comprehensive range of prophecies attributed to Muhammad. Similar, though more pared down versions of the Muslim Apocalypse appeared in the writings of such historians and thinkers as Abu Yusuf al-Kindi (801–873), Ibn Khaldun (1332–1406), and al-Suyuti (1445–1505). It was widely accepted that the Antichrist would be born in Damascus. My late friend the art critic Peter Fuller took pride in the fact that he had been born in Damascus and that therefore it might be possible that a great, though sinister, Destiny had been reserved for him. (This was not to be.) Christian astrologers and soothsayers of course made their own prophecies about the doom of Islam. When, in 1273, Pope Gregory X requested advice for preparing a new crusade, the Dominican William of Tripoli reported that a prophecy circulated widely among the Muslims that the doom of Islam was imminent and consequently the Christians should not bother themselves with preparing a crusade, but instead should send missionaries to the East.

From the late 1480s onwards (the decade of Columbus and Bartolomeu Dias), it was taken for granted by European Christians that the future belonged to them. Michel de Nostredame, also known in the Latinised form as Nostradamus (1503–1566), worked an apothecary in the South of France before turning to astrology. Like other pre-modern futurologists, he acquired status by virtue of his alleged precognitions and the events he predicted acquired status by being their allotted place in the chain of Destiny. Nostradamus's predictive account of future events, *Les premières centuries, ou Prophéties* (1555), was more than anything else a catalogue of future disasters: invasions, storms, murders, epidemics, and so forth. A remarkable number of threats to the peace and stability of Christendom originated in the Middle East. For example, these two quatrains on the Barbary corsairs and Arabs (Ishmaelites):

> Plague from Barcelona, Genoa, Venice
> And Sicily to Monaco shall race:
> Against the Barbar fleet they'll take their aim,
> And back to Tunis chase Barbar away.

> Ready to land, the Crusader army
> Shall be ambushed by the Ishmaelites:
> Marauding ships beset them on all sides,
> Ten elite galleys take them by surprise.

Prophecy only achieves true recognition retrospectively and Nostradamus's prestige grew in the centuries that followed his death, since his prophecies could be interpreted to fit all manner of triumphs and catastrophes. His quatrains were chronologically vague, cryptically phrased and they deployed a symbolism that verged on surrealism. The underlying trend was pessimistic, for Nostradamus lived in a century when, while the Christian powers quarrelled amongst themselves, the Ottomans made substantial gains in the Balkans as well as taking Rhodes from its Knights.

The Centuries, like many similar works, fed upon Christian belief and astrology. By the nineteenth century sociologists were looking for firmer ground on which to base their visions of the future. The positivist sociologist Auguste Comte propounded The Law of Three Stages, according to which mankind advanced from the theological (medieval) to the metaphysical and from there to the positive. It is possible that Comte's scientific positivism and his dethronement of traditional religion influenced the thinking of H.G. Wells. In the novel *The Shape of Things to Come* (1933), Wells sketched out the future up to 2015, in the course of which he sought to show how the abolition of all organised religions was a necessary precondition for the establishment of the Modern State. Mecca was attacked by the Air Police and its shrine was destroyed. So were almost all mosques throughout the world with only a few being spared because they were judged to be of architectural merit. The Modern State and its air force had been established by a succession of conferences held at Basra by scientific and technical workers. (We are not told why Basra was chosen.) In the longer run Islam, like Catholicism, had to give way to secular modernity. In particular the global triumph of Basic English over Arabic and other languages played a crucial role in the destruction of Islam. *The Shape of Things to Come* was a dogmatic and confident novel. But in his last book, *Mind at the End of Its Tether*, (1945) Wells had lost that confidence and the only thing that he thought he could look forward to was the replacement of humanity by another species.

Despite Wells's disbelief in the future of Islam, from the nineteenth century onwards, a number of politicians and academics took an interest in the future of the Middle East. Several were anti-imperialist. Edward Granville Browne (1862–1926), Persianist and professor of Arabic at Cambridge, worried about the declining number of independent territories in the Middle East and North Africa that were 'ever more overshadowed by the menace of European interference', and he campaigned vigorously for the remnants of their independence. Wilfred Scawen Blunt (1840–1922) the womaniser, breeder of pedigree horses and third-rate poet, published *The Future of Islam* in 1882. In this polemical work Blunt argued in favour of genuine Egyptian independence from British and Ottoman overlordship. Cairo and its intellectual centre, the University of al-Azhar would spearhead the Arab revival. Moreover, in an ideal future the caliphate should be revived and the office of caliph should be repossessed by the Arabs from the Turks. Nevertheless, taking a broader view, by the late nineteenth century most Muslims were to be found living in lands to the east of the Arabs and the manifest future of Islam, in a belated Reformation, would be in India, with perhaps a capital in Delhi or Hyderabad. Shi'ism, vulgar and superstitious, would decline, just as Wahhabi Islam evidently was on its way out.

Blunt was not a good guesser. How did he get things so wrong? First, he confused wish fulfilment fantasies with genuine precognition. Secondly, he guessed that Egyptian society and religion were undergoing roughly the same changes that European society and religion had undergone some centuries earlier. The seeds of a Reformation could be detected in nineteenth-century Egypt and Blunt thought that the Islamic philosopher,

reformer and political activist Jamal al-Din al-Afghani (1839–97) could be
its Martin Luther. Similarly, much later in 1995, Robin Wright, an
American journalist specialising in the Middle Eastern affairs, writing in
The Guardian, was to identify the Iranian thinker Abdolkarim Soroush as
the Republic's Luther. But, as Namier declared of historians, 'when trying
to gauge the future, they cite supposed analogies from the past', to which
one might add Mark Twain's dictum: 'History does not repeat itself, but it
often rhymes.' It also occurs to me that it is patronising to identify political
and religious developments in the Middle East or Africa as plodding
attempts to catch up with fleet-footed movements in Europe and America.

   After the withdrawal of the Turks from Syria and Iraq at the end of the
First World War, T.E. Lawrence experienced the sequel to his dashing raids
as a monstrous anti-climax. In the years that immediately followed he
produced a considerable amount of political journalism. As a student he
had collected brass rubbings and produced a study of Crusader castles and
later his ideas about warfare were shaped by Malory's *Morte d'Arthur*. In the
years that immediately followed the end of the First World War, he
produced copious essays and journalistic contributions, much of which was
collected and posthumously republished in *Oriental Assembly* (1939), most
notably the essay 'The Changing East'. Lawrence's medievalism made him
in most respects a hopeless prophet. His belief that the Jews in Palestine
would raise their Arab neighbours to their own level was misguided. He
underestimated Kemal Ataturk's abilities and future. He was wrong about
Feisal's holding Damascus against the French. His belief that Egypt, Iran,
and Iraq would be delighted to be offered dominion status within the
British Empire was ludicrous. The *Morte d'Arthur* was a poor guide to
twentieth-century politics (and so was his beloved *Odyssey*). Crucially
Lawrence, surrounded by ancient ghosts, had rather little knowledge about
the political thinking of the Arab townspeople.

   In his lifetime Sir Hamilton Gibb (1895–1971), the Laudian Professor
of Arabic in Oxford, was probably the grandest Orientalist in the West.
Gibb had edited *Whither Islam? A Survey of Modern Movements in the Arab World*
(1932) and was also its major contributor. He believed that Islamic society
had an essentially 'medieval constitution' and that therefore Muslims,
shackled by their medievalism, saw numerous aspects of modernity as
threats to their society. Resistance to the European hat was only a trivial

example of their resistance to modernity. Gibb took it for granted that 'real' Islam was Sunni Islam and regarded Shi'ism and Sufism as unwelcome relics of the past. He was an intensely pious man and steeped in the past himself, and he believed that Islam's problems could be solved by a new leadership. 'When Islam finds a new Saladin, a man who combines political insight with a deep consciousness of his religious vision, the rest will solve itself.' Among other things, Gibb predicted that the Orientalist would become obsolete as the Arab and other countries took over the study of their own languages and histories. It is not obvious that this has yet taken place. (Incidentally Louis Massignon was one of the other contributors to Gibb's volume and it is interesting to note that this scholar, whom Edward Said tried so hard to beatify in *Orientalism*, described South African natives of the negro race as being 'often of a very low mentality'.)

One of Gibb's students was Bernard Lewis (1916–2018). It may surprise those who are only familiar with Lewis's later publications to learn that as a young scholar Lewis was enamoured of all things Arab and was fascinated by Marxist ideas. As early as 1950, in *The Arabs in History*, which is a brilliantly condensed overview of the subject, he foresaw the possibility that the Arabs 'may try to turn their backs upon the West and all its works, pursuing the mirage of a return to the lost theocratic ideal, arriving instead at a refurbished despotism that has borrowed from the West its machinery both of exploitation and repression and its verbiage of intolerance'. But it seems clear that this possibility was not the outcome that he was then anticipating. (Oil did not feature in the final pages of this book, nor did the vitality of modern Shi'ism.)

The background of Arab-Israeli tensions prevented Lewis, a Jew, from working in Arab archives, despite his early fascination with the history of the Arabs. So, he switched to working on the fiscal and demographic data on Ottoman Palestine. As he worked in Turkish archives, he became an interested observer of contemporary Turkish politics. In *The Emergence of Modern Turkey* (1961) he praised the Turks for 'renouncing a large part of their Islamic heritage' in favour of European ways of doing things and the conclusion went on to treat the first free election in May 1950 as a political watershed. For a while, and despite the military coups of 1960 and 1980, Lewis's prognostications seemed essentially correct.

In 1974, Lewis moved to Princeton where the terms of his professorship gave him the time to produce a lot of books and articles that somewhat repetitively highlighted past and present deficiencies in Islamic society. For example, in 1997 Lewis published *The Future of the Middle East*, a little paperback that was hardly more than a pamphlet. Its open-ended presentation of future routes that the Middle East may take might seem sensible, except that, here and elsewhere in his writings, he portrayed the inhabitants of the countries of the Middle East as possessing free choices, untrammelled by the overweening ambitions of the United States, Russia, Britain, and France to make those choices for them. Moreover, it was not enough for the Arabs, Turks, and Iranians to accept the outward trappings of modernity. In the long run, Lewis held that it would be necessary for the Muslims to accept the whole package which included Western values. Often Western interventions have had disastrous results and, as Martin Kramer has noted, Lewis did not foresee the overthrow of the Shah of Iran and he was overoptimistic about the Western coalition's subsequent intervention in Iraq. Lewis and his ally Fouad Ajami believed that Western troops would be enthusiastically received in Baghdad. With respect to Iran, Lewis allowed himself to be seduced by the French Revolution paradigm and so he thought it plausible that the hard-line regime of Ayatollahs might give way to a Thermidorean reaction and that this in turn would be followed by a military dictatorship, as first exemplified by Napoleon. Here was another example of someone trying to gauge the future by citing supposed analogies from the past.

Martin Kramer was a student of Bernard Lewis. Kramer took it for granted that it was the primary job of American academics in Middle Eastern Studies to provide accurate analyses and predictions about developments that would serve government policies in the region. This they had failed to do. Notably they had not anticipated rise of Islamist movements in the 1970s. He was particularly critical of what he saw as a paradigm modelled on Edward Said's secular version of the future in which one reactionary Middle Eastern regime after another would face resistance and rebellion before being finally overthrown. According to Kramer, this had only happened in Iran with the triumph of Khomeini (though it seems a little odd to envisage Khomeini's regime as a progressive one). And that was another problem for the Saidian paradigm. Edward Said, the secularist, was unable to allocate any significant future role for political Islam. *Ivory Towers on Sand: The Failure of Middle Eastern Studies in America* (2001), Kramer's extended denunciation of an establishment of American Middle East specialists and their failure to anticipate the way things were going in Teheran, Cairo, and Baghdad scores some palpable hits and it is usually entertaining to read a hatchet job, but I do not think that university departments should be staffed by academics who aspire to become tipsters, fortune tellers, or policy shapers.

Though, like Kramer, I was a student of Lewis, I am of an older generation, and I have a different opinion of what a university should be for: it was well put by Cardinal John Henry Newman in *The Idea of a University* (1875):

> If then a practical end must be assigned for a University course, I say it is that of training good members of society…It is the education which gives a man a clear, conscious idea of their own opinions and judgements, a truth in developing them, an eloquence in expressing them, and a force in urging them. It teaches him to see things as they are, to go right to the point, to disentangle a skein of thought to detect what is sophistical and to discard what is irrelevant.

Although the political scientist Samuel P. Huntington (1927–2008) was not a student of Lewis, he was certainly influenced by him, and he borrowed the title of his most famous (or notorious) title from him. Lewis used the phrase 'clash of civilizations' in 'The Roots of Muslim Rage', a patronising and casually generalising article which appeared in *Atlantic Monthly* in 1990. Huntington's *The Clash of Civilizations and the Remaking of the World Order* was published in 1996 and attracted a great deal of controversy. It argued that future grand conflicts would not be between nation states, but between cultures that were shaped partly by religious history. It suggested that the Islamic bloc, which was experiencing a massive population growth and consequent pressure from the demands of young people, would eventually seek an alliance with China and its Sinified allies. Whereas Huntington believed that such clashes were inevitable, Lewis, in line with his belief that it was possible that Muslim territories should adopt Western values, denied the inevitability of any clash. *The Clash of Civilizations* possibly owed more to Arnold Toynbee's grandiose and long discredited twelve-volume *A Study of History* (1934–1961).

Elsewhere, wishful thinking and an unjustified faith in the virtues of secularism dominated most left-wing predictions about the future of the Middle East in the second half of the twentieth century. In *Arabia without Sultans* (1974), Fred Halliday looked forward to the triumph of secular left-wing revolutionary movements in the Arabian Peninsula (admittedly 'after a difficult and protracted struggle'). In *Iran, Dictatorship and Development* (1979), Halliday foresaw four possible capitalist futures for the Pahlavi regime: 1. its dictatorship would continue; 2. its survival after making some concessions to democratic pressures; 3. the removal of the Shah by a coup and the installation of a military dictatorship; 4. a bourgeois democracy with a purely constitutional monarchy. Four shots, but no banana. An Islamic theocracy did not appear to Halliday to be on the cards, and he placed his hopes in a socialist revolution, since 'it is in the superiority of socialism over capitalism that the argument for a new social system in Iran must lie'. One of the unhelpful premises in his thinking was that he believed that Iran would run out of oil by 2000. This then would be the Shah's main problem. What on earth led Halliday to this belief? Of course, Halliday recognised that the ayatollahs and mollahs would resist the Shah's modernist and secularising regime, but he judged that they would be incapable of managing the popular upsurge, though a military dictatorship would be plausible. Halliday saw the Tudeh communist party as leading future opposition to the Shah. (It is possible that there is a more accurate set of prophecies in Nostradamus.) Although the American-based scholar Hamid Algar successfully predicted the future triumph of Khomeini, in an essay in *Scholars, Saints and Sufis*, (edited by Nikki Keddie and published in 1972) and Khomeini did indeed return in triumph to Iran in 1979 and took over supreme power there, Algar's prophecy was as much an example of wishful thinking as Halliday's, since Algar was a long-standing disciple of Khomeini.

The wealth and corruption of many other regimes has prompted similar predictions of their imminent downfall. For example, in 1994 the Palestinian journalist Said K. Aburish (1935–2012) published *The Rise, Corruption and Coming Fall of the House of Saud* (1994). His book had no difficulty in demonstrating that the Saudis were unpopular. Aburish argued that the regime was carrying unsustainable debts which would entail a declining standard of living. The army was unreliable and the expanding youthful population was disenchanted. The Saudi Arabian Kingdom must meet its end in the 1990s or soon after, and when that happened the West must take drastic action if Saudi Arabia was not to go the way of Iran. Well, there would have been no advance kudos for a pundit if he had predicted that Saudi Arabia in the 2020s would look pretty much the same as it had in the 1990s. If a pundit is going to rise in status, he should foresee 'future disasters: invasions, storms, murders, epidemics, and so forth'.

Edward Said, who mistook his wish-list for true prophecy, was in fact not all that good at guessing how things were going to go. For example, in *The Politics of Dispossession: The Struggle for Palestinian Self-Determination 1969–1994* (1994), he wrote as follows: 'the extraordinary exaggeration of Hamas's power, is, I am firmly convinced, part of the same "Islamic threat" furor that has so dominated Western policy and journalistic commentary'. And a few pages on: 'the more I read and saw the less probable was any sign of a coherent Islamic uprising of the kind confected by Western reporters and sages'. Like Comte and Wells, Said discounted the continuing vitality of Islamism and indeed tended to write about Islam more generally as though it was something that had been foisted on the Middle East by Western experts. When one contemplates these and other duff prophecies, one may wonder why we bother to have Middle East pundits, for their record is hardly better than that of the old gang of Sovietologists.

The American academic John L. Esposito took a sunny Anne-of-Green-Gables approach to Islam's future. For example, in *The Islamic Threat: Myth or Reality?*, he wrote this: 'in recent years most Islamic movements have moved to populist, participatory, pluralistic, political stances championing democratisation, human rights and economic reforms'. Alliteration apart, there seems little to be supporting this assertion.

In France, the political scientist Olivier Roy has long maintained that political Islam was a busted flush and such manifestations of Islamist terrorism were mere manifestations of the 'dead cat bounce'. As his *The Failure of Political Islam* (English translation, 1994; original French 1992): declared: 'a strange Islamic threat indeed, which waged war only against other Muslims (Iran / Iraq) or against the Soviets (Afghanistan) and caused less damage than the Baader Meinhoff gang, the Red Brigade, the Irish Republican Army and the Basque separatist movement ETA'. Also, Islamism 'has lost its original impetus. Having social-democratised itself, it would no longer provide a model for the future.' Ah, but that was what the 1990s looked like, but the Twin Towers were subsequently destroyed in 2001 and Abu Bakr al-Baghdadi declared the Caliphate in Iraq in 2014. One would not like meet the Islamist dead cat in a dark alleyway.

In his study of twentieth-century history, *The Age of Extremes*, the Marxist historian, Eric Hobsbawm asked himself, 'why brilliant fashion designers, a notoriously non-analytic breed, sometimes succeed in anticipating the shape of things to come better than professional predictors remains one of the most obscure questions in history; and for the historian of culture, one of the most central'. Indeed, perhaps part of the answer is that fashion designers are not sitting on the side lines in institutes of politico-economic prediction and punditry. They are actively engaged in making the history of fashion. Whereas, on the other hand, academics regularly overestimate the influence of intellectuals.

Finally, it is obvious that historians must be cautious when they venture into futures studies, for the present holds many futures. I cannot resist drawing on Michael Cook's conclusion to his brilliant *Ancient Religions, Modern Politics: The Islamic Case in a Comparative Perspective* (2014) to serve as the conclusion to my own article. In the afterword to his book Cook asks himself if militant Islam is going to go on forever? Then he provides the splendidly tentative reply: 'I have no idea when Islamism is likely to lose its attractiveness. I tend to assume that one day it will, though only on the flimsy grounds that nothing is forever and ideologies in particular have shorter half-lives than religions.' Cook then went on to suggest five possible future outcomes: first, things will continue pretty much as they have been; secondly, the Islamists will win; thirdly that Islam will reduce its political profile and perhaps this might allow the triumph of an apolitical Sufi spirituality; fourthly, a new secular belief system, like Marxism but not Marxism, could arise in the Islamic world, though Cook does not think this is likely. Fifthly, in the passage of time Islam may follow a path analogous to that of nineteenth- and twentieth-century Catholicism and accommodate itself to liberalism and modernism.

Since I have strong Sufi sympathies myself, I hope for the Sufi option, though I do not foretell it.

THE NEW ICONOCLASM

Jeremy Henzell-Thomas

One of my early encounters with the erasure of history was a very literal one. In the late 1960s as a student in the English Department at University College London, I observed that throughout the department the word 'history' on all notices had been crossed out and replaced with 'herstory'. Thus, the 'History of the English Language', my favourite subject, had been altered to the 'Herstory', an act of radical revision very much in tune with the rising feminism of the time, shortly to be given powerful voice in Germaine Greer's *The Female Eunuch* (1970) which became a key text in the feminist movement through its combination of polemic and scholarly research. Whoever replaced 'his' with 'her' would doubtless have been pleased that Women's History Month, a celebration of women's contributions to history, culture and society, has been observed annually in the United States since 1987, albeit twenty years after the noticeboard revision. The National Women's History Alliance (NWHA) also promotes an annual Women's History theme, with 2022 devoted to 'Providing Healing, Promoting Hope', a tribute both to the 'ceaseless work of caregivers and frontline workers during this ongoing pandemic' and also a recognition of 'the thousands of ways that women of all cultures have provided both healing and hope throughout history.'

The current 'woke' insistence on the erasure of what is judged to be beyond the pale in history is often associated with radical 'cancel culture' and its very concrete expression in the removal of statues, especially of those with reprehensible historical connections to slavery such as Christopher Columbus and Edward Colston. The word 'iconoclasm' springs to mind, and Israeli-American writer, editor and columnist Benjamin Kerstein believes 'we are watching the era of the new iconoclasm take shape, no longer in the form of the destruction of religious icons, but in the demolition of historical memory via the toppling or desecration of statues and memorials across the West'. I see evidence of religious iconoclasm every time I pass by Wells Cathedral on my daily walk to the Bishop's Palace Gardens, for the thirteenth century west front was damaged in 1685 during the Protestant rebellion led by the Duke of Monmouth against the Roman Catholic King James II, with many carved stone figures destroyed or left headless. There were originally around 300 figures, including those of Christ, the Apostles and the Nine Orders of Angels in what has been described as one of the greatest collections of medieval sculpture in the world.

It goes without saying that in the same way as seventeenth century Puritans would not have regarded the destruction of religious figures as 'vandalism' or 'desecration', but rather as an expression of their rejection of idolatry, the same applies to the iconoclastic actions of the victorious Prophet Muhammad on entering Mecca. In his riveting book, *Mecca,* in which he traces the history of the sacred city, Ziauddin Sardar relates how, 'after performing the seven circuits of the Kaaba, he walked towards the hills of Safa and Marwah. The area was covered with 360 deities of those the Meccans worshipped as lesser gods...Using the stick he was carrying, he smashed them all, one by one, reciting the verse: "The Truth has come, and falsehood has passed away; falsehood is bound to pass away".' According to one source, on entering the Kaaba, he protected an icon of the Virgin Mary and the infant Jesus with both hands while instructing 'Uthman that all the other images should be destroyed, including pictures of Abraham painted by a Byzantine artist. It is worth noting, however, that Martin Lings, in his account of the life of the Prophet based on the earliest sources, prefers another source which records that the painting of Abraham was also exempted from destruction. Lings also notes that yet other sources say that all the paintings were effaced without mention of any exceptions.

It is important to bear in mind that the term 'iconoclast' is not only applied to one who is opposed to the depiction of idols, religious figures, and even more widely to any figurative representation, but is also applied to any individual who rocks the boat by challenging cherished beliefs or venerated institutions on the grounds that they are erroneous, regressive, obsolete or toxic. It is important to emphasise that the destruction of idols in Mecca by the Prophet Muhammad was a physical expression of the monotheism of Islam in worshipping the One God, and rejecting the worship of anything other than God. That includes our own egoic self-image, the exclusive adherence to limited formulations of the Truth and any other ways in which 'partners' are attributed to God.

Two philosophers immediately spring to mind. The first is Socrates, the troublesome 'gadfly' who was sentenced to be executed by the ruling Athenian grandees for the capital crime of 'impiety' in failing to acknowledge the gods of the state. In my essay on 'The Power of Education' in the issue of *Critical Muslim* on *Power* (CM14, 2015) I suggested that we might bear in mind that Socrates, in his philosophical, social and moral criticism of authoritarianism, was not simply 'a posturing rebel driven by anger, or a self-promoting agent provocateur captivated by his own wit and cleverness or the radical obliqueness of his own insights'. Neither did he merely play with words, or tinker with ideas. Yes, he was a 'dangerous freethinker' (the theme of CM12), a thorn in the flesh, but he had not turned freethought itself into a dogmatic ideology through which it masquerades as a supposedly 'progressive' force against religion and 'superstition'. If he were with us today we would not see him in uncritical and servile genuflection to the triumphalism of 'Enlightenment values' or 'secular humanism' or 'scientific materialism' or any other 'fundamentalism', whether secular or religious. As Ziauddin Sardar wrote in his essay for CM12, 'freethinkers are seen as dangerous simply because freethought challenges the conventional, the orthodox, and the dominant perspectives'. But authentic freethinkers are, like Socrates, fully aware of the depth of their own ignorance and the perpetual need for questioning and diligent inquiry in the service of the advancement of knowledge.

The second philosopher I had in mind is Francis Bacon who, in his book *Novum Organum* (1620), described what he called the 'idols of the human mind' that 'distort and discolour the true nature of things'. These fixations include trying to make things fit into patterns, the confirmation bias in seeking evidence to support preconceived ideas, seeing what one expects to see, believing what one wants to believe, generalising, favouring one outlook or perspective over another (e.g. antiquity over novelty, the part over the whole, differences over similarities, or *vice versa*), and failing to understand that words may have more than one meaning. The power of literalism, of words with monolithic meanings set in stone, is linked to the idea of correctness and its relationship to power invested in a priestly, social or ruling caste. It is also fitting to mention the accolade by Kamila Shamsie in the *New Statesman* that it is a 'pleasure' to be 'in the company of Sardar's iconoclastic, worshipful mind', a perceptive statement that highlights the fact that to have a mind which is both 'iconoclastic' and 'worshipful' is not an oxymoron. For my part, I relish writing for *Critical Muslim* for that very reason.

But let us return to the assault on statues as perhaps the most striking contemporary expression of the 'new iconoclasm'. In an article in *The Independent* in 2021, Gino Spocchia notes the complaint of Fox News host Rachel Campos-Duffy that Columbus was being 'cancelled' by people marking 'Indigenous People's Day' on 11 October rather than the public holiday named after the Italian explorer. As part of the Black Lives Matter demonstrations sweeping across the US after the murder of the unarmed black man George Floyd by Minneapolis police, Columbus became the focus of anti-racism campaigners and statues of the explorer were among dozens of monuments vandalised or pulled down by campaigners. Many others were removed by city officials, as were monuments tainted by association with the Confederacy and its legacy of slave ownership in the South. In response to Campos-Duffy, American comedian and talk show host Joe Piscopo said his grandparents were Italian and that erasing Christopher Columbus Day was disrespectful, although dozens took to Twitter to accuse Fox News of failing to acknowledge the historical wrongdoings of Columbus, and of denigrating Indigenous Peoples Day.

The marginalisation of indigenous (aboriginal, First Nations) peoples has become a prominent issue in mainstream news in our times, starkly brought to light most recently with the exposure of their pernicious mistreatment and abuse in Canada for more than a century from the 1880s to as recently as the 1990s, when indigenous children were removed from their families and placed in federally funded boarding schools designed to assimilate them into broader Canadian society. At these 'Indian Residential Schools' they were not allowed to speak their languages or express their cultural heritage and identities. An estimated 150,000 First Nations children suffered neglect, disease, and abuse, both physical and sexual, in these schools and the unmarked graves of dozens have been recently discovered. As Amnesty International has stated, 'aboriginal people were expected to have ceased to exist as a distinct people with their own governments, cultures, and identities'. A National Truth and Reconciliation Commission called the schools a form of 'cultural genocide'. In March 2022, Pope Francis apologised for the fact that the Roman Catholic Church operated about 70 percent of the Canadian schools. 'I feel shame and pain for the "deplorable" abuses,' the pope said. 'I ask forgiveness of God, and I join the Canadian bishops in apologising.'

In my essay entitled 'Simple Stories, Complex Facts' in the issue of this journal on *Narratives* (CM28), I related how when I was studying history at 'A' level in 1964, our syllabus identified 1492 as the year in which 'Modern History' began, the year that Columbus 'discovered' the 'New World'. I was *not* told that it was also the year in which Columbus, in his relentless search for gold and slaves, instituted shockingly cruel and genocidal policies in the Caribbean islands he had 'discovered', including the rapid decimation of the populations of indigenous Arawak Indians. Columbus's arrival in what is now the Bahamas is increasingly associated with the beginnings of the transatlantic slave trade. He himself owned more than a thousand slaves on the island of Hispaniola.

As for Edward Colston, the 5.5-metre bronze statue of this seventeenth century slave trader, merchant and philanthropist, which had stood on Colston Avenue in Bristol since 1895, was toppled from its plinth and pushed into the docks during Black Lives Matter (BLM) protests in June 2020, an event which made headline news. It was perhaps predictable that the Home Secretary, Priti Patel, described this 'completely unacceptable' act of 'disorderly and lawless behaviour' as 'utterly disgraceful' and 'sheer vandalism', and 'it's right that police make sure that justice is taken with those individuals responsible'. Prime Minister Boris Johnson asserted that 'these demonstrations have been subverted by thuggery, and they are a betrayal of the cause they purport to serve'. However, ITV presenter Piers Morgan responded in tweets: 'Does Priti Patel even know who Edward Colston was? He was a major slave trader involved in the transportation of 84,000 enslaved African men, women and young children, of whom 19,000 died on voyages from West Africa to the Caribbean and the Americas. Priti Patel thinks pulling down a slave trader's statue undermines racism protests. Have we ever had a more tone-deaf Home Secretary?' Writing in *The Guardian,* Martin Farrer confirms that Colston was a member of the Royal African Company (RAC) which had a monopoly on the West African slave trade in the late seventeenth century. The slaves, including women and children, were branded with the RAC initials on their chests.

A petition that gathered thousands of signatures during the week before the statue was toppled said that Colston had 'no place' in the 'diverse and multicultural city' of Bristol, and that 'whilst history shouldn't be forgotten, these people who benefited from the enslavement of individuals do not deserve the honour of a statue. This should be reserved for those who bring about positive change and who fight for peace, equality and social unity.' It needs to be acknowledged, however, that, as Farrer explains, the statue of Colston was actually a memorial to the philanthropic works he developed after divesting himself of links to the RAC, having sold his shares in the company to William, Prince of Orange, in 1689 after the latter had orchestrated the Glorious Revolution and seized power from King James II the year before. Colston's reputation as a philanthropist in Bristol was based on substantial funding to sustain schools, almshouses and churches.

Despite this, many might understandably side with Piers Morgan rather than Priti Patel in seeking to excuse the pulling down of the slaver's statue, but I would guess that few would applaud the scrawling of graffiti on the plinth of the statue of Sir Winston Churchill in Parliament Square, branding him a 'racist', during the same BLM demonstrations in June 2020. Banners with the words 'British Colonialism is to blame' had also been left at the base of the statue, while a Black Lives Matter sign was strapped to Churchill's body. While Churchill is venerated for leading the country to victory in the Second World War, his views on race and ethnicity have come under fire. He has been blamed for causing the Bengal Famine of 1943, which resulted in the death of some three million people in West Bengal and Bangladesh where access to international imports, including food aid from Canada, was largely denied by his War Cabinet, although this was arguably due to a wartime shortage of shipping. Churchill is reported to have said that relief efforts would be ineffective because Indians bred 'like rabbits'. His overriding concern was the war effort, and as such he was willing to divert food supplies from India to Allied military campaigns.

We might leave aside the marginal stigmatisation of Churchill, whom defenders have tended to label as a 'liberal imperialist' at the worst, but in addition to the more virulent furore provoked by statues of Columbus and Colston we might also mention the angst caused by the statue of British imperialist Cecil Rhodes at Oriel College, Oxford. Calls to remove the statue included a gathering of protestors in Oxford's High Street outside Oriel College in June 2020. Rhodes, a nineteenth Century businessman and politician in southern Africa, had been a student at Oriel and left the college £100,000 – about £12.5m in today's money. In October 2021, the BBC reported that 'an explanatory plaque "contextualising" the statue of British imperialist Cecil Rhodes' had been placed outside the college. The college had said previously that it had been prevented from removing the statue by complex planning, regulatory and financial challenges. Under the government's new 'retain and explain' policy designed to protect controversial monuments, planning permission is required before a statue can be removed from its position. The plaque states that Rhodes was a 'committed British colonialist' who 'obtained his fortune through exploitation of minerals, land and peoples of southern Africa. Some of his activities led to great loss of life and attracted criticism in his day and ever since.' It further directs readers to the college's website and an article entitled 'Contextualisation of the Rhodes Legacy', but 'The Rhodes Must Fall' campaign, which claims that Rhodes represented white supremacy and was steeped in colonialism and racism, objected on social media that 'this sign trivialises the pain and suffering Rhodes caused'. Oxford city councillor Shaista Aziz said the language used on the plaque was 'very ambiguous' and that 'at the very least what should be stated was how much wealth Cecil Rhodes made from his so-called endeavours across Africa, the human impact and the legacy that has on our high street. This is not about a statue, this is about the denial of history and representation of people of colour in our city and beyond.'

The ambiguity attributed by Shaista Aziz to the Oriel College plaque highlights the complexity of the issues raised by the controversy over statues. The controversy of course extends further to encompass iconic monuments, historical estates and collections of artefacts, as for example in the report published by the National Trust in 2020 that revealed that, after examining the sources of wealth that helped to fund its collections and buildings, one third of its properties (93 in all) have direct links to slavery and colonialism. Ruchira Sharma explains that the report, which draws on the trust's own archives and external evidence, gives details of those who acquired their wealth through the slave trade, including the links of plantation owners to specific sites, as well as the compensation paid to some for slaves freed through abolition. The report gives a full list of the properties with relevant links. Those which attract many visitors include Bath Assembly Rooms, Barrington Court, Buckland Abbey, Lacock Abbey, Glastonbury Tor, Dyrham Park, Clandon Park, Hare Hall, Stourhead, Ham House and Blickling Hall. Some others, including Peckover House, Mount Stewart and Sudbury Hall were, however, linked to support for the abolition of the slave trade.

John Orna-Ornstein, formerly Director of Museums for Arts Council England, and currently Director of Curation and Experience for the National Trust, with responsibility for leading the Trust's work to care for and make relevant and accessible its historic sites, explained that while the research was sometimes very painful and difficult to consider, it was important for raising awareness. 'They make us question our assumptions about the past, and yet they can also deepen and enrich our understanding of our economic status, our remarkable built heritage and the art, objects, places and spaces we have today and look after for future generations,' he said. Tarnya Cooper, the National Trust's Curatorial and Collections Director, said that as a heritage charity, the organisation's work is to openly share all the available information of its sites, including information about colonialism and slavery 'where it is relevant'. She explained that the report is not exhaustive, but a foundation for more work in the future. 'This is part of caring for our properties in a historically responsible and academically robust way. The work helps us all understand what's gone before; now and for future generations.'

I have been a member of the National Trust for years and derived much pleasure from visiting many of its properties. As a resident of Glastonbury for many years I have climbed the Tor countless times, previously unaware that it is one of 29 properties cared for by the National Trust which have links to successful compensation claims as a result of the abolition of slavery. Although the National Trust deserves to be commended for its historically responsible report in helping us to understand what has gone before, I have no intention of ceasing to climb the Tor or to visit nearby sites such as Stourhead or Barrington Court. This is not because I am condoning slavery or failing to question assumptions about the past, for nothing in the past would be changed if I chose to cancel all future visits. I can, however, keep the findings of the report in mind as a salutary reminder of how historical narratives inevitably change and evolve with shifting values.

One particularly iconic building which has recently been targeted is the Taj Mahal, the world-famous mausoleum in Agra built by the seventeenth-century Muslim emperor Shah Jahan to house the tomb of his favourite wife, Mumtaz Mahal. Writing in *Religion News,* Katelyn Beaty describes how, in June 2018, 'about two dozen members of the Vishwa Hindu Parishad (VHP) tore apart a 10-by-11-foot steel gate that had recently been installed for ticket collection'. The VHP is associated with the governing Hindu nationalist Bharatiya Janata Party (BJP) and was recently described as a 'militant religious organization' in the World Factbook. The leader of the VHP, Ravi Dubey, claimed that 'the gate was blocking the way to a 400-year-old temple of Hindu god Shiva', thus clearly identifying the Hindu nationalist motive for the vandalism. While police said the gate was torn down and thrown about 150 feet, Dubey said it was a 'minor incident.' Beaty explains that 'the Archaeological Survey of India, which manages the Taj Mahal, said there was an alternative route to the Hindu temple, rejecting Dubey's claim that the gate was blocking the way'. According to Apoorvanand Jha, who teaches Hindi at the University of Delhi, Hindu nationalists insist that the Mughals, who ruled India from the sixteenth to the nineteenth centuries, destroyed Hindu holy sites and converted them into Muslim memorials, many of which are now India's principal tourist landmarks. BJP leaders have variously claimed that the Taj Mahal was originally a Hindu temple dedicated to Shiva or part of a palace owned by the Hindu king Jai Singh. Shashi Tharoor, a lawmaker from the Indian National Congress party and former undersecretary-general of the United Nations, attributes the prevailing anti-Muslim fervour to 'the ascent of the Hindu-chauvinist BJP'.

'The Taj Mahal,' he says, 'is merely the latest victim of a political campaign over Indian history that seeks to reinvent the idea of India itself...Whereas for seven decades after Independence, Indianness rested on faith in the country's pluralism, the ascent of the Hindu-chauvinist BJP has brought with it attempts to redefine the country as a Hindu nation long subjugated by foreigners.'

In addition to the word 'contextualise', we might well identify the words 'reinvent' and 'redefine' used by Tharoor as keywords in our discussion about the erasure or revision of history. Writing in January 2015 in the wake of the massacre of *Charlie Hebdo* journalists in Paris, Pankaj Mishra also appealed for the need to 're-imagine', referring in this context to our conceptions about freedom and the Enlightenment: 'We may have to retrieve the Enlightenment, as much as religion, from its fundamentalists... The task for those who cherish freedom is to re-imagine it – through an ethos of criticism combined with compassion and ceaseless self-awareness.'

Kerstein points out that the 'desecration' of the statue of Churchill, whom he applauds as 'perhaps the greatest anti-fascist of them all', shows only too clearly how the new 'iconoclasm' is 'in no way confined to the punishment of historical traitors'. He also deplores the toppling of the statue of Ulysses S. Grant, bearing in mind 'his legacy as the man who crushed the Ku Klux Klan and fervently defended Reconstruction and human rights'. He makes the telling point that 'no one disputes that there is great sin in the history of our civilization. But historical sin demands a moral struggle. In their erasure of history...a new totalitarianism is being born' even though 'for the moment, this is a soft totalitarianism – a totalitarianism suited for an age of social media spectacle.' Nevertheless, as he says, 'the essence is the same: The penalty for even the weakest sin is damnation.' Dino Sossi, asking the question 'Can we cancel cancel-culture?' in *The Conversation* in 2021, accepts that 'social media's amplifying powers' are a key factor in the 'cancellation' of all manner of things, including people, brands, and even shows and movies because of 'what some consider to be offensive or problematic remarks or ideologies' but he also blames 'society's deep divisions and difficulties redressing longstanding inequities'. And we might add that if we dig deep enough into our own ancestry, we are doubtless all damned. Should modern Italians feel responsible for the acts of the ancient Romans, and pay reparations to the modern descendants of their slaves? And does the 10 percent of my own DNA defined as 'Italian' point to ancestors of my own who were likely to have been Roman settlers in Britain who oppressed the indigenous Celts?

Kerstein believes the only way forward is that 'people must begin to think again. We require a revolution of nuance.' Arguing with conviction that we should admit that 'historical injustice is real and must be addressed' and that 'there are indeed some beliefs and opinions that are beyond the pale and must be shunned', we must yet demand 'overwhelming evidence before doing so', for 'if there is one great and absolute enemy of totalitarianism, it is truth. And to reach the truth, one must think.' Only in this way can we begin 'the slow process of resistance to those who would impose their will on anyone who demands the right to choose the difficult struggle and not the easy bonfire of the vanities'.

And yes, it is true that thinking through all the ambiguities, questioning assumptions, reframing obsolete scripts, dismantling fixed mindsets, giving due attention to factual evidence, and keeping track of shifting values is indeed a 'difficult struggle'. The same struggle was implied in Plato's affirmation that the process of dialectic was immeasurably superior to rhetoric as a means of persuasion because it entails the gradual refinement of an existing 'position' through careful critical engagement with opposing or alternative ideas and perspectives. The recent request of a superintendent of a north Texas school district that libraries should remove books about transgender and LGBT+ people closes the door on dialogue and smacks of the totalitarianism that has also dictated the burning of books. From the other side, the recent 'cancelling' of Harry Potter author J.K. Rowling seems equally dogmatic. In this case, a secondary school in Essex that named a house after her has renamed it following requests from students and staff due to her 'comments and viewpoints surrounding trans people'. In short, she was accused of 'transphobia' for merely voicing concerns about allowing 'trans' women into women-only spaces, for taking issue with avoidance of the word 'women' in the phrase 'people who menstruate' and for disputing the idea that male and female sexes did not exist.

I would add to Kerstein's passionate belief in the importance of moral struggle, nuanced thinking and evidence-based inquiry the even deeper imperative of spiritual struggle, the 'greater jihad' as defined by the Prophet as the struggle with the lower self. The stark distinction between the iconoclasm of the Prophet in destroying idols and that of those driven by lower impulses is captured well in the wise words of the Catholic monk Thomas Merton: 'those who attempt to act and do things for others or for the world without deepening their own self-understanding, freedom, integrity and capacity to love, will not have anything to give others. They will communicate to them nothing but the contagion of their own obsessions, their aggressiveness, their ego-centred ambitions, their delusions about ends and means, their doctrinaire prejudices and ideas... We have more power at our disposal today than we have ever had, and yet we are more alienated and estranged from the inner ground of meaning and of love than we have ever been.' The iconoclasm of the Prophet was rooted in divine revelation and the 'maturity' invested in him (Qur'an 46:15) and it goes without saying that it was in no sense an expression of individual emotionalism or 'doctrinaire prejudices'.

Coming back to the history syllabus I studied at school that identified 1492 as the year Columbus 'discovered' the New World but failed to mention the atrocities he committed against indigenous people in the Caribbean, neither was I told that it was the same year in which Muhammad XII, the last Emir of Granada, surrendered his city to the Catholic Monarchs after a lengthy siege, bringing to an end 780 years of relatively peaceful co-existence under Islamic rule in Al-Andalus. And no mention was made of the Alhambra Decree in the same year expelling all Jews from Spain unless they converted to Roman Catholicism. Clearly, I was expected to assimilate the dominant 'narrative' from a Eurocentric perspective, a simple 'story' about modernity, progress and outreach as pivotal features of Western civilisation and hegemony.

As I related in my essay for CM 28 (*Narratives*) I was fortunate in having a very enlightened history teacher whose method of teaching was to teach as little as possible but to ask the class to research the topic at hand and think through the material. He would ask one of us to give a presentation based on our research, followed by a discussion amongst the class, with little intervention from his side. The topic given to me to research was 'Columbus and the Age of Discovery'. Budding iconoclast, subversive rebel and non-conformist myth-buster that I was, I delighted in undermining the dominant Eurocentric narrative, basing my counter-narrative on my eye-opening research into the *Convivencia* in Al-Andalus which was totally new territory not only to me and the class, but also to the teacher, especially since there were so few books on the subject in our school library, and no internet of course in 1964. I deliberately use the term 'counter-narrative' to describe my subversive presentation, because, as I realised many years later, my idealised vision of the *Convivencia* could also be legitimately described as a questionable 'narrative' in itself.

Clearly, the erasure of history is not accomplished simply through conscious acts of vandalism, iconoclasm, censorship or cancellation, but is, and always has been, built into the simple stories that become entrenched monocultural myths. In this way, the erasure of history is as much a matter of unconscious omission as it is of intentional deletion. In fact, such omission doubtless accounts for most of our reading of history. Robert Trivers refers to 'false historical narratives' as 'lies we tell one another about our past. The usual goals are self-glorification and self-justification... False historical narratives act like self-deceptions at the group level, insofar as many people believe the same falsehood', unconscious of the fallacies that went into constructing the narrative. The emotional power of such narratives can easily be harnessed and exploited by leaders in the service of identity politics, corporate power or tribal or national interests. While the ditching of the statue of Edward Colston was a newsworthy photo opportunity, it is well to realise that the erasure or revisioning of history has always been cemented in the dominant narratives, and, indeed, the narrative fallacies, that permeate the often one-sided way in which our understanding of history has been transmitted and drummed into us. As the war in Ukraine takes its toll, it is all too easy to side with the Democratic Congressman Gerry Connolly who remarked following his trip to Poland in March that Putin has a 'Russo-centric delusional view', but we also need to be aware of the way in which our own national biases have governed so much of our own reading of history and the attitudes and actions provoked by it.

As a counterpart to 'Russo-centric' delusions, it is therefore refreshing to have seen in recent times a series of books rectifying the hitherto pervasive Eurocentric bias which has studiously ignored the contribution of non-Western cultures and civilisations to the development of Western civilisation. This welcome revision of mainstream accounts of the rise of the West includes the successive critiques of this ingrained bias by Jack

Goody, the exploration of 'how the Arabs transformed Western civilisation' by Jonathan Lyons, and John Hobson's impeccably researched study of the 'Eastern origins of Western civilisation', including the assimilation of Eastern (mainly Chinese) inventions. As a review in the *New Statesman* put it, Hobson's ground-breaking work 'shows that cultures do not exist, nor have they ever existed, in isolation'. This can be most emphatically verified by the achievements of the Abbasid Dynasty, which ruled most of the Muslim world for 500 years from 750 to 1258, and marked the zenith of Islamic power and civilisation. The empire ruled by these caliphs had greater outreach than that of the Roman Caesars; it was the outcome of a flourishing creative expansion during which the Muslims integrated peoples, cultures, and inventions on an unprecedented scale. This civilisation, in total contrast to modern perversions of the concept of the 'Islamic state', drew avidly from the resources of the entire known world.

I have suggested at several junctures in this essay that our response to the various ways in which history is erased, distorted, biased, or radically revised needs to rest on a willingness to excavate the 'facts' through the rigorous evidence-based inquiry that can inform what Kerstein regards as the absolute imperative to think critically and with appropriate 'nuance'. Now this is not easy, as became only too evident to me when my counter-narrative for the year 1492, based on my assiduous research into the Convivencia in Al-Andalus, intended to debunk the glorification of Columbus, turned out on further research to be an idealisation in itself. David Nirenberg claims that the co-existence of Muslims, Jews and Christians under Islamic rule was actually in part predicated on systemic violence, and in *The Myth of the Andalusian Paradise*, Dario Fernandez-Morera confirms that the relationship between the three faith groups was marked more often than not by segregation and mutual hostility. It came as a shock to me to discover that in the massacre of the entire Jewish population of the city of Granada in 1066, the Jewish death toll was higher than in the much publicised Christian pogroms in the Rhineland thirty years later. When I visited Cordoba several years ago, and saw the figure of the Jewish philosopher and polymath Moses Maimonides (1135–1204) standing alongside Ibn Rushd and Ibn 'Arabi in the museum across the bridge from the Great Mosque, I had no idea that he was actually forced to flee from Al-Andalus to avoid conversion by the Almohads, which may have prompted his bitter statement that Islam had inflicted more pain on the Jewish people than any other 'nation'.

Is it not the case that for every narrative there is a counter-narrative, and, as more 'facts' emerge, a further corrective in yet another counter-narrative? Are there no stable or absolute historical conclusions to be drawn, or are our views on history unavoidably relative and impermanent in an ever-shifting landscape always dependent on how we update or 'contextualise' the facts?

A common narrative in our times is that we are living in very dark times, even in eschatological terms the 'End Times', the 'Last Days', or the 'Kali Yuga'. This pessimistic narrative heralds impending global catastrophe, even human extinction. An arresting counter-narrative was put forward by Swedish Professor of International Health and global TED presenter Hans Rosling in his book *Factfulness* which became an international bestseller when published in 2018. The subtitle, *Ten Reasons We're Wrong about the World – And Why Things Are Better Than You Think,* speaks for itself. Rosling showed that when asked basic questions about global trends, we systematically get the answers wrong, even so wildly wrong that a chimpanzee choosing answers at random will consistently outguess journalists and even Nobel laureates. If, however, we embrace a worldview based on facts, it turns out that the world, for all its imperfections, is in a much better state than we might think.

Let me offer a final example of narrative and counter-narrative as a supplement to Rosling's exposure of the distorted perspective which he claims underlies so much of what we believe. A common assumption is that religion has historically been the chief cause of violent conflict. Yet, even cursory investigation of the 'facts' reveals that this is a gross misconception, for it is estimated that, at worst, religious causes actually account for less than three percent of the 248 million deaths caused in the ten worst wars, massacres and atrocities in human history. Of that number, 185 million people were killed in the twentieth century alone, the overwhelming majority as a result of secular wars and oppressions, often linked to totalitarian ideologies.

To put another spanner in the works (after all, I am a self-confessed iconoclast), while 'factfulness' is of course a critical factor in honing our ability to think clearly and come to valid conclusions, it has no predictable or coherent relationship to our actions. Two people may have access to exactly the same facts about Edward Colston, including his record as a slaver, but whereas one may react by ditching his statue in the docks, another may realise that what is needed is not destructive erasure but education in raising historical awareness about the past in the light of progressive values.

Facts are not enough, but must always be evaluated in a balanced way through the lens of human values and the needs of time, place and people.

ANTICOLONIAL RESISTENCE IN MOROCCO

Abdelaziz El Amrani

It is commonly acknowledged that Islam played an important role in anticolonial resistance in different parts of the Muslim world. Muslim countries were under European colonisation for several decades and gained political independence by using Islam as a mode of resistance. But, when we read resistance narratives and major postcolonial works, we infer that religious resistance has been neglected because notions within resistance/postcolonial narratives are defined in secular terms. Instead, nationalist and Marxist anticolonial movements have been highly celebrated, leading resistance and postcolonial narratives to remain silent on Islam as a form of resistance. The failure of Frantz Fanon, due to his Marxist ideology, to link anticolonialism with Islam in his masterpiece *The Wretched of the Earth* is an excellent example to be mentioned here. In the case of Morocco and numerous other postcolonial societies, to produce a linear and uncontested history – and because of the dependence of history on the politics of nationalism – it has been necessary to silence narratives contradicting the dominant narrative. It is true that Moroccan anticolonialism was ideologically diverse, but it was Islam and not any other ideology that served as the primordial mobilising force. In order to undermine the postcolonial secular historiography that has valorised Marxist and nationalist liberation movements over religious ones, one only has to shed light on Islam as an *idélogie mobilisatrice* for the Moroccan Nationalist Movement. Put differently, it can be argued Salafism and Sufism played a greater role in framing and shaping Moroccan anti-colonial consciousness. Although Sufism and Salafism are incompatible in terms of their religious and political aims, they often cooperated in their struggle against European colonisation.

To explore the role of Islam in Moroccan anti-colonial resistance, a postsecular approach can be implemented. There is no doubt that anti-colonial/postcolonial narratives relied on the Eurocentric secular nature of historical interpretive devices, and accordingly they failed to address the fact that historical events are driven by a certain particular religious heritage. Indeed, history continues to be informed by theological narratives that mediate between the sacred and the secular, the temporal and the divine, the religious and the political. In this sense, postsecular history involves and invokes the complex confluence of theological and political ideas. In their 2019 introduction to *The Routledge Handbook of Postsecularity*, Justin Beaumont and Klaus Elder use the term 'postsecular' in a similar way, suggesting that it names both a 'complementarity of discourses' and a 'confrontation of normativities'. Based on this, postsecular history revisits and revises the secularisation of concepts in the philosophy of history and highlights the confluence of theopolitical forces that characterise historical studies. Using postsecularism in analysing historical events is a new approach in historical studies. We can find traces of it in works by scholars who published work around the 2010s, including Dominick LaCapra, Allan Megill, Dipesh Chakrabarty, and Ananda Abeysekara. In his book published in 2021 and titled *Postsecular History: Political Theology and the Politics of Time*, Maxwell Kennel claims secular ideas have a religious provenance, and agrees with Carl Schmitt's insight that many modern state concepts are really secularised theological concepts. For Kennel, postsecular history goes beyond dualistic oppositions between secular and religious ways of thinking, and instead theorises the complex mediations and entanglements between competing normative orders that structure our world. What is at issue here is that in reading Moroccan history, one may deduce the fact that in contrast to the secular ideals of Eurocentric historiography, the secular and the religious go hand in hand in a postsecular way.

As a nationalist reaction to European expansion and a reform movement originating in the late nineteenth century in the teachings of Jamal al-din al-Afghani, Mohamed Abduh and Rashid Rida, Salafism or Salafiyya made a deep impact on Morocco. The anticolonial role for early Salafist-liberal thinkers was carried over into the formation of twentieth century nationalist movements. Regarded as a theology of liberation and a protest against oppression and social injustice, the writings of Rida, Abduh and al-Afghani became the banner of anticolonialism in the Muslim world in general, and in Morocco in particular. Salafist ideas deeply affected the spirit of Moroccan anticolonial liberation movement during the first half of the twentieth century, inspiring many nationalists with new political and religious programmes. In his *Rebirth of a Nation: The Origins and Rise of Moroccan Nationalism, 1912–1944*, John P. Halstead claims Salafism permeated the thinking of the early Moroccan nationalists. Morocco provides a good example of pan-Islam in action in that Moroccan nationalists were eager to exploit pan-Islamic ideas in their struggle against colonialism.

Moroccan anticolonialism, therefore, served as a model of how pan-Islamic groups from the Middle East, particularly from Egypt, sought to intervene in support of indigenous Moroccan efforts to resist foreign imperialism. It is worth pointing out that many of the pan-Islamic textbooks and newspapers came from Egypt and played an unprecedented role in sharpening the sense of national consciousness of Moroccan nationalists. Simply put, Salafi magazines such as *al-Fath, al-Manar, Majalla al-Salafiyya,* and *al-Haq* published a series of articles in the early twentieth century urging the unity of all Muslims against the French in North Africa. They advocated the return to the simple principles of Islam and hence had a profound impact upon the Moroccan nationalists particularly in Fez, Tangier, Rabat, Sale, and Tetouan. In addition to this, there were also many Moroccan students in Egypt, studying chiefly at al-Azhar University. Among them were the future leaders of Moroccan religious anticolonialism, Abdullah ibn Idris al-Sanusi and Abu Shuaib al-Dukkali.

What is interesting is that the Moroccan anticolonial activists were thinking globally and acting locally in that they had a knack for better exploiting Salafism, as a revolutionary ideology, for propagating their cause both locally and transnationally. It is obvious that the Moroccan liberation movement was global and transnational in nature in the sense that Moroccan anticolonialists appropriated ideologies of resistance from outside Morocco. Because pan-Islamic sentiments were sweeping across the Arab world, the Moroccans wanted to establish relationships with their co-religionists in the region. Many young Moroccan activists were sent in an educational mission, mainly from Tetouan, to Egypt and Palestine where they studied the writings of al-Afghani, Abduh, and Rida. They became fully aware of the importance of Salafism in their anticolonial struggle against the French and Spanish imperial forces.

Inspired by Middle Eastern Salafism, the Moroccan nationalists, whether Salafists or modernists, had to speak the religious language and use Islam as a tactical choice or a means of popular mobilisation. Put differently, the terminology used by the Moroccan anticolonialists was partly borrowed from the *zawiya*. Even the young modernists, whose convictions were largely based on Western ideals, realised the effectiveness of Salafism as a mobilising device and, therefore, used its discourse when addressing the people. The Moroccan anticolonialists believed sticking to the teachings of Islam was very important in their struggle against Western imperialism.

It goes without saying that the Qur'an was the source of the Moroccan liberation movement. For the Moroccan anticolonialists, the French conquest was a conquest by a Christian power aiming at the destruction of Islam; the French influence was seen as detrimental to their traditional way of life which was identified with Islam. Therefore, the Moroccan anticolonialists called for jihad against the foreign colonial powers. For instance, Spanish colonisation was opposed by Muhammed bin Abdelkarim al-Khattabi, who in the early 1920s called for jihad against the Spanish occupation of the Rif. Nevertheless, al-Khattabi did not receive strong support from all the leaders of the religious brotherhoods and Salafism because of his secular tendencies. He himself acknowledged that he did not see the power of Islam and failed to use it as a mobilising tool. Al-Khattabi even regretted later that he had not used religion enough as a means of combatting his opponents. But it is an undeniable fact that al-Khattabi himself was indeed a Salafi and his resistance movement was religiously motivated; it was associated with popular Islam.

It is crucial to note that Moroccan anticolonial resistance came out of sanctuaries and mosques. The mosques were the only place Moroccans could meet and discuss efforts to change their situation. In addition to their job in educating people, mosques played a significant role in the resistance to colonialism. The lessons of ulama in the Qarawiyin school in Fes and that of Ibn Youssef in Marakesh, to mention only two, were mobilising men, women, and children to stand against external imperialism. Most Moroccan anticolonial activists studied at the Qarawiyin where they came under the influence of Salafist ideology. Regarded as the founding fathers of Moroccan anticolonial nationalism, Abu Shuaib al-Dukkali, Ali al-Sousi, Muhammed Ben al-Arabi al-Alaoui, Ahmed al-Nadiri, and Abdesselam Serghini were profoundly influenced by Salafist thinking. Indeed, Salafism came to life in Morocco under the guiding inspiration of Sheikh Doukkali, a disciple of Mohamed Abdou, the Mufti of Egypt. The first Moroccan Salafi was Abu Shuaib bin al-Dukkali, often called the Moroccan Abduh. He studied in al-Azhar and came under the influence of Rashid Rida and his *al-Manar* group. He was also a teacher at Qarawiyin and instilled in his students Salafist ideas that were a source of inspiration against colonialism. Al-Dukkali had two main disciples, Muhammed Ben al-Arabi al-Alaoui and Abdesselam Serghini. Considered as the spiritual fountainhead of the Moroccan liberation movement, Muhammed Ben al-Arabi al-Alaoui became the most influential spokesperson for the Salafi view after the First World War and through his teaching at the Qarawiyin, he influenced most of the leading nationalists.

Allal al-Fassi, the most famous Moroccan anticolonial activist, himself came under Muhammed Ben al-Arabi al-Alaoui's influence as early as 1925 when he was still a student in Fes. The task of leading the Salafi movement after the First World War fell to a former student of Muhammed Ben al-Arabi al-Alaoui, Allal al-Fassi, a Salafist who founded the nationalist Independence Party that led an anticolonial struggle against colonialism. Led by Allal al-Fassi, the post-First World War Salafism in Morocco turned out to be politically engaged aiming at establishing a liberal organisation of society with a view to enabling Muslims to lead the good life, part of which was the correct exercise of their religion. According to Allal al-Fasi, the success of Salafi ideology in Morocco was largely due to French colonial policy. Indeed, since the beginning of the protectorate, it was clear to the educated elite that French policy was directed against Islam. This French colonial policy induced the ulama to play a greater role in political life and turned early Salafists such as Abu Shuaib al-Dukkali and Muhammed Ben al-Arabi al-Alaoui into active militants. As the distinguished historian of the Maghreb, Jamil M. Abun-Nasr, puts it, the Salafists in the 1920s were deemed as 'the important religious group in Morocco with the capability of articulating a defense of the rights and cultural heritage of Muslims in Morocco in the face of growing French dominance'. They identified themselves with the Middle Eastern Salafism in their cultural and religious preoccupations, their attempted synthesis of religious and political reform, and their rejection of the separation of the mosque and state. In their view, all modernisation, be it constitutional, juridical, or educational, was to be firmly embedded in the matrix of Islam. Of paramount significance is the fact that they used Islam as a mode of resistance against the coloniser.

Interestingly, the post-First World War Moroccan anticolonialism owed a great deal to the writings of Chakib Arslan. Arslan was considered the prime mover of Moroccan anticolonialism, and his ideas and contacts were undoubtedly important in shaping the thinking of Moroccan anticolonial leaders. He influenced many of those who would eventually lead the anticolonial movement to independence, and was actually moved by his faith in Islamic nationalism as the solution for Moroccan political predicaments. Arslan established his first contacts with Moroccan students in Paris, who had graduated from the so-called 'Free Schools' that offered a curriculum designed to prompt a sense of pride in the Islamic past and hope for a modernised Islamic future in their country.

The proclamation, by the French Protectorate, of the *Berber Dahir* on 16 May 1930 was decisive in the transformation of the Salafist movement from an intellectual circle composed mostly of scholars into a popular political movement. The Dahir changed the legal system in Amazigh speaking parts of Morocco. The anticolonial nationalists made every effort to get the Dahir abrogated. What is at issue here is that the protests took a religious turn. One manifestation of this was the special prayer – *the Latif* – read in the mosques and employed to express public grief on occasions regarded as national calamities. As a spiritual form of resistance, the Latif movement started in the Great Mosque of Sale in June 1930 and spread rapidly to all the major cities. It was one of the fieriest movements in resisting colonialism, becoming a classic mode of protest in the Moroccan repertoire and a ritualised framing device. The refrain 'Oh Merciful God: We request Your Mercy in whatever destiny may bring, Oh Merciful God! Do not separate us from our Berber brethren', was repeated over and over in demonstrations over the next two decades.

The Latif prayer was used in mosques to publicise the threat and energise demonstrations, including marches and petitions, against the French coloniser. The leaders of the Latif protests shared a belief that Dahir represented an explicit manifestation of a broader French Berber policy that threatened the fundamental unity of the Muslim community in Morocco. It was an attempt, to use the words of Mohamed El Mansour, 'to construct a French tailored Islam which was supposed to better serve the French colonial project in Morocco'. Clearly, the Latif protests did have some effect and, accordingly, the French authorities tacitly allowed it to remain a dead letter.

Significantly enough, the most notable contribution of the Salafi movement in Morocco was the creation of free schools by anticolonial Salafists. The raison d'être of the free schools was to resist the French policy of assimilation as pursued through the schools supported by the French authorities as well as to preserve the cultural heritage of Islam. The free schools made it possible for Moroccan children to receive a relatively modern education in keeping with Muslim traditions. A number of Moroccan anticolonialists like Muhammed Ghazi, Mokhtar Soussi, Allal al-Fassi, Ahmed Balafrej, Ibrahim al-Kettani, Abdelaziz Bendriss, and Hachemi al-Filali were intimately connected with this movement. The founders and directors of the free schools had been educated, with very few exceptions, at Qarawiyin University, where their exposure to novel ideas was chiefly limited to the reform programme of Salafism, which stressed the purification of Islam and an educational defence against cultural assimilation by the West.

In addition to its reliance on Islam as a mobilising ideology, Moroccan anticolonialism also gravitated in a more secular direction as the liberation movement was inspired by both religious and secular ideologies. Moroccan anticolonialists considered Islam to be compatible with nationalism. Thus, in Morocco, nationalists also drew their principles from their religion. In his book *The Independence Movements in Arab North Africa*, Allal al-Fassi confirms that:

> it is a fact that the fusion of the salafi doctrine with the nationalist cause in Morocco was profitable both to the salafiyya and to nationalism. We can also affirm that the method followed in Morocco resulted in the success of the salafiyya to a degree not attained even in the country of Muhammad 'Abduh and Jamal al-Din al-Afghani. It is impossible for a historian of the independence movement in Morocco to ignore this crucial phase in the development of popular consciousness in our country. It is right and proper to emphasize that

the confluence of the salafiyya and the nationalist creeds had had the roost beneficial effect upon both of them.

What can be deduced here is that along with their steadfast adoption of Salafism, the Moroccan nationalists were open to nationalist, liberal, and socialist ideas coming from the West. This indicates the fact that religion and nationalism are constantly interacting with one another in multiple ways and should never be considered as isolated phenomena. In a nutshell, in the Maghreb, anticolonialism was based on spiritual nationalisms that amalgamated religion and secular nationalism seamlessly. Accordingly, the distinction between Islam and nationalism was blurred in the Maghreb. This blurring of the boundaries of religion and nationalism in colonial Morocco, in particular, dated back to the nineteenth century writings of the founding fathers of pan-Islamism.

The prominent thinkers of nineteenth century Islamic modernity, such as Rifaa al-Tahtawi and Jamal al-Din al-Afghani, were also early defenders of nationalism. The former defended Egyptian nationalism even as his arguments were couched in terms of Islam, while the latter defended Arabism and outlined a distinct Arab history (remarkably like nationalist Christian Arab intellectuals of the period), even as he elaborated a larger modernist message intended for a universal Muslim audience. What can be drawn here is that religion and secular nationalism were closely intertwined by the majority of the anticolonial movements in North Africa and the Middle East. In Morocco, anticolonial movement was based upon spiritual nationalism in the sense that the Moroccan nationalists used the tools of both the dominant secular discourse of the coloniser to resist its political or cultural control and Salafism in order to preserve their cultural heritage.

It is worth noting that religion in the colonial context was a cultural weapon which both the coloniser and the colonised employed to enhance their positions. European officials regularly employed religious leaders and Islamic institutions to consolidate imperial authority. Like Muslims in general, Sufis reacted in different ways to the advent of European colonialism. Some Sufi orders had an active role in the resistance to the foreign invasion. In other cases, however, Sufism sustained colonialism and negated resistance. In many countries where Sufi orders and movements emerged, the colonial authorities felt the need to incorporate Sufi orders into the political system. After pacifying the Sufi orders, the French and the British turned them into collaborating institutions, hoping to foster an 'official' Islam that would promote European colonisation. In Morocco, the Darqawiya zawiya or tariqa supported and legitimated colonialism. It ordered its disciples not to resist French colonialism as long as it was the Sultan who signed the Protectorate. The zawiya thought it was its duty to justify the advent of colonialism and this was seen as a sign of obedience to the Sultan. In fact, the Darqawiya zawiya was against Mohamed Ben Abdelkarim el-Khatabi's resistance to both Spanish and French colonisation and refused to cooperate with the Riffian resistance. It had a positive attitude towards French colonialism and cooperated with it politically and militarily. More starkly, the Darqawiya mobilised the tribes to fight Mohamed Ben Abdelkarim al-Khattabi and suppress his uprising against colonialism. It did so because it thought the Moroccan Sultan had given France the green light to 'protect' Morocco.

Yet, it is important to note that not all Sufi orders were complicit with colonialism; there were others which were very active in their resistance to colonialism. In Morocco, some Sufi orders were, at certain historical junctures, fierce opponents intellectually and militarily against colonialism. While Salafi beliefs gained support among many religious and political leaders, Sufi orders maintained a presence in the political sphere of society, often challenging colonialism, as well as the domestic political leaders. Indeed, unlike the assumption that Sufis were quietest and non-political forces, Sufi orders had a long history of involvement in politics and community affairs that include specific political and military campaigns against colonialism and authoritarian regimes. For instance, the Shadhili tariqa was the forefront opponent of the Portuguese in the fifteenth century, the most notable of the Sufis being Imam al-Jazuli. In addition to the zawiya of Shadhiliya, the zawiya of Raisouniya contributed to the success of the Battle of Wadi Al-Makhazin, also known as the Battle of the Three Kings, in 1578. Thus, since the sixteenth century, the Moroccan Sufi orders had been playing a significant role in resisting European colonialism, continuing to act as a great source of strength and inspiration for anticolonial movements in the nineteenth and the early part of the twentieth century. Many of the major wars against expanding colonial powers in the nineteenth century were fought by individuals and movements that were inspired by Sufism. Moroccan cities and countryside were littered with marabouts, holy shrines of local saints. The shrines of the *sharifs,* or local saints, were places where revolutionaries and rebels met. Overrating the *baraka,* a spiritual power, of saints was an incentive to the subalterns to stand their ground against oppression and not to give up the fight. Maraboutic belonging was a socially accepted channel of exorcising one's fears and anxieties about social injustice. It is worth noting that the Sufis were amongst the foremost leaders of *jihad* against colonialism in Morocco.

The Sufi sheikhs' emphasis during colonialism was to increase the faith and piety of citizens, as this was seen as one aspect of anticolonial resistance. The Sufi orders offered the strongest resistance to the triumphant military forces of colonialism and showed more vitality in combating, and more lucidity in understanding, its pernicious cultural influence. Just as the orders fought against the initial material onslaught of the French, so they were the most tenacious fighters against the cultural imperialism that came in the wake of the French victory. For the purposes of illustration, the zawiya of Darqawiya contributed actively in the Battle of el-Hri against French colonialism in 1914. Moreover, the Shareef Moulay Ahmed Raysouni managed to unite many tribes in his resistance against colonialism in the late nineteenth and early twentieth centuries. Along similar lines, when the French colonisers occupied Oujda in 1907, the Boutchichi Sheikh Mukhtar Ben Hajj Muhyi Eddine, apparently relying on his baraka, led a jihad against the French for several months before being captured and imprisoned. Along with the zawiyas of Raysouniya and Darqawiya, the zawiya of Boutchichiya valiantly resisted the colonial enterprise.

Wazzani zawiya, founded by an Idrisid shareef Mawlay Abd Allah Ibn Ibrahim in 1678, played a remarkable role in the liberation struggle against colonialism. It joined the Nationalist Movement and contributed to the mobilisation of people against colonialism. The sheikhs of the zawiya educated and mobilised their disciples to fight the colonisers and raised the consciousness of the Moroccans about the danger of colonialism. The Wazzani zawiya's resistance to French colonialism was particularly fierce in the second decade of the twentieth century, with battles led by the shareef Sidi Mohamed Oueld Sidi Hamani al-Shahidi al-Touhami al-Wazani, leader of the Wazzani revolution and a legitimate representative of Wazzani shareefs. Moreover, the Wazzani zawiya participated in the Riffian War (1920–1927) against Spanish colonialism.

In addition to the Wazzaniya, the Kettaniyya zawiya was also a crucial actor within Moroccan anticolonialism. While using the doctrines and institutions of Sufism, the Kettaniyya mobilised the Moroccan masses from different social classes and various regions in defence of the nation's sovereignty. The convergence of the Kettaniyya zawiya and resistance against foreign occupiers in Morocco is illustrated by examples of its prominent sheikhs, Mohamed ibn Jahfar al-Kattani, Mohamed al-Kattani, and Mohamed ibn Abd al-Qadir al-Kattani. While the shareef Mohamed al-Kattani played a significant political role in Moroccan society and its political scene at the end of the nineteenth century, classical national history continues to overlook his contributions. This indicates that Sufi forms of resistance have been eclipsed in Moroccan historiography due to the fact that the history of Moroccan anticolonial nationalism has been written by those who were inspired either by Salafist or secular ideologies. Undoubtedly, al-Kattani had an impact on his society, not only in his native city Fes, but also beyond, where he had extensive allies, disciples and followers among northern tribes and in cities such as Tangiers. Keenly discerning the danger of European encroachment on Moroccan sovereignty, Mohamed al-Kattani abandoned his ascetic life and engaged in political activism, calling both for *tajdid*, Islamic renewal, and resistance against all forms of foreign dominance in Morocco.

Throughout Moroccan history, the most significant movements of protest and resistance against colonisation had a religious character. The Moroccan anticolonial movement developed out of two main religious movements: Salafism and Sufism. It transformed Islam into a purely ideological resistance movement. Moroccan religious forms were transformed as tools of local empowerment and modes of resistance against colonialism. Islam was an inspiring force for most Islamic liberation movements. Yet the study of anti-colonial jihad movements remains a neglected history. We need to develop a postsecular critique of historical imagination. We need to question and deconstruct the historical consciousness that has influenced the philosophy of history over several centuries.

HAMKA'S REFLECTIONS ON IGNORANCE

Khairudin Aljunied

He was an intellectual giant. But, apart from Southeast Asia, his thought and works are little known. His full name was Haji Abdul Malik bin Abdul Karim Amrullah (1908–1981), but he was more popularly known as 'Hamka'. He belonged to a genealogy of thinkers and reformers whose intellectual formations and reformist visions were linked to the wider world of Islam and whose tireless efforts left an enduring mark on the history of Southeast Asian Islam.

One of Hamka's paternal ancestors was Tuanku Nan Tuo (1723–1830), a respected Sumatran scholar who returned to Minangkabau after years of studying in Mecca to lead the 'Padri movement' in the early nineteenth century. The movement aimed at ridding heterodoxies that were rampant in Malay society then and, in the process, endeavoured to end Dutch dominance in many sectors of the local economy. Hamka's grandfather, Muhammad Amrullah (1840–1909), was the leader of the Naqshabandiyyah Brotherhood in Sumatra; his followers came from many parts of the Malay world. He was a known expert on Qur'anic exegesis, Islamic jurisprudence, Sufism, and Arabic linguistics. His son, Abdul Karim Amrullah (1879–1945), chose a different, reformist path. Also educated in Mecca, he, however, shunned Sufi practices and mystical beliefs. Like his grandfather Tuanku Nan Tuo, Abdul Karim was a fiery orator, a fearless polemicist, and a combative writer. He promoted freedom of thought and expression among his followers and espoused modernist interpretations of Islam. Active in reformist organisations such as the Muhammadiyah, Abdul Karim's ardent critiques of the traditional ulama and conservative elites had earned him imprisonment on a few occasions. Hamka was certainly moved by the efforts of his forebears, and more so, by the steadfastness of his father. He saw that amidst their differences, they were all devoted to uprooting one fundamental cause of Muslim backwardness: ignorance.

Indeed, the will to undo the effects of ignorance in Muslim societies became Hamka's lifetime passion and promotion. In the span of five decades, he authored more than a hundred novels, Islamic books, and thousands of essays as well as opinion pieces, covering a wide range of topics, including history, theology, philosophy, Islamic jurisprudence, and spirituality. Most of these works have been republished and a number have been popularised in the form of stage plays and movies. Hamka was more than a writer. Father of ten children, he joined many Indonesians in the revolutionary struggle against the Dutch during the Indonesian Revolution (1945–1949). He was, at the same time, actively involved in a few Muslim institutions and parties such as the Masjid Agung Kebayoran Baru, Muhammadiyah, and the Parti Islam Masyumi. In 1958, in recognition of his intellectual and grassroots activism, Hamka was conferred an honorary doctorate by Al-Azhar University; among the few Indonesians other than his father to have received such a prestigious award. After he was appointed, in 1975, the first chairman of the Majilis Ulama Indonesia (MUI, the Indonesian Ulama Council), his views were solicited by politicians and scholars alike. Lectures and interviews with radio and television channels were almost daily ritual for him up until his dying years. By the time he died, on 24 July 1981, several books and articles had already been published discussing and honouring Hamka's contributions in so many areas of Muslim life. It is not unwarranted to claim that the history of Muslim thought in Southeast Asia cannot be properly articulated or presented without, at least, a passing reference to Hamka. His commitment to exposing the ramifications of ignorance among Muslims, and the avenues that could take Muslims out of that conundrum, was phenomenal and is rightly remembered.

Hamka personifies the gamut of cutting-edge ideas produced by modern Southeast Asian Muslim intellectuals. It is unfortunate that these ideas are generally disregarded, or otherwise ignored, by scholars researching on global Islam. Such indifference towards the expansive contributions of thinkers outside the Middle East and North African region highlights the jarring gap in the field of Islamic and Muslim studies today. The second-tiering of non-Arab scholars underlines the old Orientalist trope of Islam as, quintessentially, an 'Arab religion'. In such a formulation, all thought that emanates from the 'Arab world' is representative of the entire Islamic world. We need to challenge and remedy such rampant and unproductive conceptions. It is necessary to reposition Southeast Asian Islamic thought so that it resides at the heart of Islamic and Muslims studies, to agitate for the rethinking of Islam in Southeast Asia and elsewhere as equally important and as prolific as that found in the Middle East.

Hamka was particularly attentive to the problem of ignorance in Muslim societies. How was ignorance manifested? Why did it prevail? Who were the agents of ignorance? How did they entrench it? What could be done to overcome ignorance? These are the crucial questions that concerned Hamka in his endeavour to reform a region he called home. A cosmopolitan thinker and reformer, he drew on the works of European scholars which he deployed alongside the Qur'an, hadith, and scholarship from a host of Islamic scholars. He sought to utilise what was germane from these different wellsprings of knowledge to diagnose, critique, and deconstruct ignorance in Muslim societies. This approach was not unique to Hamka. It was common among most modern reformist-thinkers across the Muslim world, including Muhammad Abduh (1849–1905), Muhammad Iqbal (1877–1938), Rashid Rida (1865–1935), Mahmud Shaltut (1893–1963), Ali Shariati (1933–77), Malek Bennabi (1905–73), and Muhammad Natsir (1908–93). For these thinkers, the pathways out of ignorance in the Muslim world was by no means easy. It had to begin with a profound acquaintance with and critical reading of landmark works written by scholars and intellectuals outside the Muslim world and then to judiciously select and harmonise these ideas in the light of sacred sources. Only then could fresh solutions to the crises of thought among Muslims be comprehensively offered.

Hamka elucidated a typology of ignorance that was more palatable to the lay readers and was based on astute observations of his immediate environment. His deliberations were filled with analogies and examples that were appealing to his audiences. In other words, Hamka provided a practical and grounded typology rather than a philosophical one divorced from the harsh reality of actually existing social problems. The master concept he used to describe ignorance was *jahil*. He wrote a thirty-volume commentary of the Qur'an – the *Tafsir Al-Azhar* – where he was attentive to the varying usages and meanings of the word *jahil*. As M. Ashraf Adeel nicely summarises it, the root word j-h-l is used in twenty-four places in the Qur'an.

> The following attitudes or ways of mind are characterized as ignorance in these usages: refusal to accept (even overwhelming) evidence in favor of an idea (6:111), adopting others' customs thoughtlessly (7:138), inability/refusal to see the worth of people because of their (lowly) station (11:29), satisfying desires unnaturally (27:55), lack of openness to evidence combined with arrogance (46:23), thinking other than the truth about God (3:154), false vanity (of tribalism) (5:50), showy behavior (33:33), zealotry (for wrong causes) (48:26), accepting reports of unrighteousness without investigation (49:6), taking unprecedented moral risk beyond one's capacities (at the time of creation) (33:72), lying on behalf of God (2:67), taking the poor to be self-sufficient, i.e., social insensitivity (2:273), misplaced impatience for results (6:35), asking for a favor for your family (from God) without knowing its real meaning (11:46), falling prey to temptation (12:33), harming your brother out of jealousy (12:89), aggressive attitude and arrogance towards the humble (25:63), vain talk or ill speak (28:55), and attributing partners to God (39:64).

Hamka simplifies such complex denotations of ignorance in the Qur'an. This simplification could be motivated by his desire to make plain the effects of ignorance. To be sure, Hamka's writings were, by and large, didactic and performative. Hence, he gave new meanings to typologies developed by medieval Muslim philosophers and theologians who wrote about the challenge of blind-following (*taqlid*) in their societies. The first type of ignorance, Hamka wrote, was 'thin ignorance (*jahil tipis*)' or simple ignorance. The Arabic term for such an ignorance is *jahil basith*. Such ignorance is borne out of a person's low intellectual aptitude and their dearth of experience as well as socialisation. According to Hamka, those with thin ignorance usually have pure souls and sincere hearts. They were open to reminders when they erred. They showed an acute willingness to listen, to learn, and to engage in reasoned discussions because they were aware of their weaknesses. Hamka was not specific about who these people were nor did he name names. We may infer that he was referring to the masses in his milieu. He further divided them into groups. Foremost were those who do not have any stand on things and were thereby easiest to guide. He likened them as 'fertile soil that has not been cultivated or planted'. The second group were

Muslims who held to a mistaken mindset but do not know they were wrong. Using the same analogy, which was familiar to Muslims who were mostly involved in agricultural activities, Hamka described this second group as being akin to a land that was fertile but had overgrown weeds that needed trimming. He criticised this second group for being oblivious of their failings. Like the first group, these people may be open to new knowledge and information even if the process might take years.

The second type of ignorance was far more dangerous than the first. He dwelled extensively on this topic which revealed his trepidation over how such ignorance brought about backwardness in many modern Muslim societies. Hamka termed it as 'thick and layered ignorance (*jahil tebal dan berlapis*)' or, to put it differently, compounded ignorance. Again, this term was taken from Arabic, *jahil murakkab*. Unlike simple ignorance, one who was enveloped by compounded ignorance would be totally averse to any forms of knowledge, advice, and reminders. He is often consumed by his hubris. Two groups of Muslims embodied such compounded ignorance. The less severe group were those who had erroneous presumptions about texts and contexts and may be initially adamant about their standpoints. They took years to change, sometimes achieving this only at the brink of death. The hardcore ones were those that fully discern their ignorance and unjust assumptions but they were unwilling to change. They shun the truth and, for the same reason, were malevolent towards anyone who showed them the truth. They were predisposed to becoming *fasik* (one who violates religious laws and norms). Compounded ignorance as explained by Hamka, parallels with the notion of 'protective ignorance or stupidity' as outlined by George Orwell in *Nineteen Eighty-Four*. Hamka read this and other Orwell's novels which were translated and circulated widely among budding novelists and movement activists in 1950s Indonesia. By protective ignorance, Orwell meant 'the faculty of stopping short, as though by instinct, at the threshold of dangerous thought. It includes the power of not grasping analogies, of failing to perceive logical errors, of misunderstanding the simplest argument....and of being bored or repelled by any train of thought which is capable of leading in a heretical direction'.

For Hamka, the two types of ignorance have affected modern Muslims. Such ignorance did not emerge in a vacuum but rather, it was a product of the schemes of certain agents in society, both local and foreign. The agents of ignorance may not work in tandem with each other. Still, the overall effects of their words and deeds sustained and ensured the continued sway of simple and compounded ignorance so much so that Muslims were unable to think and act rationally. Nor would they seek knowledge as their minds were held captive. Their worldviews remained constricted, their visions truncated, their willpowers broken. This provided the essential foundations for colonisation and exploitation.

Who were the agents responsible for the rise of ignorance? Hamka blamed the *ulama* above all others. His arguments were drawn mostly from his father, Abdul Karim Amrullah, who reprimanded the ulama for their regressive mentality. Hamka equated the ulama, during his time, with the priests in Christian churches during the Dark Ages of Europe. They were dictatorial and claimed the sole right to interpret religious texts. They blocked access to many areas of knowledge by issuing edicts that outlawed the teaching of philosophical sciences. Their justification for such moves was that the masses would be led astray if they were overly reflexive about their own faith. We can detect here the influence of Francis Bacon (1561-1626). Hamka mentioned Bacon among the many European philosophers that influenced him. In *The New Organon*, Bacon wrote: 'finally you will find that some theologians in their ignorance completely block access to any philosophy....No wonder the growth of natural philosophy has been inhibited, since religion, which has the most enormous power over men's minds, has been kidnapped by the ignorance and reckless zeal of certain persons, and made to join the side of the enemy.' Hamka added that 'the threats that came with the closing of the doors to learning philosophical sciences was intellectual lethargy and being lost in an age of change'. Most ulama in the Malay world, Hamka exclaimed, were *ketinggalan zaman* (archaic), a stinging criticism that resonated with the views of the Egyptian thinker Rashid Rida (1865–1935) on the sterility and ignorance of the ulama in the modern age. Hamka drew a great deal of inspiration from the writings of Rashid Rida, especially the *Tafsir Al-Manar*, for his own exegetical works.

However, the ulama did more than block access to knowledge. Hamka castigated them for corrupting knowledge to keep the masses subservient to them. Instead of encouraging the growth and formulation of new ideas, they taught their students to be uncritical and remain ignorant of the deeper intents of Islamic legal and ethical codes. Hamka's critique of the ulama was obviously directed toward the followers of the Nahdlatul Ulama (Awakening of the Ulama), which was an organisation of traditionalist Muslim scholars founded in 1926. Until the 1970s, the leaders of Nahdlatul Ulama upheld the practice of *taqlid*. They discouraged the use of reason in discussing matters pertaining to Islam and relied heavily on the interpretations of selected eminent scholars that were in line with the conservative views. Their approach to Islamic texts was motivated largely by their desire to entrench their intellectual authority rather than the pursuit of higher truths. Consequently, reformist and modernist writers in Indonesia tended to scathingly describe the Nahdlatul Ulama as 'a herd of buffalo in tow'. In other words, Hamka censured the ulama, to use the words of Daniel DeNicola, for being culpable of 'strategic ignorance' which involves 'gaming the system, in that the individual who chooses ignorance for strategic reasons often has more than an inkling of the content of the information being refused'.

The roots of the ignorance of the ulama, according to Hamka, was found in their understanding of the verses of the Qur'an and the functions of the scripture. In *Tafsir Al-Azhar*, he gave the example of how most traditional ulama misinterpreted verse 21:7 in the Qur'an. The verse reads, 'and We did not send before you any but men to whom We sent revelation, so ask the people of knowledge if you do not know'. The ulama used this verse as a rationale for the closing of the Muslim mind. They contended that the Qur'an, the hadith, and the works of the past ulama had everything that the Muslims needed to survive in the modern world. No other avenues of learning was necessary. To Hamka, the view that the Qur'an and other Islamic sources were the only useful sources of knowledge, contradicted the spirit of Islam. Many verses in the Qur'an encourage thinking, learning, pondering, reflecting, and travelling in search of wisdom. In choosing to ignore such Qur'anic injunctions, the ulama constructed an intellectual barrier that kept the masses beholden to them. The masses became unremittingly averse to all useful domains of knowledge, beginning with the Greeks, the Chinese, the Indians, and the advances in thought and philosophies coming from the West.

Moreover, the ulama stressed that only *they* could understand the verses of the Qur'an and that the masses must steer clear of any attempt at appreciating the scripture. The ulama propagated a narrow version of Islam and its sacred sources arguing that 'the words corresponding to "Knowledge" and "Wisdom" in the Quran relate to religious knowledge and religious wisdom only'. Hamka argued otherwise. The 'people of knowledge' (*ahladz zikri*) in that verse were not only the ulama which all Muslims should follow blindly. It includes any persons of knowledge who had expanded the frontiers of knowledge and who had made the masses more acquainted with the divine. More importantly, the keyword in 21:7 is 'ask' (*fas'alu*). Muslims must probe and ask those with knowledge until they too became knowledgeable. The same keyword suggests that to be ignorant is not an option.

Despotic states were another factor that contributed to the two types of ignorance in Muslim societies. Hamka exposed states' strategy at imbibing ignorance to maintain their control over the populace. The kingdoms which used to rule over Southeast Asia for centuries were guilty of manufacturing ignorance. Both they and succeeding colonial and postcolonial states co-opted the ulama and the intelligentsia through rewards of lofty titles and positions. These literate elites then made pronouncements and issued religious edicts that served to further weaken Muslim minds. They hid the truth, justified oppression, validated authoritarianism, and labelled anyone who strove to enlighten public minds as deviant. Hamka added that the defeatist posturing of these literate elites had tainted their teachings. By teaching the Muslim masses asceticism that rejected worldly success, they mandated rulers and states absolute authority and allowed ignorance to reign supreme. The masses were left uneducated, uninformed, and subjected to indoctrination. In Southeast Asia, this situation lasted for centuries.

The colonial and postcolonial states, in Hamka's eyes, kept Muslims mired in ignorance through education. Hamka showed how, through books written by Orientalists and ultra-nationalists as well as teachers in schools, education steered the Muslims away from seeing Islam as an essential part of their traditions. Muslims educated in these schools looked at their religion and their societies either in neutral terms without a sense of commitment and responsibility, or in disdain. These emasculated Muslims became ignorant of their heritage and identity. They prided themselves as more progressive than the pious ones and equated piety to fanaticism. It was however ironic, Hamka writes, that the families of these westernised Muslims would call upon the 'fanatics' to pray for their deceased loved ones during funeral services because they were ignorant of the litanies.

How then can simple and compound ignorance in Muslim societies be unmade? Hamka acknowledged that transformations at all levels must occur for the masses to be more enlightened. Those in positions of authority can effect such changes by pursuing the agenda of producing societies that are populated with *ulul al-bab* or men and women who are 'conscious of and maximize their rational faculties to delve into domains that are congruent with their respective talents'. Above and beyond the roles of the powerful, Hamka poured hopes on socially engaged intellectuals. They can shape minds through written works, the media, and grassroots activism. Hamka appealed to them to inculcate in all Muslims guided reason (*akal yang berpedoman*); basically a type of reasoning directed by revelation through the sacred sources of Islam, by good character, and by adapting to changing contexts, as well as by new understandings of how life as human beings should be practised and lived.

The Qur'an and hadith, Hamka maintained, encourage Muslim to think, imagine, and explore all sorts of knowledge about the world. These texts call for the eschewing of all sorts of irrational and outmoded traditions. Muslims are enjoined to explain the laws governing God's creation through postulation, observation, and experimentation. The Qur'an and hadith forbid humankind from following those who promote ignorance. But reason alone cannot comprehend everything. Hamka was against the preponderant idea during his time that science could uncover all secrets of the universe. There are limits to scientific reasoning and yet these limits should not hinder Muslims from delving into incisive research in all fields of study. Hamka explained,

> The more advanced our thinking and knowledge become, the more we are amazed by the strange and incredible laws or order that is found in nature. Our knowledge can only uncover the laws of nature. But we are unable to create something better than nature itself. We can only devise new arrangements, without departing radically from the original laws of nature. From whichever doors we may enter! Be it through logic or through higher mathematics. From geometry or chemistry, and from anywhere else.

In addition, Hamka saw guided reason as a form of rationality that is directed by the exigencies of changing contexts and constant encounters with new knowledge. He believed that people with sound minds must be sensitive to the changes in the world around them. A person with guided reason will not be mentally stagnant or allow his or her mind to be enslaved by totalitarian ideologies, retrogressive habits, outmoded customs, and stagnated traditions that have no relevance in an ever-changing world. This is why the Qur'an describes human beings as the vicegerents of God on earth. Guided by their rational faculties and their sensitivity to their shifting surroundings, human beings can gain mastery over nature and society. To shape their realities, people have to embrace what Hamka called 'the liberty to exercise *itjihad* which includes the freedom to think and the freedom to articulate thought'. While some scholars of Islamic jurisprudence define *ijtihad*, as Imran Nyazee states, 'as an activity, a struggle, a process to discover the law from the texts and to apply it to the set of facts awaiting decision.' Hamka viewed *ijtihad* as more than just a tool for deriving laws. That was a specialised form of *ijtihad* in which scholars from different disciplines would deliberate extensively and consult one another to formulate new laws and frames of reference for emerging challenges. Such *ijtihad* was, to him, imperative. But he also regarded *ijtihad* as the ability to reason based on a comprehensive understanding of texts and contexts encountered by individual Muslims in their struggles to deal with the problems they faced in their lives. It was therefore a 'personal *ijtihad*' meant to resolve the challenges of daily life and to keep Muslims dynamic and guided in their thinking.

Hamka's sapient reflections on the ignorance that has affected modern Muslims deserve our fullest attention. By putting into sharp relief the two types of ignorance – simple and compound – what he had done was to provoke both the scholarly class and the laity to reflect over their shortcomings in the road to recover the culture of learning and knowing in the Muslim civilisation. We are poised to question: what more could be done to address and remedy the state of ignorance in contemporary Muslim societies? For Hamka, it all begins with the pen, which to him, is the mighty sword that can cut into the heart of ignorance and demolish its incarnations.

PAKISTAN'S CONSTITUTIONAL TURNS

Raza Ali

We start at the beginning. The founder of Pakistan, Muhammad Ali Jinnah, also known to Pakistanis as Quaid-e-Azam (the great leader), in his first address to the constituent assembly of the nascent country, said some words that I can easily call his most well-known. He spoke to a gathering whose job was to write the constitution of Pakistan on 11 August 1947.

> You are free; you are free to go to your temples, you are free to go to your mosques or to any other place of worship in this State of Pakistan. You may belong to any religion or caste or creed – that has nothing to do with the business of the State...We are starting in the days where there is no discrimination, no distinction between one community and another, no discrimination between one caste or creed and another. We are starting with this fundamental principle: that we are all citizens, and equal citizens, of one State... Now I think we should keep that in front of us as our ideal, and you will find that in course of time Hindus would cease to be Hindus, and Muslims would cease to be Muslims, not in the religious sense, because that is the personal faith of each individual, but in the political sense as citizens of the State.

Anyone reading this would immediately get a sense of secularism in these words. A promise from the founder, that this land will be a land of equal opportunity, of equal treatment, to all faiths and all castes, as equal citizens. A lofty vision to launch a country with. Any modern reader would be filled with a heart-warming feeling that the founders had such a forward-looking and progressive view of this nation to be. A thousand angels fill the air with uplifting songs as the words are spoken. But was that situation really that rosy?

In December 2013, a column appeared in a popular Urdu newspaper by a right-wing Islamist columnist and playwright. Orya Maqbool Jaan claimed that these words were never uttered; that the speech never existed! He looked at the 12 August 1947 edition of the newspaper *Civil & Military Gazette*, which by all accounts was a 'secular' newspaper, founded and run by the British. Apart from run of the mill coverage of the event, there was nothing special in it. The famous sentences that were separating Islam and State, that are hyped up so much by the secularists, are nowhere to be found in it. He claims that it was a lie and a hoax perpetrated on the nation. As evidence, he states that in his last speech on 1 July 1948, Jinnah asked the State Bank to formulate policies on Islamic principles. He also cites that no recording of this speech is available. Third, the claim that it was published by the newspaper *Dawn* on 12 August is incorrect, as its offices in Delhi burned down a few months back. His main source for this assertion is *Secular Jinnah & Pakistan:What the Nation Doesn't Know* by the little-known writer Salena Karim, which debunks Jinnah's secular stance. Sounds like a moon-landing conspiracy.

According to A.H. Nayyar, there was an attempt to censor this speech from the beginning and it was not discussed publicly for decades in Pakistan. It came out of its dusty archives in the eighties to support the struggle to resist General Zia-ul-Haq's attempt to Islamise Pakistan. Journalist Zamir Niazi, in his book *Press in Chains*, details the attempts to censor this speech. He quotes from Jinnah's biographer, Hector Bolitho, that he worked on this speech for hours. Establishing the significance and attention given to each word used. Niazi says that as soon as Jinnah left after giving this speech, covert hands were active in attempts to change the speech. He quotes from an article written by Hamid Jalal in the weekly *Viewpoint*, that the establishment gave 'advice' to the press to not publish those parts of the speech, as it conflicted with the 'Ideology of Pakistan'. The then editor of *Dawn*, Altaf Hussain, threatened to take it up with Jinnah himself and they backed off and allowed them to publish. The case of newspaper offices burning down can be fact-checked as well. The report can be seen in the archives of *Dawn*, on 20 September 1947, that the office was attacked on 11 September, long after the speech, the fire was controlled and 'the damage to the *Dawn* Office that night was not much'.

While the *Civil & Military Gazette* did not publish the speech, the newspaper, *The Hindu*, did.

These attempts to suppress the speech continued in later decades and represented the Pakistani establishment's uneasy relationship with its minorities and its clash with their own ideological goals. In a *Guardian* article, Jon Boone interviews Murtaza Solangi about his attempts to locate the audio recording of that speech. Solangi was appointed the Director General of *Radio Pakistan*, the state-owned radio channel, by the last secular government of the People's Party. *Radio Pakistan* apparently has a complete collection of Jinnah's speeches, except this one. And no one else has a copy. He reached out to the *BBC* and *All India Radio* (*AIR*) for it without success. *The Hindu* reports that at the time of this speech, *AIR*, which was the primary radio channel of the territory, was responsible for recording it. AIR had three radio stations in Pakistan, east and west, but the west Pakistan stations did not have recording facilities. So, a team had to be sent from Delhi to record this inaugural speech. Other attempts to trace the recording also bore no fruit.

Whether Pakistan was going to be an inclusive, secular country or an Islamic state with second class non-Muslim citizens, one thing was clear: it was going to be democratic. Jinnah made that clear numerous times and clearly denied any intention for it to be some theocratic state. Democracy had to be the assumed system in Pakistan, and all its constitution-making, but it continues to be a journey to get there. In that journey lie multiple military coups and martial laws. Jinnah was speaking to the constituent assembly in 1947, but it took nine years for the first constitution of Pakistan to appear. A document that would represent the contract between Muslim and non-Muslim citizen alike, with the state of Pakistan.

The history of constitution-making in Pakistan has gone through four events: The Objectives Resolution, the first constitution of 1956, the constitution of 1962, and the constitution of 1973. The Objectives Resolution has some controversy around it, but it forms the guiding principles behind all the subsequent constitutions. It was introduced by the first Prime Minister of Pakistan, Liaquat Ali Khan in March 1949. The Objectives Resolution had a key article that 'sovereignty belonged to God'. These words in Pakistan are seen as a kind of struggle between the authority of God and the people as lawmakers. The Islamists, such as Abul

A'la Maududi, have always championed God as the lawmaker, but this creates practical confusion. The late noted Muslim scholar, Fazlur Rahman, explained this confusion:

> While, therefore, making a compromise under the pressure from the rightists, the modernist in reality succumbed to the conceptual framework of the rightists inasmuch as he accepted 'God's Sovereignty' rather than asserting, as he should have done in honesty, that sovereignty belongs to the people of Pakistan, who, being consciously Muslims, willed that Islam be implemented in Pakistani society both at the individual and the collective level...Thus, when the Constitution of Pakistan talks about the Sovereignity of God, it commits sheer confusion under the impact of revivalists and the rightists in general who had little idea of the modern concept of political sovereignity.

The tensions between right-wing Islamists and secularists developed from the very beginning. Before the first constitution could be produced, Liaquat Ali Khan was assassinated in October 1951. Two Prime Ministers changed by the time of the first draft arrived in October 1954. Before its presentation, the Governor General dissolved the government. The dissolution was taken to the courts and the court upheld it, setting a precedent for many such dismissals to come later. In 1955, another assembly was formed to take on the job and it included the decision to have parity between East and West Pakistan, even though the East wing had a greater population. And so, the first constitution was produced in 1956.

We move on to the next phase. The government is structured according to the constitution from the previous phase, but only two years later, in 1958, the president Iskandar Mirza abrogated the constitution, dissolved the democratic setup, and declared martial law.

With the words:

> The constitution, which was brought into being on 23rd March, 1956 after so many tribulations, is unworkable. It is full of dangerous compromises that will soon disintegrate Pakistan internally if the inherent malaise is not removed. To rectify them the country must first be taken to sanity by a peaceful revolution, then it is my intention to collect a team of patriotic persons to examine our problems in the political field and devise a constitution more suitable to the genius of the Muslim people. When it is ready at the appropriate time it will be submitted to the referendum of the people...

General Ayub Khan is brought in as the Martial Law Administrator. But he quickly realises that he does not need Iskandar Mirza, removes him, and takes over. He appoints another commission to write the constitution in 1960. As opposed to the previous one, the aim here was to create a presidential system instead of a parliamentary one. In 1962, this new model was implemented but it too turned out to be short-lived. Strangely it also takes a curious 'Islamic' turn, on which Fazlur Rahman comments:

> The 1962 constitution, on the other hand, not only charged the Advisory Council of Islamic Ideology with the Islamization of law but also called upon it to make recommendations for the Islamization of life and also examine and evaluate legislation in progress from the Islamic point of view (something which the 1956 Constitution completely ignored).

What does a secularist like Ayub Khan, known for his love of drink, have to do with Islamisation? It is a mystery. But, as troubles continue between East and West Pakistan, top-down authoritarian governance, and democratic freedoms, Ayub Khan resigns, the constitution is abrogated again, and martial law is imposed again. General Yahya Khan takes over and conducts the famous elections of 1970. Things could have turned for the better, if the democrats, Zulfiqar Ali Bhutto from West Pakistan and Sheikh Mujibur Rahman from East Pakistan, stuck to democracy. But the country was polarised. Due to these 'grave political differences' and a military operation to maintain control over the Eastern wing, Pakistan breaks up in 1971 and Bangladesh is born. A partition, soon after a partition. Ironically, the partition did not come about as a result of the 1956 constitution as Iskandar told us, but due to the imposition of martial law that he initiated.

The Objectives Resolution has the article: 'wherein the principles of democracy, freedom, equality, tolerance and social justice as enunciated by Islam shall be fully observed'. With such a guiding light, how could Bangladesh have happened? Explaining the various reasons, which included political, economic, regional, social, and cultural, historian G.W. Choudhry writes:

> After the fall of Ayub, General Yahya made a number of gestures to try and win the confidence of the Bengalis. He allowed free and fair elections on the basis of 'one man, one vote', and Mujib won an absolute majority. Yahya also acknowledged the fact that the Bengalis had no share in decision-making

processes and that this state of affairs must be ended. But these measures were too late. Another analogy can be made with the period of British rule. In the 1940s, the Congress tried to make a number of concessions to Jinnah and the Muslims. But by that time the Muslims had already decided to have a separate state. Similarly, the scheme for a transfer of power as formulated by Yahya in 1969 was too late; the Bengalis had already decided to have a state of their own.

After the break-up of Pakistan, Zulfiqar Ali Bhutto became the president 'as well as the first civil Chief Martial Law Administrator'. The authoritarian streak was so strong within the Pakistani establishment that even after this 'second partition' and the bad decisions of the past two decades, this role-playing game did not stop. Another Constitution Committee was formed in 1972, which prepared the third constitution, which was presented and unanimously passed in 1973. This is where our journey of making new constitutions ends. There have been many amendments since then, but that was the last one to be created. This constitution returned Pakistan to the parliamentary form of government. Just because the parliamentary system was back did not mean that we will learn a lesson from our experiences. History continues to repeat itself in the 'Groundhog Day' that is the Pakistani experience. The debates to return to a presidential form of government still happen in 2022. Writing in *Dawn*, journalist Fahad Hussain says:

This latest debate on the presidential system — choreographed or otherwise — is as useless as the one before that, and the one before that. It is useless because it misdiagnoses what ails our governance, and more importantly, who ails our governance. It is in fact depressing to realise that after all these decades the only lesson we have learnt from our presidentials and their choir boys, and the parliamentarians and their chorus girls, is that we have learnt no lesson. But then, you already knew that.

Just because democracy returned to Pakistan, does not mean that it was going to stay that way. A key article that was added in the 1973 constitution was Article 6, on abrogation of the constitution. It reads:

6) High treason

(1)   Any person who abrogates or subverts or suspends or holds in
abeyance, or attempts or conspires to abrogate or subvert or suspend or hold
in abeyance, the Constitution by use of force or show of force or by any other
unconstitutional means shall be guilty of high treason.

This was clearly a product of the constitutional upheaval over the past
few decades – an added deterrent to anyone thinking of breaking the
constitution again. But Article 6 did not prevent future abrogation of the
constitution. It did not take very long, after the last constitution, when
Zulfiqar Ali Bhutto ran into problems with his own authoritarian style of
government. He announced early elections, which were not accepted by
the opposition and General Zia-ul-Haq abrogated the constitution and
imposed martial law. Yet again we had a president in charge. Elections were
held on a non-party basis and assemblies were restored but the power was
held by the president.

This was formalised into official constitutional power with the
introduction of Article 58(2)b, which empowered the president to dissolve
parliament at their discretion. And this article will get used multiple times
by presidents in a bizarre 'game of thrones', until it was removed by the
13th Amendment. In yet another round, General Parvez Musharraf
overthrew the government of Nawaz Sharif in 1999, held the constitution
'in abeyance', and suspended parliament. He initially entered as a Chief
Executive but later became President, and so the power was back in the
hands of one. A National Security Council was established, and one of its
goals was 'to achieve the aims and objectives as enshrined in the Objectives
Resolution 1949'.

We now return to the Objectives Resolution and the cyclical form of
history that governs Pakistan. But I want to look at some of the freedoms that
are promised as fundamental rights, in the constitution of Pakistan and how
they have played out in its history. Article 19 of the constitution states that:

19. Every citizen shall have the right to freedom of speech and
expression, and there shall be freedom of the press, subject to any
reasonable restrictions imposed by law in the interest of the glory of
Islam or the integrity, security or defence of Pakistan or any part thereof,

friendly relations with foreign States, public order, decency or morality, or in relation to contempt of court, [commission of] or incitement to an offence.

In regard to this, three periods are particularly noticeable, namely, the Martial Law of General Zia-ul-Haq, the 'War on Terror' years, and, oddly and surprisingly, the years of Imran Khan's latest government – during which no war is taking place and on technical grounds, it was a democratic government. This is not to say that before Zia, freedom of expression looked any better. As we have seen earlier, suppression of the press and efforts to concoct a specific narrative out of it have been going on from day one. Even the founding fathers of the nation were not exempt from it. Yet, some periods have had special significance.

Far too much has already been said about the Zia years in Pakistan and there is plenty of literature available on it. The Zia years perfected the art of pre-censorship; employing draconian laws to control what was being said. Veteran journalist Zamir Niazi's *The Press in Chains* is a good account of the challenges. Journalists were arrested and flogged, print newspaper editions were blanked and redacted wherever content appeared that was not in accordance with the policies of the state.

The 'War on Terror' years were a different beast altogether. All the tools were already in the tool chest but on top of it, there was a deadly war going on in Afghanistan and numerous terrorism incidents happening within Pakistan. The stakes were already too high and there was little room for manoeuvre. These were, roughly, the years 2002-2016. According to the Committee to Protect Journalists (CJP), as many as eighty-nine journalists were killed during this period. And the United Nations declared Pakistan 'the most dangerous country in the world' for journalists. So, Pakistani journalism fell under extreme repression and found itself in a deadly environment. What more could happen? As it happened, the ceiling was nowhere in sight.

A new, multi-dimensional brand of press suppression was later put in place. While the government in front was led by Imran Khan, the media at no point believed this to be the case. In a barely veiled manner, the military establishment was simultaneously ruling the country and making policies. One had to witness the bizarre spectacle. At one moment the information minister of the state would give a press conference and then the military spokesman would hold their own press conference. The public was hearing constantly from two sides – two concurrent, parallel governments.

In this new 'hybrid' model, journalists were still being killed. The CJP database reports that seven journalists were killed during the period 2018–2022. Far too many at a time when there was no active war or terrorism taking place. But what was different was the way the two different streams – authoritarian suppression and populist suppression – met and created a doubly toxic environment. The authoritarian suppression used all the tactics that have been matured by governments, intelligence agencies, and the military establishment in the past. The advertisements and funding of media houses were squeezed, their channels were taken off-air, moved on to the cable network numberings to cause confusion, journalists were muzzled or employers compelled to fire them from their channels if they refused to comply. The media suppression during the military dictatorship of General Zia set the gold standard, but one would have to be unusually extreme to beat that record. But, Imran Khan's government accomplished just that incredible feat:

> Journalists, activists, authors and politicians spoke to the *Guardian* of a climate of 'extreme fear and self-censorship', and the suppression of opposition political voices, even worse than during the military dictatorship of General Zia, who oppressively ruled Pakistan between 1977 and 1988.

I could dwell further on this and talk about how journalist after journalist was picked up, roughed up, even shot, and killed. Or, how Pakistan stands at 157 out of 180 in the current Press Freedom Index ranking put out by Reporters Without Borders. But there is a more advanced and sinister attack on journalism in Pakistan that we must appreciate. This comes from the populist narrative of Imran Khan, mimicking the on-going populist nightmare we are witnessing across the world from Thailand, India, Turkey, eastern Europe, and Latin America to the United States itself. This narrative polarises the population, and divides journalists between good and evil. There is really no room for the middle ground. Either you support and legitimise the government and its policies, or you are a sell-out, working for the corrupt internal enemy or the ruthless foreign conspiring one. You must choose; to be a patriot or to be a traitor.

This is not a polemic. These are the words heard every day, on TV channels, on social media posts and videos, and among the public at large. Every family has a WhatsApp group these days. I have been reading and hearing this on my own family group every day for the past few years. The population has been transformed. They are angry and they are fed a precise narrative, endlessly repeated to the point that everything else in their harsh light pales in comparison. A powerful manipulation technique that was perfected by Imran's government. Because the general population is usually not capable of physically suppressing journalists, they resort to other tactics, mainly social media harassment. I was astonished to see people in my own family, who did not have a Twitter account, join Twitter, just so they could go online and abuse people who were speaking against Imran Khan!

Male journalists are generally able to handle this abuse, but female journalists have had a much harder time dealing with it. A 2020 report in *Dawn* talks about the experiences of female journalists where they were trolled in an orchestrated and organised way, by the governing party. Apart from general accusations and psychological abuse, there can also be specific misogynistic threats as made clear by a statement prepared by the women journalists:

> the online attacks were instigated by government officials and then amplified by a large number of Twitter accounts, 'which declare their affiliation to the ruling party'... According to the declaration, personal details of women journalists and analysts had been made public as part of a 'well-defined and coordinated campaign' while in some cases, their pictures and videos had also been morphed... In addition, they were referred to as peddlers of 'fake news', 'enemy of the people' and accused of taking bribes in order to discredit and intimidate the journalists, it said... The persons involved in the campaign also targeted the journalists for their gender, posting gender-based slurs and threats of sexual and physical violence on their social media timelines.

Let us switch our attention to a different form of free expression, the freedom to be a free person, unafraid of being 'picked up' and disappearing without a trace. The Constitution of Pakistan says in Article 10(2):

> (2) Every person who is arrested and detained in custody shall be produced before a magistrate within a period of twenty-four hours of such arrest,

excluding the time necessary for the journey from the place of arrest to the court of the nearest magistrate, and no such person shall be detained in custody beyond the said period without the authority of a magistrate.

This is the norm in all civilised countries. The constitution grants this right to the ordinary citizen of Pakistan but, particularly since the days of the 'war on terror', there has been a pandemic of people going 'missing' in Pakistan. Unidentified people would come and pick someone up from their home or place of work and no one knows where they went or what became of them. No one can even talk about it. People at the highest level could lose their job if they tried to raise the question. This was seen in the case of Iftikhar Chaudhry, Chief Justice of the Supreme Court, during the Musharraf era. He was deposed for misconduct, but he had also taken up the cases of 'missing persons'. Things have not changed much since then. Many of the missing are still missing, some have been 'traced' and some have been assumed dead.

In 2018, the Muslim Institute's Sixth Annual Ibn Rushd Lecture in London featured the Pakistani journalist Mohammad Hanif. He is famous for his novel, *A Case of Exploding Mangoes*, loosely based on the reign of General Zia. But in that presentation, he had a different topic, the case of the 'missing persons':

> Baloch started disappearing first, then Sindhi activists, then Shias, then young men from Karachi, then God-fearing patriotic citizens from Lahore and my home town Okara too. Many of them were political activists, separatists we call them and the state told us, they were anti-state and not good enough Muslims and the state denied having anything to do with their abductions. But amongst the missing, there were lots of people, who were very good Muslims. Who were ready to kill us, or get killed, in order to make us slightly better Muslims…In Urdu, we struggled what to call these people? We said, '*la pata afraad*', which basically means 'lost people'. It sounds as if they were coming home and took a wrong turn and lost their way…We in the media in Pakistan pretended that nothing was happening…then the families of those missing started appearing at our doorsteps…they set up camps outside press clubs, where journalists often hang out…These families had pana-flexes, with the names and pictures of their missing…asking the same questions day after day. 'But where is my son?'. 'What have you done with him?'. 'Why don't you put him on trial?'.

Hanif cites two cases, one of Sabine Mahmood and the other of Mama Qadeer. Sabine was a social activist from Karachi, who created this little hangout called The Second Floor. I had the pleasure of meeting her there myself. It was an odd and eclectic place with random art, and they organised music, talks, lectures, and discussions. One such discussion was with Mama Qadeer. He was a 'missing persons' rights activist. Soon after that, she gets shot, in her car, outside the same place. Qadeer as a demonstration of protest, walked 1,200 miles between 2013 and 2014, from Quetta the capital of Balochistan province, to the federal capital of Islamabad. When he tried to speak at LUMS (Lahore University of Management Sciences), one of the top universities in Pakistan, the event was forcefully called off by the military authorities. Sabine's event followed this cancellation, and it was called 'Unsilencing Balochistan' (Take 2). The things that happen in Balochistan have dangerous vibes. Vibes we had felt from East Pakistan, before it broke away from West Pakistan. So, this topic makes authorities nervous. Breaking the constitution never makes them nervous.

We return to the Objectives Resolution and its words, 'wherein the principles of democracy, freedom, equality, tolerance and social justice as enunciated by Islam shall be fully observed'. The words social justice became the driving force behind Imran Khan's campaign to bring back *Riyasat-e-Madina* (The State of Medina). It is an idealised conception of what Prophet Muhammad and his companions had established in Medina 1,400 years ago. An imaginary place where there was complete social justice and one had difficulty finding someone to give charity to. This place, for all practical purposes, never existed. The 'state', especially the 'nation-state', is a modern concept. What existed then was a government over a territory with a loose boundary. Prophet Muhammad became the leader and ruler of Medina, but his years there were very tough. Things became better after the conquest of Mecca, but he died soon after. His companions expanded this territory far and wide, and the government was called a Caliphate, delegated from God to man, and from the Prophet to his companions. It was slowly organised but remained a tumultuous business. In its organisation, it was more like a presidential system, with governors ruling over different territories.

When everything one needs is written in the constitution, invoking an imaginary concept like the State of Medina is nothing but political sloganeering. Imran was borrowing from the Islamists. They were there from the beginning of Pakistan and steadily asking for a more 'Islamic' state. Their interpretation of the Objectives Resolution also hinted at this, but it did not hold up consistently. Fazlur Rahman captured that inconsistency of Islamists:

> When it enunciates the principles of 'Islamic social justice' and 'freedom, equality and tolerance in accordance with the teachings of Islam', such statements are Janus-faced. To the Modernist they mean values that are valid in the progressive liberal modern societies and which, in his view, Islam stood for in its pure and pristine teaching; to the revivalist, secondly, they mean values as acted upon in the early history of Islam (implying the Muslim community's special status as distinguished from non-Muslims). It should be noted that Mawdudi explicitly affirmed his conviction in the status on non-Muslims as Dhimmis [protected minority].

Imran was simultaneously and in a contradictory manner using religious language of the Islamist along with the progressive interpretation of the Modernist, as described by Fazlur Rahman. That was not going to work, just as it has not in the past. It was only good as an opportunistic move, to use Islam to give Muslims of Pakistan something Islamic to look forward to. To add Islamic credentials to, otherwise, simply a political project. Rather than engaging in the misuse of Islam, if one just sticks to delivering the provisions of the constitution and focuses on bringing the promises made in the constitution to fruition, one may have a better chance to making a difference to the lives of the ordinary citizen of Pakistan. But, as some say, the constitution is just a piece of paper.

MEMORY CENSORED

Anna Gunin

The past. Each of us has a rich and complex personal history. The word itself denotes that which has gone, elapsed – and yet the past continues to shape us and live within us. We dwell on the past; our perception of the world is coloured by it. Sometimes we yearn to return to a bygone era – nostalgia has a powerful grip on the human mind. And at other times we long to obliterate the past. Memory can be a prison, a source of trauma. Or it can offer a wellspring of comfort, a release from the present, sustaining us in difficult times with the hope of something happier. And alongside our individual pasts, we also carry a collective past. The body of memories shared by our family, our community, the societal groups we belong to.

The adage 'History is written by the victors' is commonly attributed to Winston Churchill. In fact, the sentiment predates Churchill, with pronouncements closely resembling it made by various people in the nineteenth century. There can be no doubting that collective memory is of immense political importance, shaping how members of a society conceptualise the past. In totalitarian systems, the government will maintain a tight control on historical narratives, dictating the memories that are allowed in schools and universities, the press and the public domain.

The deliberate erasure of a people's collective memory is called historicide. During the twentieth century, the USSR engaged in historicide on several fronts. Under Joseph Stalin's rule, the Soviet authorities would designate individuals undesirable, sending them to the firing squad or the concentration-camp network known as the Gulag. They also persecuted entire social classes, professions deemed ideologically inimical, and minority ethnicities. Top members of the Party could become pariahs overnight, and this would lead not only to their arrest, but also to the erasure of their faces from the official photographs and the school textbooks. If a person was declared an 'enemy of the people', the consequences for the other members of their family would be devastating. There was a high chance the spouse would be sent to the Gulag and their children brought up in an orphanage. The Stalinist state followed an official policy of separating brothers and sisters with the purpose of severing family ties. These children would come under intense pressure to forget their own parentage. Their surnames were frequently changed, thus making it difficult for the parents who survived the Gulag and were released to trace their own children.

In such times, the mere writing of a diary would be fraught with danger. The acclaimed Soviet writer Yuri Nagibin, who lived from 1920–1994, buried one of his stories in a box in the forest. Over the course of thirty years, he would periodically dig up the box, take out the manuscript and retype it on fresh paper, before putting it back in the box to be reburied. Nagibin began writing a diary in 1942 and continued adding to it until 1986. It only became safe to have his diary published when the Soviet Union fell in the 1990s; by the time the diary finally came out in 1996, Nagibin was no longer alive.

My husband Alexander is Russian. He was born in the USSR. Alexander attended a Soviet school named after Pavlik Morozov, a boy who achieved fame through denouncing his own father to the secret police. As in all Soviet schools, the curriculum was taught through the prism of Marxist-Leninist ideology. In parallel with his history lessons at school, Alexander also learnt an alternative history at home from his grandmother, who had lived through the October Revolution, the Civil War, Stalin's Purges and the German occupation of their city during World War II. As a child, she kept a diary, recording the dramatic moments her family underwent: the arrest of her father by the Bolsheviks and his later release; the execution by firing squad of one of her brothers; detailed stories of how the Bolshevik Red Terror affected their daily lives. One day, in the early 1920s, one of her brothers discovered her diary and flung it into the stove. Had it been found during a search of their home, the whole family would have been placed in grave danger. And yet the act of recording her memories on paper helped Alexander's grandmother to recall those scenes with clarity well into old age. She would tell these stories to Alexander when he was a boy, thus keeping alive their family history. In many Soviet families, however, the generation who had survived Stalin's repressions were so terrified of sharing anything even slightly subversive that they would maintain total silence even in the privacy of their own homes with their own children and grandchildren.

While collectivisation, the brutal persecution of the prosperous peasant class known as the kulaks and the Stalinist purges affected people across the entire Soviet Union, there were also policies aimed more narrowly at particular ethnicities. Along with other areas on the fringes of the historic Russian Empire, Ukraine had been a hotbed of resistance to Bolshevik rule. In 1876, under the decree of Tsar Alexander II, books and newspapers in the Ukrainian language had been banned. The restrictions were lifted after the Russian Revolution of 1905, and Ukrainian national consciousness began to prosper. Following the 1917 October Revolution, the new Communist masters in Moscow were facing a growing threat from Ukrainian aspirations for independent rule. In 1933–34, an artificially created famine that later became known as the Holodomor (meaning in Ukrainian 'the extermination by hunger') took place. Laws were brought in making it a punishable offence to store even a few ears of grain from the harvest, and soldiers would inspect people's homes, searching for hidden food. Blacklisted villages were encircled by troops, placing the inhabitants under siege and condemning them to starvation. Cases of cannibalism began occurring, and horrific scenes unfolded, as areas of rural and urban Ukraine were slowly depopulated. Memories of the Holodomor, alternatively named the Terror Famine, were strictly taboo.

My husband's friend Zhenya was born in Kyiv in 1980. He remembers how his maternal grandmother would cry whenever she spoke of 'the Hunger'. She used to curse Stalin as 'a total demon'. Due to the pervasive Soviet propaganda which in those days under Leonid Brezhnev was already softening its stance on Stalin, Zhenya's mother refused to believe the horrors depicted by her own mother, instead thinking her stories must be heavily exaggerated. Meanwhile, Zhenya's paternal grandmother only spoke of Communism in glowing terms, but when the Perestroika reforms were brought in, she began to recall memories from her early life that had been suppressed for decades, such as the occasion during another famine in 1947 when a Party activist requisitioning food had even confiscated a scarf she was sitting on, snatching it from right under her. The trauma of the Holodomor slowly induced in many Ukrainians a fear of speaking Ukrainian and identifying with Ukrainian culture. Over the decades, Ukrainians gradually assimilated into the dominant Russian culture, many families switching entirely to the Russian language. This process was actively encouraged by the authorities, who would pay teachers who taught in Russian a higher salary than those teaching in Ukrainian. Zhenya recalls being frightened to speak Ukrainian on the streets in the early 1990s because the other lads could attack boys for doing so. It was considered the language of the underclass. Whereas Russian was the language of the top dogs.

For a first-hand account of Ukraine in the 1930s, we may look to Vasily Grossman's remarkable work *Everything Flows*. This unfinished novel contains harrowing scenes of the Terror Famine that will sear indelibly into the reader's mind. Grossman is famed in particular for his magnum opus *Life and Fate*, but in the opinion of Anthony Beevor, '*Everything Flows* is as important a novel as anything written by Solzhenitsyn.' In the story, the character Anna Sergeyevna unburdens herself from the terrible reality she not only witnessed, but was complicit in.

> We all thought that no fate could be worse than that of the kulaks. How wrong we were. In the villages the axe fell on everyone – no one was big enough, or small enough, to be safe.
>
> 'This time it was execution by famine.
>
> [...]
>
> Who signed the decree? Who ordered the mass murder? Was it really Stalin? I often ask myself. Never, I believe, in all Russian history, has there been such a decree. The decree meant the death by famine of the peasants of the Ukraine, the Don and the Kuban. It meant the death of them and their children. Even their entire seed fund was to be confiscated.

Grossman was born in Berdychiv (written as Berdichev in Russian), a city in north-western Ukraine. He witnessed the effects of the Holodomor, and while the narrative in *Everything Flows* is fictional, many passages throughout the novel capture the historical reality in stark, distressing detail. 'And the children's faces looked old and tormented – it was as if they'd been on this earth for seventy years. By the spring they no longer had faces at all. Some had the heads of birds, with a little beak; some had the heads of frogs, with thin wide lips; some looked like little gudgeons, with wide-open mouths. Nonhuman faces. And their eyes! Dear God!' As Grossman's translator Robert Chandler writes in his introduction to the novel, 'Grossman is simply doing what he can to remember the lives and deaths of millions who have been too little remembered.'

Another witness account of Ukrainian history comes to us from Anatoly Kuznetsov, born in 1929, who began recording scenes from his life in a notebook at the age of fourteen. These writings would later form the basis for his book *Babi Yar*, which earned him worldwide renown. Kuznetsov's mother was a teacher, and in the memoir he describes her constant fear of the nocturnal knock on the door that would signal arrest. Many of his mother's colleagues were already arbitrarily disappearing during Stalin's purges. 'My mother had practically no sleep at all at night. She would go from corner to corner, listening carefully to every noise. If she heard the sound of a car outside she would jump up, turn pale and start rushing about the room.' One of the most striking aspects of *Babi Yar* is the parallel he draws between the oppressive existence under Stalin and life under the Nazi occupation in Kyiv. The memoir is subtitled 'A Document in the Form of a Novel'. When Kuznetsov attempted to get it published, he was told 'not to show it to anybody else until I had removed all the "anti-Soviet stuff" from it.' So he took out a quarter of the text, and then the Soviet censors expurgated a further quarter. The resulting heavily censored version was published in the USSR in 1966. As Kuznetsov writes in his introduction: 'the manuscript became so seditious that I was afraid to keep it at home, where I was often subject to searches, so I photographed it and buried it in the ground.' Three years later, he escaped from the Soviet Union, carrying with him the films containing the unabridged text of *Babi Yar*, which could finally be published as the author intended. Kuznetsov issued a plea for his readers 'to consider this edition of *Babi Yar* as the only authentic text'. His memoir revealed to the world the horrors of the Nazi mass killing at the Babi Yar ravine. The slaughter of Kyiv's entire Jewish population took place over a two-day period in 1941; it has been described by historian Wendy Morgan Lower as 'the largest single massacre in the history of the Holocaust'.

The first time I personally heard an account from the Holodomor was in secondary school. Katrina Rowland, our Russian teacher, was a Ukrainian who ended up in Britain after the Second World War. Mrs Rowland was not only a gifted and inspirational teacher, but she could also hold the entire school spellbound whenever she gave an assembly. One of her stories in particular I shall never forget. She told us how during her childhood a terrible famine was taking place. A man with a horse and cart would appear each day to gather the new corpses, heaping them on to his cart. Katrina's garden had an apricot tree. A young girl who was mere skin and bones saw a green apricot growing on the tree and offered to swap her silver ring for it. The next day, Katrina spotted the girl's skeleton among the bodies on the cart: the apricot had proved too rich for her weakened digestive system and it had killed her. Mrs Rowland had clearly been haunted by this episode ever since.

For many years, little consideration was given to the Holodomor in the West, with Robert Conquest's *The Harvest of Sorrow*, published in 1986, being the prominent work dedicated to it. Anne Applebaum's *Red Famine: Stalin's War on Ukraine* has since appeared in 2017, and this terrible event in twentieth-century history is finally receiving due attention. Since Ukraine gained independence in 1991, not only have Ukrainian families been free to talk about it – and no longer in whispers – but also the Ukrainian state has erected monuments in memory of the victims of the Terror Famine and introduced awareness of this dark episode into Ukrainian schools and the public arena. This trend accelerated under the government of President Viktor Yushchenko, which came to power in 2005 following the Orange Revolution. It did not escape the notice of the men in the Kremlin that neighbouring Ukraine was not only enjoying a free press as well as free and democratic elections, but it also was granting its citizens freedom of memory.

The forced deportation of entire ethnicities is another harrowing and hidden chapter in Soviet history. In 1944, the Crimean peninsula was ethnically cleansed of its indigenous population, the Crimean Tatars. Similarly, in the North Caucasus the Chechen and Ingush people of Chechnya and Ingushetia were forcibly transferred, as were the Balkars and the Karachays. The Soviet authorities justified the mass displacement of these non-Slavic, ethnically Muslim peoples as collective punishment for their alleged collaboration with the invading German forces during World War II.

At first, the Bolshevik revolutionaries had been welcomed in the North Caucasus as saviours, unshackling the local peoples from Russian imperialist rule. During the 1920s, the indigenous ethnicities were allowed a degree of autonomy. Soon, however, the Soviet policies coming from Moscow began to cause tension due to their incompatibility with local traditions and religious sentiments. During collectivisation, there were attempts to introduce pig farming, much to the outrage of the pious

Muslim population, and the confiscation from the local men of illegal weapons and the imposition of mandatory military service proved unpopular. Rebellion against Bolshevik rule began to emerge. By the time the Germans invaded the Soviet Union, discontent was simmering in the form of sporadic armed resistance to Soviet power. There was a higher rate of draft-dodging and desertion from the Soviet Army in the North Caucasus compared to other regions. In Chechnya, there was no collaboration with the invading German troops due to the simple fact the Wehrmacht never reached Chechen soil. Despite this, the Soviet authorities successfully propagated the myth that the Chechens were traitors who sent a white horse as a gift to Hitler.

Stalin's mass deportations were carried out with ruthless efficiency. Entire communities were encircled by troops, rounded up and herded into cattle wagons. An extremely high proportion of the deported peoples died of hunger and disease during the journey or in the early years of their exile. At least a quarter of the deported Chechens died in transit, and it is estimated more than half the total Chechen population perished as a result of the population transfer. It was only in 1989 that the Supreme Council of the USSR finally condemned these genocidal deportations as 'illegal and criminal'. Discussion of these mass expulsions on ethnic grounds was not tolerated under the Soviet system, and following the collapse of Communist rule, families finally became free to talk and write openly about these episodes. The publication in 1988 of Anatoly Pristavkin's novel *The Inseparable Twins*, which touched on the topic of the Chechen deportation, marked a turning point. Under Putin, however, the Kremlin has begun persecuting historians and closing down historical organisations dedicated to exposing the crimes of the Stalinist state. The human rights organisation Memorial, founded in 1989, was dissolved by the Russian authorities on 5 April 2022. The Gulag historian Yury Dmitriev has been handed a fifteen-year custodial sentence in what is clearly a politically motivated case masquerading as a criminal prosecution.

During the 1990s and early 2000s, the Chechen nation underwent a new wave of trauma, as they fought two bloody wars for independence. The First Chechen War began in 1994, and the Chechens emerged victorious. It was an unpopular war among the Russians, and the mothers of the fallen Russian soldiers organised a large and powerful anti-war movement. This was one of the factors pushing President Boris Yeltsin to sign a peace treaty with the Chechens, ending the conflict. The Second Chechen War was begun by Vladimir Putin, although its planning preceded his taking office. Historians have been unable to establish a reliable figure for the total death toll, but upwards of a fifth of the population of Chechnya died during these wars. Both conflicts began with invasions by the Russian Army.

One of the most moving and lyrical works to be written on the First and Second Chechen Wars is the memoir of the Chechen poet and journalist Mikail Eldin. He wrote his story in exile in Norway, where he now lives. In the Russian Federation, it would be illegal for his book to be published, due to Russia's 2013 censorship laws prohibiting the circulation of works that promote separatism. After penning his memoirs, Eldin showed the manuscript to the head of Norwegian PEN, who sent it on to English PEN, one of whose committee members was the publisher of Portobello Books. Thus the memoir *The Sky Wept Fire* found its way into English, despite never appearing – and having no imminent prospect of doing so – in the Russian original.

For Eldin, the trauma of two brutal wars, the genocide of his people and his horrific torture in a Russian 'filtration camp' profoundly changed him, creating another self. In *The Sky Wept Fire*, many passages are dedicated to reminiscences of the past and reflections on the power of memory. As Eldin writes in the book:

> The most important thing in war is not the past, not the future, but the present moment. And if in the present something delightful is happening, even if it's nothing exceptional, why not be happy? Teetering between life and death, you were always living in the present. Not glancing over your shoulder at the past or peering into the future. That made things easier. But the snowfall doesn't know and doesn't care about what is easier for you. It simply jerks you out of your diabolical present and for a brief time leads you by the hand – like when you were a child and your mother led you back home from the streets after you'd become lost in play – to a distant, joyous past. This past is an illusion. What you so bombastically refer to as your past is in fact the life of some other guy, someone you thought of as yourself. But he is not you. You and he are two different people; as unalike as a crystal and a stone.

This other persona, the pre-traumatic self, is referred to by Eldin as 'your reflection in the unshattered mirror of the past'. So strong is the effect of this splitting into two distinct people that Mikail takes to regarding himself in second-person narration.

Eldin's imprisonment and torture in a 'filtration camp' and a Russian military base takes up one third of the memoir. According to the (now banned) Russian human rights organisation Memorial, more than twenty percent of Chechnya's population passed through the notorious Russian 'filtration camps', which, as Mikail writes, should more accurately be termed 'concentration camps'. During this period, Eldin faced a terrible battle with depression, trying desperately not to succumb to its siren call. Depression becomes personified, and it attempts to ensnare Mikail in a potent net of nostalgia. 'With a savage ferocity you rip away the cobweb of memories in which depression has entangled you and blot out all the idyllic images. In their place you paint ugly abstractionist pictures of your past.'

In a later section of Eldin's story, we read about how memories of the past fortified the resistance fighters in dire circumstances.

In conversations among themselves, they often talk about the past. All their memories are of peaceful life before the war, when they were ordinary guys in the countryside or city, studying and working, having friends and falling in love. There are plenty of conversations about memories and just as many about future plans for a peaceful post-war life. They dream of ordinary bread as if it were the most exquisite of dishes. They name the precise addresses of cafés and restaurants and the time of day they plan to visit them, listing what they'll order after the war. It is, of course, a very bad idea to think about food when you're hungry. It only makes you hungrier. But then again, these dreams help them live, striving towards an objective that perhaps seems prosaic: eating. Yet was it not through mankind's desire to eat nice food and work less hard that modern progress was born?

And in the memoir's Epilogue, Eldin returns once again to the extraordinary importance of keeping the flame of memory alive.

I am fated to long, endless conversations with the ghosts of my memories. And these ghosts will only die when I die. Unlike the characters in so many films and books, I don't want to forget the past. For there is nothing degrading in it, and it deserves to be remembered. This is not only my past: it is also the past of those who will never be able to talk about it or return to it in their memories. Their pains and hopes are reflected in me as in a mirror. Since it was my lot to survive, I have a duty to remember the past of those who burned in the nation's sacrificial fire. And not just to remember, but to tell their story as best I can.

Over the course of the centuries, exile has been a key theme for the Russians and the other peoples of the former Russian Empire and Soviet Union. The tsars used to send prisoners, whether political or criminal, into exile in Siberia. Stalin transferred entire ethnic populations to Central Asia and other regions far from the European-Russian heartland. Many successive waves of emigration took place, from the Whites fleeing during the Civil War to the Soviet dissidents who escaped during the decades of the Cold War. The particular pain that exile causes is separation from the places and people that feature in one's memories of the past. Just as Palestinians continue to feel the distress of being unable to return to the places of their childhood that now fall within the Israeli state borders, Crimean Tatars are now exiled from Crimea due to ongoing persecution by the occupying Russian authorities. Chechens such as Mikail Eldin cannot visit Chechyna, even when a parent dies. They cannot set eyes on the landscapes and communities that formed their sense of self. They cannot breathe in the smells that act as such a powerful trigger for nostalgia and are so individual to each place. Instead, they are fated to long, endless conversations with 'the ghosts of their memories'.

In his book *La Russie en 1839*, the French writer Marquis de Custine wrote the following words:

> In Russia history forms part of the domain of the crown; it is the moral prop-
> erty of the prince, just as the people and the land are his material property; it
> is kept in the storeroom along with the imperial treasures, and only that part
> of it which the ruler wishes to make known is displayed. The memory of what
> happened yesterday is the property of the Czar; he alters the annals of the
> country according to his own good pleasures and dispenses, each day, to his
> people the historic truths which accord with the fiction of the moment.

Custine could have been describing Russia not in 1839 but in 2022. Let us hope that this time Russia's war on memory will be doomed, and the many peoples living in the Russian Federation and living under Russian military occupation will soon enjoy the freedom to remember their family stories and national narratives in years to come.

HERSTORY:
FEMINIST ERASURES

Sunera Thobani

History has been written by, about, and for men, western feminists have argued for some time now. Consequently, History has been a largely patriarchal, as well as male, enterprise. Building on the works of European women's writing of the eighteenth and nineteenth centuries, and the activism of the suffragettes of the early twentieth century who are credited with winning the vote for women, the feminists of the mid-twentieth century began unearthing and documenting the historical and contemporaneous experience and political perspectives of women. They also turned their attention to how it was that women had been written out, silenced, or simply disappeared from most accounts of history. Reclaiming the stories of these silenced women became a major feminist project in its own right. To rewrite origin stories thus became a critical aspect of the politics of contesting the patriarchal order, and of challenging the power of men to shape History in their own image. The tradition of Herstory was hence developed by feminists as they sought to highlight the centrality of gender to the politics of knowledge production *as well as* to the organisation of the social world. This is Herstory's foundational narrative. It remains firmly entrenched within the political universe of western feminism. However, this narrative is as much *western* as it is *feminist*.

The power vested in these twin aspects of the feminist narrative – reclaiming history and transforming the present – was viscerally brought home to me as the drumbeats for the war in Afghanistan were quickening across North America following the 9/11 attacks in the US. I was scheduled to speak at a national conference on 'Ending Violence Against Women' that had been organised by Canadian feminists. Using the occasion to speak out against the looming invasion of Afghanistan, as well as the larger war on terror, I revisited significant moments in the well

documented history of US foreign policy. I highlighted the point that the
brunt of this war would inevitably be borne by Afghan women and
children. The Canadian feminist movement, I argued, should actively
organise against Canada's involvement in the Afghan invasion, as well as its
support for US foreign policy more generally. This argument, I believed at
the time, should be a no-brainer for feminists.

The backlash to my speech was instant. The mainstream media whipped
up a storm of public condemnation, provincial and federal ministers
denounced me. I was inundated with hate mail and threats of violence. I had
not expected such public vitriol, even less was I prepared for the 'internal'
response from the feminist movement. Prominent feminists lauded the
Canadian government for its role in the war on terror, defining this
imperialist aggression against a country already ravaged by decades of war
as an honourable attempt to 'save' Afghan women and girls. More
disturbing, the larger women's movements across North America and
Europe, not to mention in many parts of the Global South, enthusiastically
embraced and reproduced the Islamophobic constructs of Islam as an
inherently fanatic and murderous religion, and of Muslim men as
irredeemably fanatical and misogynistic. Muslim women appeared in this
ideological framing of the war on terror as hapless victims of their families,
communities, and religion. In the ensuing media furore, I repeatedly made
the point that European empires had developed their colonial policies
through these very kinds of constructs of the peoples and cultures they
were colonising. So, for example, the British had used the rationale that
they were 'saving' Indian women in their colonisation of South Asia, much
like the French argued they were 'protecting' Algerian women in their
occupation of Algeria. While some feminists did take a critical stance
against the war on terror, they were but a handful. They defined the war on
terror, especially the subsequent invasion of Iraq, as imperialist in nature
and opposed it on these grounds. Yet even those feminists who opposed the
wars were reluctant to challenge the damaging constructs of Islam as
promoting violence and of Muslim men as pathologically woman-hating.
These constructions became rapidly institutionalised in state practices as
well as political and public cultural discourses, often with feminist leaders
promoting them. Rather than learn from the histories of past imperialist
wars and occupations on women's lives, feminist movements instead

advanced the idea that western cultural values were equality oriented, especially on the question of women's rights. War against Muslim men hence became defined as the way to promote Muslim women's equality.

These recent developments demonstrate how firmly ensconced in global politics has become the idea that Western culture is exceptional for its commitment to women's equality. Most feminists were so invested in this idea that they did not mount any organised feminist movement to oppose the global war on terror. The war has resulted in a profound restructuring of the nation-states that waged it, as well as the international order that they continue to dominate. I use this state of affairs as an entry point to revisit – in broad terms – 'the history of feminism'.

Herstory, like the feminist ideologies, politics, and practices that constitute it, has been fraught and contentious, since the very emergence of feminism as a historical phenomenon. Although feminism is presently treated simplistically in political as well as public discourses as always-already on the right side of history, in actuality, its story is far more complex and contradictory, both in terms of 'external' responses to feminist organising as well as 'internal' contestations within and between communities of 'women'. Indeed, feminism's very construction of the category 'woman' has been challenged by non-western communities of women, as has been the feminist ideal of a 'global sisterhood' that shapes its political horizon. In short, the construction of the 'woman' who is the subject of feminist concerns was reliant on universalising the experience of western, white, middle-class women. This 'woman' remains, even now, at the heart of feminist politics, which posits, explicitly or implicitly, this figure as representing the experience, perspective, and future of all 'women' across time and space, that is, in History and in Culture.

Broadly speaking, feminism is defined as the intellectual and political movement to transform gender inequalities and achieve all the rights and entitlements for women as those endowed upon men. Like any other political and cultural formation, feminism is constituted by a range of ideological traditions and practices. Feminist political objectives have ranged from equality for women to women's liberation through social and economic transformation to a matriarchal future shaped by women's unique qualities.

Feminism's accounting of its own history, Herstory, generally organises this into three major phases. The first wave, beginning in the latter half of nineteenth century and continuing into the mid-twentieth century, was characterised by feminist struggles for women's political rights, centred on the right to vote. First wave feminists considered this to be the key to women's full participation in political life. Women's right to education was also an important objective during this wave. The suffragettes - as the feminists who organised the struggle for the right to vote are known - believed women's right to education along with their access to the vote would open the doors to their full inclusion in socio-political institutions. Moreover, the right to vote, which is at the centre of liberal-democratic forms of governance, would ensure the state's recognition of women as full and equal citizens, entitled to every opportunity offered by their society. With this right, women would change everything that was wrong with a world that undermined their status by actively barring the realisation of their potential. As the early feminist movements mobilised around this political vision, feminism became closely aligned with liberal-democratic ideologies and politics.

The activism of these early European and US feminists was met with public ridicule, stringent opposition, or a deafening silence by most western male intellectuals and political leaders, as is well documented. Prominent male politicians heaped scorn on the suffragettes, as well as on those feminists who dared to speak publicly of the oppression of women within the home and family. Certainly, these feminists had their male supporters, but the undoing of male power and domination remained the task of the feminists.

Feminist movements across Europe and North America were successful in achieving the right to vote for women, although this right was initially won only for white women. These movements also began the long and arduous process of transforming social attitudes towards the status, and treatment, of women, which in the case of western societies, were steeped in early Christian concepts of 'women' as the embodiment of sin and sex. Yet, contrary to the expectations of the first wave feminists, achieving the vote for women did little to change the political and economic organisation of the social world or its patriarchal power base. Although this right did allow women to participate in the political process, they ended up voting for established political parties, and even then, mostly along the same lines as the men in their families. The stage was thus set for the second wave of feminism, although this would not emerge until the global upheavals of the 1960s.

Second wave feminism was shaped by a range of social, political, and cultural traditions, which were broadly grouped into liberal, socialist, and radical feminist traditions. There was considerable overlap among these traditions, which does need to be taken into account in studying the concrete expressions given to feminist politics and campaigns during this phase. Liberal feminists focused their efforts on achieving equal rights for women in the spheres of politics, education, and employment, such that they reproduced the earlier feminist alignment with liberal-democratic ideologies. Their political vision was thus centred on achieving the rights of full citizenship for women.

Socialist feminists, in contrast, concentrated their efforts on addressing the economic aspects of women's inequality, primarily within the workplace as well as the institutions that represented working-class interests. Arguing that gender divisions crosscut with class divisions, the efforts of these feminists were directed at identifying and contesting the relations of capitalism as well as patriarchy. Drawing attention to the sexual division of labour that shaped capitalist economies, these feminists defined women's labour within the home and family as underpinning capitalist class relations. Women's 'reproductive' labour – unrecognised and unpaid – was thus the necessary condition for men's wage labour, defined as 'productive labour' within Marxist and related left political frameworks. Among the campaigns organised by socialist feminists were those for equal wages for women in the workforce as well as wages for housework. Equality of access to employment for women was a key concern, as was the development of specific social programs that recognised women's work within the family as socially necessary labour. Contesting the patriarchal privileging of the interests of male workers by unions, labour movements, and left political parties, these feminists worked for the transformation of patriarchy along with capitalism. Socialist feminists (and Marxist-feminists) thus underscored the vital role of class within feminist politics. Their role in advancing the larger feminist movement's understanding of the importance of women's unwaged as well as waged labour, and of the need for large scale economic change in the struggle for women's rights, cannot be underestimated. These feminists also shifted the focus of feminist organising to the struggles of working-class women, thereby critiquing and expanding the liberal-feminist focus on women's equality to include issues of equal pay, childcare, and redistribution through the social programs of the welfare state.

Equally influential in shaping second wave feminism was the envisioning of a radical female-centred future. Radical feminism, as this tradition was known, identified the control of women's bodies, sexuality and reproductive capacities as central to patriarchal power relations. The means of this control was organised through male violence against women, and radical feminists prioritised the issues of rape and sexual assault, male violence within the family, and the imposition of compulsory heterosexuality on women in their organising. The historical record of patriarchal society was replete with such violence against women, which was tolerated if not explicitly sanctioned, now by the liberal-patriarchal state and its political, social, and cultural institutions, argued the radical feminists. The building of safe spaces for women, including rape crisis centres, shelters, transition houses, and women's centres became the hallmark of their feminist organising.

In the early 1990s, feminist thought and politics were further complicated by what became known as 'the turn to theory' a trajectory influenced by the prominence of 'continental theory'. In dialogue with the unfolding of the post-structural and postmodern theories that grew out of the ruins of post-war Europe and the post-independence Third World, the work of French feminists had a far-reaching impact on feminist traditions. This new development within feminist thought – postmodern feminism – questioned the separation of the idea of 'sex' (as biological) from 'gender' (as cultural) that underpinned the earlier feminist traditions, which had all treated gender as a social construct and hence subject to change. Arguing that 'sex' as well as 'gender' were constructed in language, the postmodern feminists focused on the politics of knowledge production, and its relationship to power. Furthermore, they challenged essentialising ideas about 'woman' by embracing the idea of 'difference'. Postmodern feminists hence interrogated the very foundations of feminist political campaigns by treating these as unattainable, even redundant, given the post-structural approach to subjectivity/ies and identity/ies as multiple and fragmented. These arguments would profoundly undermine feminist political activism as they made 'high theory' the preeminent site of feminist politics.

Another significant theoretical as well as political development during the 1990s would further destabilise the earlier feminist traditions. This was the development of Queer Studies as an independent field that was both connected to, yet critical of, feminism. This emergent field approached the politics of sexuality as previously formulated by lesbian and gay intellectuals and movements as based on conventional approaches to sexuality and committed to achieving respectability for its constituencies. Queer theorists argued against these conformist approaches to gay and lesbian organising by highlighting the fluidity and multiplicity of the experiences, identities, and desires of gender and sexual minorities. These could not be contained within the gay or lesbian politics of a 'homosexuality' that reproduced the binary formation of sexuality, i.e. heterosexuality vs homosexuality. This binary imposed sexual conformity onto a range of 'queer' sexualities and genders which queer politics rejected. The quest for sexual 'respectability' as represented in, for example, the struggle for gay marriage, was now considered a reflection of the conservatism of gay and lesbian communities.

Second wave feminism certainly helped shift mainstream ideas, values, politics, and cultural forms cross Europe and North America, particularly with regard to the status of women. Since the 1960s, the basic idea of women's equality has generally become socially and politically acceptable, indeed even popular, across the broad spectrum of these societies. Second wave feminism also had an impact on other social movements of the period. There is, of course, a debate about the extent to which this wave was itself sparked by the anti-Vietnam War, Civil Rights and radical, including student movements of the 1960s, in the US, Europe, and beyond. And although the gains of the second wave were not distributed evenly among 'women', the feminist movement made significant advances in building public support for the general acceptance of the idea of women's rights. Upper- and middle-class white women benefited from the most lucrative of these gains as well as from the powerful economic, legal, and political positions that were now within their reach.

As these women moved up the social and economic ladder, their political and economic empowerment began to impact the family and male privilege in the home and the workplace. Soon enough, an angry backlash against these changing conditions gained ground among white men, including from the working classes, in western societies. Susan Faludi famously called this backlash, which had become a potent political force by the 1990s, 'an undeclared war against American women' in her bestselling book with the same title. Faludi identified the media as 'leading' this anti-feminist backlash, which has only intensified since then, by feeding the anger of angry white men who blamed feminism – and the women who worked outside the home, ran shelters, and provided abortions – for pushing men out of the workplace, undermining their authority, and destroying the family. This backlash became more visible as organised political opposition grew to women's increased social and economic rights, legal protections against violence and sexual harassment, access to abortion and contraception, and changes in family laws related to divorce and child custody. Men's groups led campaigns to ban abortion, deny women access to child custody and destroy the anti-violence women's centres, transition homes, and rape crisis centres. Under the banner of 'family values', this deepening anti-feminist backlash soon entered the political mainstream. The platform of protecting the family attracted significant support from right-wing political parties and conservative and right-wing Christian women, who were often at the forefront of the 'pro-life' attacks on feminism.

Furthermore, the popular feminist casting of women's rights in individualist terms, and in the language of women's choice, was soon co-opted into neoliberal consumerist discourses. Right-wing anti-feminist movements also promoted their version of 'women's choice' by promoting women's right to arm themselves, for example. The feminist linking of women's empowerment to women's individual 'right to choose' allowed the gains of the women's movement to dovetail with neo-liberal political values; this discourse of 'choice' did little to foster a sense of social solidarity or collective responsibility among women. Indeed, the right-wing appropriation of this language was turned against feminists by the right-wing women who used it to promote the political visibility of their explicitly anti-feminist causes.

This was the context for the emergence of third wave feminism in the late 1990s. It was led by a younger generation of women who grew up in the context of the social and cultural transformations brought about by earlier waves of feminist activism. Third wave feminists defined themselves as more radical than the older feminist generations, including that of their mothers. These earlier generations were considered by the third wave to have accomplished important rights for women, but were now entangled in outdated political worldviews and outmoded organising practices. Turning to the cultural field and using zines and social media to organise disruptive 'guerrilla' actions, the third wave feminists soon transformed themselves into various political manifestations of 'social justice warriors'. Committed to 'anti-oppression' politics, this wave was however soon overtaken by the profound shifts in gender and sexual politics at the geopolitical level brought about by the war on terror.

I have described here in very broad and general terms the evolution of the feminist waves that have shaped, and been shaped by, the telling of Herstory. The astute reader will have recognised that feminism's Herstory has been centred on the politics, experience, and perspectives of western feminists. Given that these feminists represented their versions of feminism as universal and progressive, and even now dominate feminist narratives, unpacking the centrality of their politics in the formulation of Herstory becomes necessary to understand the power that remains invested in this narrative.

The early western feminists took the view that their experience defined the female condition, and that they were deserving of the same rights and privileges enjoyed by western men. In the process of making their claims, they represented themselves as speaking for all women, across time and space. Following the path well-trodden by the male architects of European colonial ideologies, the early feminists considered the societies and polities, spiritual and religious traditions, and cultural practices of enslaved and colonised peoples as misogynist and anti-women. In the name of feminism, western feminists took upon themselves the White Women's Burden to 'civilise' colonised and enslaved men and to train the women into respectable femininity. During the periods in which the three feminist waves were unfolding across Europe and North America, and often beyond, the lot of the vast majority of women in the world – Indigenous, Black, Third World, and Women of Colour – improved only marginally, and in many cases, actually worsened as colonialism transmogrified into globalised neoliberalism.

The first wave of feminism unfolded in the context of the colonisation of much of the world by European empires. As first wave feminists argued for women's access to education on the basis that they would help produce enlightened families and future generations, these feminists identified the women of their societies as forward thinking and responsible 'Mothers' of the great European races and nations. In the case of Canada, for one example, first wave feminists considered Indigenous women to be 'squaws', not yet developed into 'woman'. The most famous among them supported the genocidal and eugenicist politics of their states. Demanding independent access to equality, mobility and migration rights, these women became an indispensable resource for the colonising missions of their societies. In the settler colonies, these women's role in reproducing white families and communities was as critical to the building of European institutions on indigenous lands as it was to the Christianising, 'civilising' and governing of enslaved, indentured and colonised women. The location and position of western women – mainly from the bourgeois and emerging professional classes – within their societies, as well as their close familial, social, and other ties to white male politicians, intellectuals, and administrators, enabled feminists to articulate their gendered experience and feminist vision in the language of the universal. With such a casting of a generic, ahistorical 'womanhood', these feminists took upon themselves the task to speak for, and represent the interests of women in their own societies as well as in those dominated by European empires.

In the colonised world, women from the higher ranks in these communities eventually began to emulate western women and adopted their approaches to women's 'equality'. The internalisation of these approaches helped reproduce emergent hierarchies within native societies. However, women from the exploited and dispossessed sectors challenged the former's embrace of feminist politics by exposing the relationship between western feminism, slavery, and colonialism. One very famous example comes from Sojourner Truth, who exposed the racism of the US slave-owning class. Her critique was directed at white American women as well as the white men who profited from the dehumanisation and slave labour of black women and men. Indigenous women likewise challenged the dehumanising invisibility thrust upon them by European Christian settlers in North America, Australia and other settler societies. Their struggles were against the reduction of their communities to the status of 'savages', doomed by their very nature to extinction.

These women, elite and subaltern, played an indispensable role in the rise of the anti-colonial movements of the later nineteenth and early twentieth century. They contested the power of European colonial states across Asia and Africa, and they defined as vital women's contributions to the fight for independence. In this context of anti-colonial upheavals, the classes of women newly emergent as intellectuals, activists, and leaders within nationalist movements challenged the western feminist privileging of their own experience. The alignment of these classes of women with white feminists thus remained tenuous and uneasy. This, however, did not stop native elite women from replicating the white feminist erasure of the experiences, perspectives and struggles of the masses of women from colonised and indigenous societies. Like the western feminists, these elite women in the colonies likewise elevated their own interests and status over those of the subaltern and subjugated communities, women as well as men, situated lower on the socio-economic hierarchies within their own societies. In short, if first wave western feminists constructed their own rights in tandem with the extension of western power over the colonial order, the women from elite classes shaped their own feminisms within the context of the nationalisms of colonised societies. Notably however, the political expressions of subaltern women in the west and in the colonised world ranged from the abolitionist activism of black women, which supported the suffrage of black men, to the anticolonial mobilisations of indigenous and native women, which demanded self-determination of their own societies. First wave feminism continued to remain *western*, whereas the feminism of black, indigenous, and Third World women was entangled in the tensions between anticolonialism and its various forms of nationalism – self-determination, neo-colonialism, and modernisation.

The evolution of western feminism into its second wave during the 1960s was notable for its unfolding in the context of the larger political turmoil of that period brought about by the anticolonial movements, the Civil Rights, radical Black and Students movements, as well as the anti-Vietnam War movement. Winning the vote for white women had not brought about the social transformations in the home and family envisioned by feminists, nor did this transform male domination at the national level as hoped for by many of the suffragettes. Instead, the subject of feminist politics, the middle-class white woman, was now mired in what Betty

Freidan called 'The Feminine Mystique'. Drowning in the miseries of the suburban family lifestyle, this Woman was determined to win for herself not only economic independence but also sexual freedoms, considered now the pathway to women's liberation. Women's consciousness-raising groups formed the building blocks of this feminist wave; the slogan developed through this mode of organising – 'the personal is political' – reflected the feminist mood of the period. Second wave feminists also made the university a preeminent site for their activism as they began to offer courses that would become the precursor to the Women's and Gender Studies Program that would become established by the 1990s.

But much like the first wave, the subject of concern in the second wave remained the upwardly mobile white, middle-class woman. This subject's privileged status was met with sustained, and significantly expanded critique in the politics of resistance developed by black, indigenous, Third World, and women of colour. In the US, Angela Davis, for example, tracked the historical role played by white women in the reproduction of slavery and its institutions, in the extraction of slave labour as well as the sexual exploitation of black women and men. She demonstrated how white feminists had actually opposed the enfranchisement of black men, played a key role in the lynching of black men, and in the post-1960s era, helped nurture the myth of the black rapist. Such racial pathologisation of black men and women, and of the black family, legitimised the criminalisation and incarceration of black men and youth in the 1990s' war on drugs. These constructs also furthered the sexualisation and exploitation of black women. Police brutality against black communities remained a constitutive feature of the country's racial politics, and Davis, along with other black feminists, developed an abolitionist perspective as central to the struggles of black women. In Canada, Lee Maracle reformulated Sojourner Truth's question, 'Am I Not a Woman', into the political assertion, 'I Am Woman', to expose the role of white women in the colonisation and genocide of indigenous women in Canada and the US. The sexual brutalisation of indigenous women and children had not been a matter of concern, let alone urgency, for the Canadian feminist movement, Maracle argued.

Over in the UK, Pratibha Parmar and Valerie Amos linked feminism to imperialism by confronting the institutionalisation of western feminism as the 'only legitimate feminism'. This 'imperial feminism', they argued, severely limited the possibilities of feminist political alliances across racial divides as it relied on making black feminists and their political struggles 'invisible'. Parmar and Amos argued the racism of the British state was directed against black communities in the UK through its immigration and policing practices, while the feminist movement ignored this targeting of the black family. The issues of family reunification and black women's access to education, employment, and housing did not feature among mainstream feminist politics. Whereas white feminists continued to treat the family as primarily the site of women's oppression, black feminists often experienced the family and community as a site of protection from the racism that permeated British society at every level. Moreover, it was black men who were the allies of black women in their struggles against racism and the racist state.

In her critique of feminist studies of development in the Third World, Chandra Mohanty showed how western feminists essentialised the 'third world woman' as a passive object of oppression. Casting her as incapable of agency, these feminists erased the very real class and other social divides in post-independence countries that shaped the actual hierarchies among unequally situated communities of women. By flattening out the status of 'the' Third World Woman, and attributing this to the 'cultures' of these societies, western feminists working in the field of feminist development studies were constructing themselves, and by extension, 'the' Western Woman, as liberated and the agent of her history.

I have mentioned here only some of the well-known critiques of western feminist politics of representation and their domination over 'feminism'. Herstory had no place for Third World, indigenous, and other women of colour. The gatekeeping role of white feminists over feminist knowledge production extended to their delineation of the issues elevated for feminist political organising. Each of these critiques has led to persistent and ongoing contestation of the universalisation of white experiences by the vibrant traditions of indigenous, black feminist, and women of colour intellectual work and political activism. Within western feminisms, these critiques were largely met with silence, and eventually led to the adoption of a pluralist approach based on the tokenisation and inclusion of women of colour in what remained the former's 'feminist' projects.

There is one further development in this anti-racist critique of western feminism that needs attention, notable for its impact on the larger field of 'feminism'. In 1991, black legal scholar and feminist activist, Kimberley Crenshaw, wrote an article advancing the concept of 'intersectionality'. Although most political iterations of what can be defined as counter-hegemonic 'feminisms' (anticolonial and anti-racist feminisms) were developed on the recognition that women's experiences of 'gender' were shaped by race, class, ethnic, national, regional, linguistic, religion, caste, and other relations of power, Crenshaw theorised these entanglements to demonstrate how they were mutually at work in state policy as well as feminist praxis to reproduce the privileging of whiteness. Feminist movements, Crenshaw noted, were centred on the experiences of white women whereas anti-racist movements were largely based on the experience of men of colour. Women of colour were marginalised in both sites. Intersectional approaches, she argued, were crucial in order to address the experiences and status of women of colour, and to contest their marginalisation in society as well as movement politics. While Crenshaw's essay was another anti-racist attempt to decentre gender by highlighting the role of race and class in the construction of gender, her development of the concept of intersectionality was unusual for the impact it had on white feminist politics. For Crenshaw's essay became influential not only within anti-racist feminist movements, but also across a range of western feminist and queer intellectual traditions. 'Intersectionality' has of course now become part of the larger terrain of social movements; it is also popular in public lexicons. Analysing this western feminist uptake of the concept of intersectionality is illuminating, in terms of the long-standing patterns of erasures and silencing that have shaped Herstory.

Crenshaw's theorisation of 'intersectionality' demonstrated how race and class functioned together in shaping black and immigrant women of colour's experiences of gender, yet as she also showed, feminist politics and practices arising from the experience of middle-class white women were unable to comprehend the levels of marginalisation that arose from the poverty and related exploitations of the former. For example, anti-violence state legislation that was lobbied for by feminists and enacted in immigration legislation to protect migrant women against fraudulent marriages actually increased these women's dependency on men. The legislation required migrant women remain married to their spouses (migrant as well as citizens) for two years in order to become eligible for permanent status. Instead of this requirement protecting migrant women from abusive fraudulent marriages, it tied these women even more firmly to their abusive spouses for fear of their own deportation, or of their non-citizen spouses, if they left their marriages. Crenshaw's point was that race as well as immigration status created this vulnerability to gendered violence in these women's lives. The concept of intersectionality had an immediate impact on black and women of colour theory and practice, and was subsequently also taken up by white feminists. However, in contrast to black and women of colour's deployment of this concept, the white feminist use of intersectionality highlighted the intersections of gender with sexuality, but ejected race as a central constituent of both. Intersectionality, as developed within black feminist theory, was thus turned on itself by white feminist and queer scholars and activists to restabilise the whiteness of their politics and movements by simply ejecting the issue of race from the concept of intersectionality as development by Crenshaw.

Turning to the contemporary turn taken by feminism in the war on terror demonstrates how deeply entrenched remains the privileging of whiteness in its treatment of gender inequality. The twenty-first century was inaugurated with the war on terror and its impact on gender politics has been profound. From the vantage point of two decades of this war it is clear to see how central gender politics were to the ideological framing of the war as a fight for 'freedom' and the protection of western civilisation.

As has been widely documented, the Bush administration and its allied states reframed 9/11 as an attack on western civilisation by hate-filled Islamic fanatics. This Islamophobic framing identified terrorism and violence as a peculiarly Islamic phenomenon; it also defined misogyny and sexual violence as part of the essential nature of the Muslim men who had waged the attacks. The war on terror, its key architects and political supporters argued, was being fought against an enemy that was global in nature — 'Islamic fundamentalism' — and in defence of freedom, democracy, and gender egalitarianism, which included the protection of Afghan/Muslim women and girls. The western state discourses and practices deployed in this war (securitisation, militarisation, increased border control, etc.) institutionalised Islamophobia in national as well as global politics. US nationalism took on an explicitly western supremacist turn, which would become more rampant with each defeat suffered by US and allied forces, eventually culminating in the Trump presidency.

The political focus in the US and Europe shifted to the ultra-right as white supremacists moved into mainstream politics as the war on terror came to an end, but we would do well to remember the role of feminists in shaping Islamophobic constructions of Muslim men and women. Feminists did not contest the Islamophobic war discourse. Instead, they integrated this into their gender and sexual politics which served as key aspects of the demonisation of Islam. While the neo-conservative Bush administration, the Liberal Canadian government, and the UK Labour government all deployed Islamophobic constructs to fight what was basically an imperialist war, feminist movements grounded these constructs in their intellectual and theoretical traditions as they supported the invasion and occupation of Afghanistan. In my earlier work, I identified three main ways in which feminists integrated Islamophobia into feminist politics as they developed new concepts in their theory and praxis: these included the ideas of a 'new anti-Semitism', 'gender apartheid' and 'precarious life'. The first of these constructed Muslims – male and female – as virulently anti-Semitic and identified this as a 'new anti-Semitism' that was the 'real cause' of the 9/11 attacks on the US. What was 'new' about this anti-Semitism, in this view, is that Muslims hated Christians as well as Jews, and that Islamic fanaticism was out to destroy western civilisation which was now defined as 'really' Judeo-Christian in nature. Conflating western culture with Judeo-Christian civilisation, as forged in the post-World War II western alliance with Israel, this culture was now identified as singularly progressive in its treatment of women and its support for gender equality. Any critique of Zionism was thus also an expression of this 'new' anti-Semitism against Judaism as well as Christianity, argued Phyllis Chesler, one of the founding figures of second wave feminism. Muslims, particularly Palestinians, were the most odious proponents. This development within feminist politics cast Palestinians as fanatics, and Palestinian women, in particular, as hate-filled and murderous. The concept of the 'new-anti-Semitism' has since been used by western states and their institutions to officially redefine anti-Semitism along these lines as they have intensified their support for the Israeli settler state.

The second concept, that of 'gender apartheid', was developed in close association with the earlier idea of 'global sisterhood' that was popular among western feminists from the 1970s to the 1990s. The older concept – based on the idea that women around the world were oppressed by patriarchy – was now rejuvenated to argue that women in the US and in Afghanistan were oppressed by a patriarchy that took the form of sexual terror in the US and gender apartheid in Afghanistan. Women in both countries needed to struggle together to overthrow this patriarchal power structure that was embedded in imperialist, masculinist militarisation. The concept of 'global sisterhood' that was popular into the 1990s had elevated gender as a primary social relation to posit all women as natural allies. In the context of the global war on terror, 'global sisterhood' was based on the claim that US and Afghan societies were dominated by violent masculinities of which women were the main targets. Developed by Zillah Eisenstein, a well-known proponent of second wave socialist-feminism, this feminist argument made invisible the North/South divide that created the immense inequalities between the US and Afghanistan. Such a feminist construction of the global war hence conflated not only the position, but also the interests, of white women in the US (itself a racial hierarchy) with those of women in Afghanistan (also a hierarchal society). The renewed idea of 'global sisterhood' hid the asymmetries of power *among women*, it also erased the actual effects of the US-led invasion of Afghanistan and its resulting destructions on the lives of Afghan women.

The third conceptual advancement in feminist knowledge production and praxis was that of 'precarious life'. 9/11 had exposed the precarity of all life, argued Judith Butler, a leading figure in the development of postmodern feminism. Indeed, precarity was the human condition, as symbolised by the infant who is utterly reliant upon others for her wellbeing and protection, for the conditions that sustain her life. Here, the violence of the US-led war and occupation was conflated with the vulnerabilities of the condition of infancy, which of course, is one of innocence. Approaching the violence of the war as a reflection of the condition of infant dependency, Butler's notion of 'precarious life' made invisible the imperialist interests and forms of 'precarity' served by the war on terror.

These three feminist concepts, and the politics arising thereof, were developed from the experience and perspectives of middle-class white women and universalised their fears, anxieties, and interests as the general condition of gendered humanity. The power relations of race, colonialism, imperialism (historical and contemporary) were thus jettisoned from these feminist conceptual frameworks. The point here is that such *feminist practices of power* can be traced back to first wave feminism. Indeed, these practices are foundational to the formation of feminism. That these practices extended the Islamophobic ideology and imperialist ambitions of western nation-states through the war on terror is no anomaly, oversight, or, indeed, coincidence. Such gendered Islamophobia has not only set up Muslim women, men, and sexual/gender minorities for particular kinds of violence and disciplinary projects. This gendered Islamophobia is also the grounds for the remaking of western gender, feminist, and sexual politics and identities as vulnerable, under attack for their inherently progressive politics by an irrational and fanatical Islam.

In the two decades of the global war on terror, the core elements of Islamophobia became entrenched in geopolitics as well as the politics of nation-states around the world. The backlash generated in response to my speech against the Afghan war came from the media, politicians, members of the general public *as well as feminists*. The narrative of the superiority of western gender and sexual politics fed by such attacks on anti-war activists was part of the backlash that mobilised public support for the war, as well as for a closer alliance between feminist politics and western state discourses. This political shift in gender politics continues to inform most contemporary feminist approaches to national and global politics, and to international relations, even as women's rights in the west have come under unprecedented assault by the political and economic changes wrought by the global war. Certainly, more critical assessment of the feminist collusion with the imperialist politics of the global war is now emerging, but we have yet to see a thorough accounting for the role of feminist thought and practice in remaking the racisms and Islamophobic discourse that have now overtaken mainstream political discourses, both inside feminist movements as well as in the larger social world. Feminism and Herstory remain, as has been the case since their historical emergence, deeply contested terrain.

MUSEUM ISLAM

Hassan Vawda

What would you like to see in an exhibition on Islam? I asked this question to a warden in one of Britain's prominent museums. The warden had worked within the institution for decades, guarding the artworks, speaking to visitors, navigating the public that visit the collections, so their institutional memory of the museum was profound; and also occupied the space as a Muslim. Yet, when asked this question, the warden said they wished to see an exhibition that would really explore 'Islam' and 'Art', as this was something the warden had yet to see in all their time working on the exhibition floor. Why did this answer surprise me? Was it the fact that the museum in question had a reference point of Islam in its recent history? Since the 2000s, there had been two exhibitions in which Islam was heavily, explicitly referenced. Yet, this staff member, with their daily experience on the gallery floor, over decades, as a Muslim, voiced that they had not seen a show that explored Islam.

It speaks volumes to the way museums have versed themselves in presenting on Islam, yet, seemingly an Islam that is far removed from the Muslims that practice it as their faith – as their worldview. What and who have been cast as the experts of the museum logic of Islam? Are the historical actors who have helped define and continue to inform the Islam of the museum, ignorant to the Islam of Muslims? The British Museum's long serving curator, Venetia Porter, in her latest title as curator of Islamic and Contemporary Middle East art, speaks of the term 'Islamic Art' as 'very reductive'. She emphasises that the term 'was created by western scholars and to a certain extent we are stuck with that now'. Porter is speaking about her 2021 curated exhibition at the British Museum, 'Reflections: Contemporary art of the Middle East and North Africa' – that a categorising focus on the geographical elements allows for 'more flexibility' rather than using this idea of 'Islamic art'.

This overt resignation of 'Islamic Art' being a problematic category, from an institutional dialect may seem like some serious decolonial street cred. But to then confidently use something like geographical location as being a solution to the problem is at the heart of these consistent phases of orientalising orientalism that has been flourishing in museums over the last few decades. In fact, it is representative of an institutionalised spin-cycle that has sought to continuously attempt to re-energise the framing of 'Islam' in the museum over the last century, but largely creating stagnation instead. The displays and framings of today are hardly different to that of the early twentieth century, when 'Islamic Art' in the museum grew its confidence as a category. It is always pushed and pulled between re-inventions of focus on 'geography' or the 'pre-modern' then back to 'geography'. Porter's own space that she occupies in the British Museum has seen discursive changes, from once called the Department of Oriental, to the Department of Asia – but how do these discursive shifts really impact or innovate on the framing of Islam in the museum? Is 'Islam' in the museum just one long continued dance with the spectre of Islam in relation to the Christian/secular worldview? The very worldview that formed this idea of the museum as an authoritative societal meaning-making and cultural compartmenting organism.

These attempted re-articulations or acknowledgments of the problematics of 'Islam' in the museum, by the museum, seems in hyperdrive in recent years. I really felt the frustration in Raha Rafii's recent lament on what she called the 'repackaging' of orientalism by modern museum curatorial cultures. Citing another British Museum show, 'Inspired by the East: how the Islamic world influenced Western art', she observes how the show, which literally opens with a quote from Edward Said, goes on to present an exhibition that emphasises 'orientalism as artistic exchange and benign observation of domestic and religious life rather than as the justifying ideology of violent European colonialism and expansion'. It is acknowledging orientalism on the museum's terms. It is situated in a museum professionalism that has become a Jannat-ul-Firdaus of liberal conscious clearing. A space that has become entrenched in the language of inclusion, yet still holding histories and current realities of exclusion – the museum as a vestige for the dominant culture.

I remember visiting this exhibition after Jummah in 2018. Walking into the dimly lit exhibition space, I felt hyper-minoritised as I was surrounded by a packed visitor cross-section that did not feel a semblance of familiarity in comparison to the mosque I had just come from. I heard well-trodden comments in upper-crust dialects such as 'what a beautiful vase' that I am sure has been uttered in every exhibition about 'Islam' in museums over the last two centuries. I felt my experience in this space was situated closer to the objects on display, not with the visitors. It made me think: why am I, as a Muslim, feeling uncomfortable in this exhibition supposedly on the cultural influence of Islam, yet the dominant culture is comfortable? There were rave reviews of this show from institutional press voices, with Jonathan Jones calling it 'a glorious show Boris Johnson really ought to see'.

It is the logic that this framing of the cultural value of the so-called 'Islamic' past is as rich as our European histories, and thus will relinquish any prejudice of 'Islam' being a backward or lesser reference point, from someone like the once-prime minister. It is an exhibition in a museum that can alleviate this, rather than meeting any 'Muslim', in the present, in the everyday. In the logics of this culture, the mosque I had just come from was the space of the ignorant Muslims while the museum is showing the light of the enlightened Muslim. The logic of the museum has produced a confidence that can boldly claim that they are pioneering the reframing of problematics, without reflecting on the very way that the knowledge producers and values that structures validifying knowledge production in the museum are themselves part of the problematic. We have exhibition, projects, and museum practice consistently finding footing that is put forward as the latest expansion and innovation in re-invigorating the framing of Islam. We even had the Victoria & Albert Museum taking a faux 'British mosque' to be put on display for the 2021 Venice Architectural Biennale, with institutional pride in the fact that it is including British Islam in its category of 'Islamic art and culture'.

Yet, take a step back and look at whether these innovations are critically expanding the conceptual realm of what Islam has come to represent in the museum. It is largely all re-inventions of the orientalist exhibits that put Islam in the grip of the museum in the first place. Wendy M. K. Shaw, author of *What is Islamic Art?* points explicitly at the narrow modes of constructing meaning that museum knowledge and categorisations rely upon – of a Eurocentric display culture of post-Enlightenment attributes. In this structure of meaning making, 'Islam' falls to a consistent pattern of being presented to 'learn about' a 'culture' rather than 'learn from' a 'culture'. This creates re-inventions, without looking to bring in different epistemological roots, different approaches to meaning making and/or storytelling – it just creates a consistent 'discovery' culture. It is then forever the 'other', forever the 'orient', forever the Muhammad in the Mist for the curatorial class to present – in all its exoticism, danger, and anti-modern romanticism. Forever holding the power of categorisation, what may seem like inclusive museum practice to take a faux mosque to Venice, in fact is also an act of positioning the 'British Muslim' into the lens of their exotic Muhammadan today. What difference is it in the display of the faux British mosque in Venice to the 'Muhammadan' pavilions at the 1851 Great Exhibition?

This push for 'repackaging orientalism' may seem like a trend that is a natural part of the continuous wave of new museology that made Foucault and Bourdieu father figures in their reflexivity. A wave that has found itself in a twenty-first century museum matrix as a liberal self-digesting culture that capitalises on activist trends whilst still entrenched in inequalities, exclusions and established canon formation cultures. There is such fine work happening across museums, with innovation and challenge to dominant cultures ripe through the presence of those with skillsets that look to histories outside the museums walls as much as within, who bring positive disruption. But all too often this falls secondary to the narrative control of post-Enlightenment categorisation and rituals of experience that the structure of these institutions has baked into its functionality. In this point, there is a particular texture to the way framings of 'Islam' has been stagnated – that is in the way religion and belief itself was ejected or reformatted by the museum, and in the unreflective, without criticism sacralisation of secularism that still haunts the museums walls as an ever present.

When Shaw speaks to museums going beyond their own epistemes in the context of Islam, she suggests that meaning making should be drawn from expertise of the Qur'an, Hadith, and all aspects of theology, culture, and the lived experiences people have with 'Islam', its material cultures and its intangible, everyday significances in their lives. What would it look like for an Imam, Shiekh, or Mufti to curate a show at the V&A or the British

Museum? This is a radical proposition for the museum space, whose formation is tied to the reformatting of religion and belief into rational categorisations in relation to a colonial structuring of the world. More specifically, in how the museum's foundational modes of meaning making and structuring the world represented a European synergy between the Christian worldview to a secular civilising world view. For instance, icons of the Church were literally placed in the new categorised space of the museum, alongside the expanding enterprise of constructing categories of cultures, communities, and beliefs of the 'other'.

For most of the eighteenth and nineteenth century, the display of 'Muhammadans' in the museum categorisations were largely geographical – related to the region, to the orient, to specific place and time. If we take Britain for instance, the nineteenth century saw collated exhibitions of largely private collections put into public display such as 1854's 'The Oriental and Turkish Exhibition' at the St Georges Gallery in Knightsbridge. Speaking in the context of the British Museum's non-categorisation of 'Islam' in the nineteenth century, Ward says its curatorship 'saw the Islamic realm as both a geographic and cultural buffer between Europe, Asia and Africa and as a bridge linking the artistic achievements of antiquity with renaissance Europe'. It was utilised in this chronological sense of progress, a modernity of colonial restructuring.

From the turn of the century, something begins to emerge. Exhibitions with the central focus and tie being 'Islam', being 'Muhammadan art' came about across Europe – for instance in London, you have the Whitechapel Gallery's 1908 show 'Muhammad Art and Life' and in Munich, the monumental 1910 show 'Masterpieces of Muhammadan Art and Life'. Eva-Maria Troelenberg has provided vital assessment of the latter, in what is arguably the most significant major announcement within exhibition and museum cultures that a category of 'Islam' emerges as the defining categorical tie – diffusing geographical identities and presenting an essence of an art, a craft, a cultural existence that is linked through a belief system, from historic materials through current craft and cultural object and experience.

Troelenberg makes a particular observation of the use of the word 'Masterpieces' in the exhibitions title. The curatorial motivations of this exhibition came from an increasing trend amongst orientalist scholars at the time of turning to anti-modernists positions, romanticising the past and lamenting the industrial futures. In the current terminology we can even say they had decolonial re-orientation motivations. The use of the word 'Masterpiece' was a specific challenge to the authorities of canonical knowledge production within museums, in which the 'Masterpiece' was designated to art and artefact in the European tradition. The masterpieces of Leonardo da Vinci, for example, bring into the museum a liminal space that holds the tensions and smoothness in handover of shared power between a Christianised worldview and the secular civilising worldview. The motivations of the Munich 1910 show were to highlight that there are different histories as important as that of Europe, that masterpieces existed in the histories and presents of 'Muhammadan cultures' yet were tainted by tradition-shattering modernity. Yet, Troelenberg presents an argument that by bringing in this broad, cross-geographical, cross-cultural plethora of material cultures (vases to paintings) around this idea of 'masterpiece' it also brought this concept of 'Islam' into the very framework that had brought the icon from the church into the art museum. De-godded while retaining a renewed societal-cultural value.

And so 'Islamic Art' was born and a framing of 'Islam' museumified. A framing that then brought a few generations of experts and continues to. An expertise that exists within the dominant culture logics and flexes of the museum. A flex that has created a museum professional that is largely homogenous in terms of the backgrounds and cultures that occupy its space. A professionalism often in an institution that even today struggles in deep desperation to come to terms with itself being an exclusive space. No matter how inclusive in language it attempts to be. Report after report, book after book, over the last few decades have created this versed language of inclusion, where 'diversity' is talked about non-stop, yet, museums are some of the most un-diverse workplaces in the societies they find themselves in. The name of a department may change from the department of orientalism to the department of Asia – but the skills, experience, and dominant culture within these spaces largely has remained in many ways enshrined – drawing from the very same epistemological trough that 'Islam' in the museum found its framing within. So, when Shaw speaks of expanding the values of knowledge that contribute to the framing and bring in different epistemes, the shutters often come down. If for instance, traditional and practiced expertise and insight on Qur'an or

Hadith are to be brought into the way museums hold 'Islam', this could mean for the neo-orientalist profession, a reality shattering nightmare in which the 'Muhammadan in the Mist' appears in a curatorial meeting. The fear of no alcohol at the private view or the Qur'an being read over the interpretation label of that Qur'an on display.

But who are the traditional Muslim scholars and voices that can be brought in? It is a testament to the power of the museum, that 'Islamic Art' now also exists as a category within Muslim lives, societies, and everyday cultures – a concept in many ways drawn from this very same framing of what the museum decided in the early twentieth century. The Munich 1910 show is not just reflective of what is still the 'Islam' in museums – but is also now the anchor of what constitutes 'creative' expression within Muslim spaces. Throughout the twentieth and into the twenty-first century, we perform calligraphies and architectures, holding a nostalgia for the golden age of an 'Islam'. With secular embassies (art galleries) and Euro-categorisation centres (museums) across the world, the sparsity of Islamic thought in thinking about creative expression, or even conceptualising 'art' outside of the power of these spaces, emphasises the domain of seized power on the framing of 'Islam' and its material cultures. The pre-modern, the geographical, the distant – the Muhammadans in the Mist. It is this seized power of meaning making and structuring the world that should be at the centre of museum practice in any attempt to reorientate framings.

The power of the museum's seized territory of being the authority of 'Islam' as art or material cultures today can be further seen in the proliferation of European museum brands and structures being imported and present within the skyrocketing skylines of the Gulf states. The most symbolic example being the Louvre brand of museum being imported into Abu Dhabi. In fact, all excursions into art, from biennales to ground zero museum builds take the blueprint of meaning-making and cultural value from the very mechanisms that forged Muhammadans to exist in the Mist of modernity. It follows a tradition of Islamicate money investing in European museums, to pursue the showcase of a culture and history that *needs* to be valued by the West. From the oil money that made the 1976 'World of Islam Festival' a reality, to the recent Albukhary patronage at the British Museum or Jameel Foundation support of 'Islamic Arts' at the

V&A. Whilst all have facilitated incredibly important work and continue to do so – are they really making the museum work in a different logic to re-considering their framing of Islam? Or is it investing in continuing its authority on structuring what constitutes its framing of 'Islam'?

If the fundamental aspects of 'Islam' in European museums either flit between the historical pre-modern or as a cultural 'other' – not of Europe but to be admired with value through European thought – then, it is no surprise that an incongruent reality that unfurls the museumified 'Islam' is the attempt (and lack of) in bringing the presence of 'Islam' in Europe into the frame. Both historic and present. The Albukhary display of the 'Islamic World' in the British Museum, is not where you find King Offa's coin inscribed with a faux shahada, often cited as one of the earliest Islamic reference points in Britain. In fact, most museums with 'Islamic' collections or displays today, do not have any room for Islamic presence, practice and realities that allow Islam to be present outside of geographical or chronological distance.

There is an interesting observation to make on the V&A's recent display of a 'British Mosque' at Venice – as the entire piece exists as a 'special project'. Rather than sitting in their categorical section 'Islamic art and design' it sits in contemporary architecture – and the discursive framing of the exhibition is one which is 'contemporary multiculturalism through three adapted mosque spaces'. This explicit engagement acknowledges, through the museum, an Islam that exists beyond geographical or chronological distance, is a disrupting act. But by detaching it from the very heart of categorical boundaries in the museum – detaching it from the space of 'Islamic art and design' and exceptionalising it for an exploration on multiculturalism, it mirrors the very same dynamics that birthed 'Islamic Art'. I wonder where this exhibition would be displayed in the permanent collection galleries of the V&A once it is done in Venice – could it be placed in the Jameel Gallery? I doubt it, unless pushed to think beyond its current categorisation culture. The constantly re-aligning perspectives to attempt new ways of displaying/framing 'Islam' is ripe, but as discussed, each time always without critical reflection on the very basis that the museum functions as a meaning-making organism of Westernese. The rest, then the West; the futures of the West is the future of Islam. It is a contestation Yasir Morsi asks of the museum, that 'do they need to explain the East through a western lens to make the former's achievement legitimate through the language of the dominant?'

Morsi asks this question after visiting Melbourne's 'Islamic Museum of Australia', opened in 2010 to attempt to make relevant the reverence of Islamic civilisations and their presence in relation to Australia. Museums across Europe, the United States, and Australia, in a post-9/11 context, and with the Euro-crucifixion of multiculturalism on a cross made of the 'Muslim question', saw great energies pour into attempting to find purpose in the conversation. Exhibitions, new display wings and even new museums emerging to challenge narratives of Islam being incongruent to the values of liberalism, the values of civility. Yet, just as the original formulation for what motivated 'Islam' to be framed in the museum – the *decolonial* challenge to European canonisation by saying 'Muhammadans' can create masterpieces too – it creates a formulation that for Islam to be accepted, it must be ordered within the meaning-making comforts of the museum. Rather than turn to a critical reflection on the meaning, it remains just a recycled approach for continuity. To find an inclusive place that feels like a liberal achievement of welcoming the Muhammadan into the realm of study, the lucky realm of being organised by the West.

Morsi uses a Nietzschean musing that put forward two cosmological ways of structuring the world – the Apollonian and the Dionysian. The Apollonian represents 'the desire for symmetry, the rational order, teleology and optimism'. The Dionysian is 'the wilderness, drunkenness and our sense of letting go, of abandoning ourselves to the unknown'. It is the realm of the ignorant to the enlightened. Morsi takes these cosmologies and argues that the museum is engaged in presenting an Apollonian 'Islam' – structured and ordered into post-Enlightenment meaning makings and as a by-product, intentional or not, it casts the Islam in the world and in the realities of people's experiences as Dionysian – a spectre in the wilderness.

It is hard not to approach any museum framing that references 'Islam' from anything other than a starting point of suspicion. No matter how many times Said's *Orientalism* is referenced or claims that the problematics of 'Islamic Art' are being acknowledged – the formula of meaning-making that the framing emerged from is still very much in place. So, what do we look to do? Is there any possibility of the museum being a space that reflects and relinquishes authority in its meaning-making by bringing in different experiences, and realities into its space? The starting point for any possibility of this, is for the logic and professionalism of the museum to relinquish its Apollonian aspirations using Morsi's analogy. It must cast itself as a space for Dionysian cosmology – unfurling itself to be an uncontrollable challenge to its rationalist sensibilities that lock itself, its structures, and its professionalisms to always work within parameters. In this Dionysian Museum, the facilitation and support of new ways of meaning-making can be prioritised – new experiences and even professionalism can be brought in. A structure of re-orientation can truly begin, and an Islam unbound by time and geography can begin to be engaged with. This would mean that the dominant culture of that space, the professionals who maintain Apollonian authority would be made to feel out of place, in a confusion without the reference points they need for comfort. But why would the dominant culture cast itself into the wilderness that it has assigned for the 'other' – with its specially designated place for the 'Muhammadan'? Perhaps it needs to be forced.

REMEMBERING KERBALA

Masuma Rahim

It is no exaggeration to say that the death of the Prophet brought turmoil to the followers of Islam. According to Shia traditions, the Prophet made it clear, during the final pilgrimage, that he wished his son-in-law, Ali, to be his successor. Despite his request that all those who witnessed his declaration offer Ali their allegiance, the hours following his death brought fissures and divisions amongst the faithful into plain sight. Several groups from Mecca and Medina asserted their case for taking the role of caliph, with Abu Bakr eventually being selected as leader. When Ali refused to pledge allegiance to the newly elected caliph, his home and family were threatened. When his wife Fatima refused to leave their house, it was raided and set alight, leaving her with serious injuries, causing her to miscarry, and leading to her eventual death five weeks later.

After the death of Uthman, who was Abu Bakr's and Umar's successor, Ali was finally able to realise the wishes of the Prophet and governed for five years. Following his assassination in the mosque of Kufa, his son, Hassan, became caliph. Almost immediately, the Umayyads, led by Muawiya bin Abi Sufyan, mounted an army to march on Kufa. The besieged Hassan agreed to cede control on condition that, after Muawiya's death, the leadership return to the household of the Prophet. Muawiya died in 60 Hijra, having declared his son, Yazid, his heir apparent. Yazid was well-known for being corrupt, for sowing discord, and for neglecting vulnerable members of society. Horrified at the character of the usurper, Hussain refused to offer his allegiance. Shortly after Yazid's accession, Hussain and his family sought refuge in Mecca, assuming that Yazid would not attack them there. They were wrong, and shortly before the commencement of the Hajj, they were forced to flee, having discovered that Yazid's followers had entered the city disguised as pilgrims, with the intention of killing him. Hussain had no desire to violate the sanctity of Mecca, but he also wished to expose Yazid, and remaining in Mecca would have allowed the culprits to remain undetected.

Hussain announced that he was embarking on a journey to Iraq, and that he would be martyred, while also calling for volunteers to join his army. He received letters of support from the citizens of Kufa and set off, but was intercepted by Yazid's forces and forced to travel north to Kerbala. He arrived with his family on 2 Muharram and ordered that their tents be set up on the banks of the Euphrates. His companions were prevented from doing so by the army of Yazid, and from 7 Muharram, they were prohibited from obtaining any water.

On the night of Ashura the Imam and his companions spent the night in prayer and contemplation of what lay ahead. Ha gave anyone who wished to return to their homes, permission to do so, saying: 'The covenant I overlook. The oath of allegiance you have taken which bonds you to me is lifted. You are free, there is no obligation to bind you and I shall hold you no longer. You can go and leave me to myself. Leave this land under cover of night. These soldiers of Yazid's army have business with me, not with you.' There is no evidence that any member of his army left, but it is documented that soldiers in the opposing forces defected to Hussain's army; most notably Hurr, who had been responsible for diverting the Imam on his journey to Kufa.

The following day, the Imam gathered his army, numbering fewer than 100, and over the course of the morning, all the companions were killed. After the Zohr prayer, Ali Akber, the son of Hussain, was martyred. One by one, every male member of his family met his death in battle. In desperation, Abbas, the defender of the Imam's camp, went, unarmed, to plead for water but was attacked on his return, leaving him blinded, and his arms severed.

By now, there were no men left to fight, and the Imam's children had not drunk water for three days. Hussain took his baby, Abdallah to the banks of the river to ask for water. He left his sword in his tent and begged for water for the child. But Yazid's commanders, seeing that the soldiers were moved by the baby, and by his thirst, ordered him to be killed in a show of no mercy. And so it was that Abdallah was shot through the neck with an arrow large enough to kill a fully-grown animal.

The only one to remain was Hussain. He went to say his final farewells to his sister Zainab, and his son, Sajjad, who was too ill to fight. Riding courageously into battle he was attacked by the full might of Yazid's army. Arrows and swords rained down upon him, and he fell from his horse. He performed one last prostration before Shimr severed his head from his body.

Hussain was gone, but there was someone who watched every moment of this terrible day: Zainab, sister of Hussain and daughter of Ali and Fatimah. It was Zainab who observed the bodies of the martyrs being trampled by horses. And it was Zainab who protected the family of Hussain when Yazid's forces set fire to their camp and looted their hijabs. Zainab witnessed everything that had happened following the death of her grandfather. She had seen every member of her family come to an untimely end, often in unimaginably violent circumstances.

Zainab became the guardian of all those who survived the day of Ashura. She endured the humiliations which followed: she and her family were whipped and chained and dragged through the streets. They saw the heads of the martyrs paraded on sticks. They were imprisoned in Damascus, where Yazid ruled from. And despite all that she had witnessed, it was Zainab who gave the famous speech in Yazid's courtyard, in which she spoke out against the corruption of his regime, noting 'how amazing it is that the virtuous people, sons of the divine prophets and vicegerents are killed at the hands of liberated slaves, evil-doers and sinners'.

That speech, delivered not only to the caliph but to his entire court, led to revolution. Word rapidly spread through the empire that the family of the Prophet had been imprisoned and Yazid began to fear for his position. He released the remaining members of the family and returned to Medina. It was in Medina that Zainab started the tradition of *majaalis*, or commemoration of the events at Kerbala, and it is due entirely to her that the story continues to be told. Even after the release of the family, Zainab was persecuted. Her activities in Medina were closely monitored, and it is said that she was eventually exiled to Damascus, so that those in power could limit her influence. It is likely that she died less than two years after that infamous battle at Kerbala.

Growing up in an observant Shia Muslim family, Muharram and Safar were, without a shadow of a doubt, the most revered of months. Ramadan offered a different pace of life, but the mourning period at the beginning of the Islamic New Year was when almost everything stopped. Televisions were switched off. Trips to the cinema were, at least in our household, frowned upon. Birthdays went unmentioned; announcements of engagements were embargoed. The buying of new clothes or furniture – anything that suggested celebration or enjoyment – was delayed until *Milad un Nabi*, the formal end of the mourning period. Although majaalis were typically at their most regular during the first ten days of Muharram and the middle ten days of Safar, there would be several opportunities to attend commemorative programmes both at the mosque and in private homes each week.

Women were present at virtually all these events. The Khoja Shia community – Indian in origin but inhabitants of East Africa until they migrated to the UK in the 1970s – never restricted women's access to collective worship, but nor did it encourage their participation in the public-facing sense. Women probably made up the majority of mosque attendees but, at least at that time, they were not part of the committees that made the decisions. Nor were they the people who sat on the pulpit during the main evening programmes or who recited the lamentations. That privilege was reserved – as it still largely is – for men. Only the morning majaalis was exclusively for women, where the speaker would be a female and could recite lamentations in a single-sex environment. Interestingly, the male speakers who preached to the entire community were usually well-known and there would be a sense of anticipation at the prospect of hearing them speak. That anticipation was not usually extended quite so enthusiastically to the female daytime speaker.

Even as a child, this made little sense to me. Male speakers, a mixture of scholars who had been to seminary and lay preachers, would sit on the pulpit and tell me the stories of Fatima and Zainab, but what could they possibly know of the female experience? And why did they speak so little about prominent women of Islam in comparison to the men? And when they did speak of them, why did they always describe them as role models only for women? There was never any consideration of the possibility that contemporary Muslim men might learn something from key female figures in Islamic history. And when they did talk about the achievements of women, why did they only ever talk about hijab, as though the female experience was only about covering up? I came from a family in which the women had observed hijab for decades and I knew that their female-ness was not just about choosing to cover. It was obvious to me that their experience as displaced people who had survived the racist, misogynistic

Britain of the 1970s and 1980s – and who were continuing to survive it – was about much more than the clothing they wore; it was plain to see that the women of my family had found a way to maintain their faith and to instil it in their children despite everything they had experienced. Women, it seemed to me, were the key figures in family and society, and their influence was immense.

But somehow that link was never made in the sermons I heard, and the courage and conviction of Zainab was never offered as a lesson for the men of our community. And that was a shame, because it was a disservice not only to key figures in our history, but it was a disservice to the congregation, who were denied the opportunity to think about women as strong and courageous and principled in and of themselves, rather than simply being peripheral to men.

Looking at how that community has evolved over the past thirty years, and considering the ways in which it has perhaps failed to evolve, I wonder what would be different now if those sermons had offered a more distinctive narrative.

The truth is that the history of Islam is really a history of women's courage and dedication. Islam flourished primarily because of Khadija, an entrepreneur who invested her resources – financial and otherwise – in the fledgling faith. After the death of the Prophet, the land of Fadak, which had been left to Fatima by her father, was seized by his companions. In an under-acknowledged chapter of history, Fatima objected to the theft of her land, bringing witnesses to testify on her behalf, and advocating for her rights under Islamic law, she said:

> O Muslims! Will my inheritance be usurped? O son of Abu Quhafa! Where is it in the Book of Allah that you inherit your father and I do not inherit mine? Surely you have come up with an unprecedented thing. Do you intention-ally abandon the Book of Allah and cast it behind your back? Do you not read where it says: 'And Sulaiman inherited Dawood?' And when it narrates the story of Zakariya and says: 'So give me an heir as from thyself (One that) will inherit me, and inherit the posterity of Yaqoob.' And: 'But kindred by hood have prior rights against each other in the Book of Allah.' And: 'Allah (thus) directs you as regards your children's (inheritance) to the male, a portion equal to that of two females.' And, 'If he leaves any goods, that he make a bequest to parents and next of kin, according to reasonable usage; this is due from the pious ones.' You

claim that I have no share! And that I do not inherit my father! What! Did Allah reveal a (Quranic) verse regarding you, from which He excluded my father? Or do you say: 'These (Fatima and her father) are the people of two faiths, they do not inherit each other?!' Are we not, me and my father, a people adhering to one faith? Or is it that you have more knowledge about the specifications and generalisations of the Quran than my father and my cousin (Imam Ali)?

Her sermon went on to accuse the companions of tyranny and oppression, of betraying the Prophet, and of plotting against his family. The parallels with the events that took place at Kerbala are evident. Indeed, it would not be unreasonable to suggest that the murder of Hussain and his companions on the day of Ashura had its genesis in the usurping of the rights of Fatima immediately following the death of the Prophet.

If anyone were to ask me today why I am still a Muslim, I would say without hesitation that it is, in no small part, because of Kerbala, and because of what it inspires in me. It is because of the values – justice, courage, strength, dignity – that speak to me. And I do not think that is unusual: there is something about Imam Hussain that pulls people back towards Islam. It is a rare thing for someone to be remembered more than 1,300 years after their death; rarer still for them to be mourned, annually, by millions of people around the globe. Visitors to the shrines of Hussain and his brother, Abbas, surpassed 21 million on the day of Ashura in 2022. It is incomparable to any other gathering of humans on earth.

But it was not always so. For many years, pilgrimage to Iraq was not possible under Saddam Hussain's Ba'ath regime. Until his deposition in 2003, all commemorations of Ashura were banned. It was a strategic decision: Saddam had come to power in Iraq during the period immediately preceding the Revolution in Iran. He saw at close quarters how Shia clerics could mobilise citizens by invoking Hussain's legacy of rising up against tyranny. He witnessed first-hand how fragile even the Pahlavi dynasty was in the face of mass action. He became ferocious in his persecution of Shias, both civilians and clerics. One of the leading intellectuals of the time, Muhammad Baqir al-Sadr, an outspoken critic of the Ba'ath party, and touted as the leader of the 'Iraqi Revolution', was imprisoned, tortured and executed by Saddam's regime. Interestingly, he was not the only member of his family to undergo such violence: his sister, Amina Sadr, an academic and political activist in her own right, suffered an almost-identical fate.

Nevertheless, some pilgrims continued to visit Kerbala and the other holy sites: the city of Najaf, home of the shrine of Imam Ali; Masjid-e-Kufa, which is reputed to have been visited by Adam, Ibrahim, and Khidr; and Samarra, the place from which the Mahdi entered the period of the Minor Occultation. Such journeys were not undertaken without considerable risk: in 1990, during an ill-timed trip to Iraq, my father, a lay preacher who often gave sermons during Muharram, was held hostage by the regime for some three months.

My own trips to Iraq, in 2009 and 2010, were less fraught, although they did coincide with the ongoing war, and I remember clearly the sound of explosives detonating alarmingly close by. They were not my first experience of this sort of pilgrimage: in 2005 I had been to Mashhad, where the Eighth Imam, Ali bin Musa Al Ridha, had been lured to his death by the Abbasid caliph Mamun and where his sister, Masuma, who had followed him to Iran, had also perished. And I had been to Syria several times since 2003. What was most striking in each case was the sheer scale of the mosques which housed the shrines. So vast were they that entire cities had built up around them. Despite that, they were constantly under construction, being expanded in all directions. In 2018, I went to Iran once again. Building works were, unsurprisingly, in progress, but the enormity of the complex was quite unexpected: the shrine covers an area of some 2.8 million square feet, but when considered alongside the seven courtyards which surround it, the site as a whole takes up 6.5 million square feet. In Kerbala the complex is built with two mosques – one housing the shrine of Hussain; the other his brother Abbas – are built opposite each other, with an area 378 metres long, and known as *bayn al haramayn*, connecting them. The courtyards of these shrines are effectively for the public to use however they wish, and it is common to see people praying or reading there, and, not infrequently, picnicking or napping. Coming from the UK, and from a community which saw mosques as places to escape daily life, this easy relationship between living and worshipping struck me as odd, perhaps even disrespectful. But a decade later, I can see the beauty in places of worship allowing congregants to go about their business as required. In any case, many of the people who go on pilgrimages such as this lack the means for comfortable and convenient accommodation, and it makes sense that, if a religion is designed to meet all of your needs, mosques should do the same.

The story of Islam, as I said, is a story of women fighting for their rights, and of refusing to be silenced by tyrannical, oppressive regimes. A shame, then, that women are still denied the opportunity to participate fully in civil and religious life in many Muslim communities and countries, not least in Iran, a majority Shia country, which has seen considerable unrest and dissent over the past decade. The recent protests were prompted by the death in custody of twenty-two-year-old Mahsa Amini, arrested for failing to wear her hijab 'correctly'. Of course, the protests will be suppressed brutally, with great loss of life. But the protests are not about hijab at all, of course: they are about what it represents in a patriarchal system, where women's freedom to choose how they dress – and how they live – is restricted. Anyone who thinks such policing of women's bodies and lives is justified clearly understands little about Islam, or what the women who fought for it stood for. Women have been diminished, and we have all been complicit in allowing it to continue. Somehow Khadija, Fatima and Zainab – and those who came after them – have come to play a supporting role in the evolution of Islamic thought, rather than being given the place they deserve as central characters and stateswomen in their own right. One could easily draw parallels between them and the women fighting for their rights in present-day Iran – and I wonder what they would think of those women, as they rise up against police brutality and clergy-sanctioned state violence. Khadijah and her daughters refused to submit to men in positions of influence; they had ample power and influence of their own, and they were not afraid to wield it. In doing so, they shaped the course of Islam.

The scale of the problems Muslim women face is overwhelming, and it is easy to feel powerless, or to become insular. But power – as Ashura teaches us – is about more than numbers. From its inception, Islam was built on struggle and it flourishes only because of that continual struggle. If we are to truly understand and practice Islam through the lens of Ashura we have to be alive to these issues. Remembrance is not enough: action is what counts. The stories of what happened to the family of the Prophet are not stories; they are lessons. They teach us the consequences of power that is wielded unjustly, and they show us that resistance is not only possible but necessary, because liberation is a human right.

FINDING ANNA

Leela Prasad

I had not imagined that my obsessive search for twenty years for a hundred-and-fifty-some-year-old grave would teach me something about the meaning of history. Few would have cared about the discovery of this grave. It was, after all, the grave of a low-class Indian woman who was practically a nobody in the grand annals of nineteenth-century colonial India. But that was precisely the question: *was Anna Liberata de Souza a nobody?*

Anna Liberata de Souza was an ayah to Mary Eliza Isabella Frere, the daughter of Bartle Frere, the legendary governor of Bombay in the 1860s, who at one point in his career, had been tipped to be the governor-general of India. Bartle Frere came from a distinguished political family (his grandfathers had been MPs for Norwich and Arundel) and he had graduated with distinction from East India College, the East India Company's recruitment-and-training school at Haileybury. Landing in Bombay in 1834 after an adventurous land passage through Egypt, Bartle Frere rapidly scaled colonial ranks—private secretary to the governor of Bombay, political resident of Satara, chief commissioner of Sind—to finally become governor of Bombay. His heavy footprint in India is visible in those things that colonialism congratulates itself for: irrigation canals, trade fairs, the Sind Railway, the Oriental Inland Steam Company, and even the first adhesive postage stamp in India. His role in suppressing the Indian Uprising of 1857–58 earned him a knighthood and a coveted appointment to the Viceroy's Executive Council, a position in the cabinet of the British government in India. In 1864, Frere's wife, Catherine and his eighteen-year-old daughter, Mary, the oldest of five siblings, joined him. When Catherine shortly returned to England to be with the younger children, Mary took charge of the domestic management of Government House in Bombay (or their monsoon residence in Ganeshkhind, Poona). Her sister Georgina credits Mary with performing the task 'with a tact and power singular in so young a girl…owing to a very human interest in her fellow creatures, which took no narrow view of life and of its possibilities under all sorts of conditions, and she enjoyed the opportunities of meeting Native ladies in their Zenanas and Missionary workers at their Stations, as much as "Society" in its more usually accepted sense'.

One of these 'fellow creatures' was Anna, the ayah, who worked for the Frere household in Ganeshkhind for eighteen months. She started work in 1865, around the time when Government House began to be built. By the time it was finally completed in 1871, Government House, with its hundred-foot tower, had broken all budget and project timelines. It occupied the centre of a 512-acre colonial development where British-style bungalows for officers nestled amidst tree-lined roads and terraced gardens. The four-hundred-foot-long Government House itself stretched north-south and had two double-storied wings connected by a central portion. A durbar area, a formal dining room with an arched ceiling, a ballroom, and an arcade opening to a large conservatory hosted banquets, receptions, and ladies' socials. One wing was reserved for guest bedrooms, the other for the governor's office and his private residence. A 250-foot underground tunnel connected the main building to the kitchen, the store, and the servants' quarter. In addition, four bungalows for the governor's staff, a guardroom with an ornate clock tower, European-style barracks for the governor's band, stables, and coach houses were placed around the main building. There was apparently no problem housing servants in these mansions, because, according to Edmund Hull's vade mecum for Anglo-Indian domestic life, the great advantage with Indian servants is that 'no provision has to be made with regard to their board or lodging'. Hull instructs that only one servant should sleep in the house at night—on a mat in the veranda. The cook could sleep on a shelf in the kitchen. The horse keepers should sleep with the horses in the stables, 'always'. Anna would either have lived in one of the servant outbuildings or slept in the verandas of the north wing of Government House in Ganeshkhind, where Mary could have called her at will.

In the winter of 1865, Mary accompanied her father on an official journey through the Deccan. Bored, she persuaded Anna to tell her stories, and *Old Deccan Days; or, Hindoo Fairy Legends, Current in Southern India*, was thus made. It was published in 1868 by John Murray, the publishing house that had published Charles Darwin, Jane Austen, Henry J. Coleridge, David Livingstone, and Lord Byron and all the trademark guides that were used by travellers to Britain's colonies. I discovered *Old Deccan Days* in a secluded aisle of a university library in the American Midwest.

Attracted by a thumb-sized image of a golden Ganesha donning a British crown on a maroon cover, I had serendipitously pulled out a yellowed book from the stacks. I leafed through the first pages. A hand-drawn picture captioned 'Government House' startled me. At the bottom of the page, it said, 'Anna Liberata de Souza died at Government House, Gunish Khind, near Poona, after a short illness, on 14th August, 1887'. An unexpected nostalgia overpowered me.

Ganeshkhind was where I had spent all my childhood. I had lived in what had once been the palatial house of a British officer. The house had been assigned as residential quarters to my father, a professor, by the University of Poona (now called Savitribai Phule Pune University) which now occupied the Ganeshkhind campus. The campus' giant pipal and banyan, neem, and tamarind trees, and abandoned outbuildings provided for encounters with ghosts. There was the story of a British memsahib who had fallen off her horse and died. It was rumoured that her ghost still roamed the grounds in search for her saddle and hat. In later years, I recalled this spectre as symbolic of the empress searching for her lost throne and crown. I have often wondered if ghost stories about colonial India were a masterly way for formerly colonised people to assert justice, poetic and other. The colonial past lived here, exhaling 150 years of irreconcilable history. The Main Building – near the site of the bloody battle of Khadki in 1817 between the Marathas and the colonial British – was now the administrative hub of the University of Poona. It was a majestic Italian-Gothic building with Romanesque arches and a central tower surrounded by sprawling lawns. I had played on these lawns.

The converted quarters were too large for their modern, middle-class occupants. Each house had a tiny kitchen and a tinier dark and airless storeroom, evidently designed for the Indian cook and the ayah of the colonial British household. Domestic manuals written by white women of the time cautioned the neophyte English wife in India: 'the kitchen is a black hole, the pantry a sink'. In the disused stables attached to my home, I had summoned ghosts with my brother and his friends on a self-designed

Ouija board. We had even talked to Mahatma Gandhi on this board about upcoming exam results.

So, when I saw a picture of the Main Building and a portrait of the narrator in this yellowed book, I saw history being woven back and forth on the loom of time. Mysterious, enigmatic, compelling, intuitive connections. Mesmerised, I turned the pages and saw a pencil-sketch of Anna Liberata de Souza. The next page was Anna's autobiographical narrative, titled 'The Narrator's Narrative'. A first reading told me her story: two generations before her, Anna's family had been Lingayats, members of a Hindu sect that worships the deity Shiva. Her grandfather had moved from Calicut to Goa, at that time a Portuguese territory, where he had converted to Christianity, and consequently become ostracised by his family. Like many Goan Christians, Anna's grandfather and father had served in the British army; her grandfather had been a havildar (sergeant) and her father a tent lascar, and both had won medals in the battle of Khadki. The family had settled in Poona. After a childhood that lacked nothing, Anna's destiny changed when she was married at twelve and widowed at twenty. With two children to raise, she became an ayah to British families. Already fluent in Marathi, Malayalam, Portuguese, and Konkani, Anna quickly learned to speak, read, and write in English. A year before Anna narrated the stories, her only son drowned in a river accident in Poona. Anna's narration ends on a philosophical note about these turns in her life.

The 1881 edition of *Old Deccan Days* fixed a structure that gave the book its permanent identity. It contains a 'Preface' that Mary Frere wrote when she was thirty-six years old in which she recounts the circumstances in which Anna narrated the stories and describes the way Mary recorded them. Then there is Bartle Frere's 'Introduction', full of glib assertions for an English audience about Hindu beliefs and practices supposedly underlying Anna's stories and tying his personal experiences in the Maratha country to European ethnology. Next comes 'The Collector's Apology' by Mary Frere, containing her guarded defence of the stories against perceptions of Indian character. She provides a brief statement on transcription and orthography. The tour de force is 'The Narrator's Narrative', in which Anna tells her life-story. Mary assures the reader that it has been 'related as much as possible in [Anna's] own words of expressive but broken English'. We learn that the life-story was compiled and edited over many conversations with Anna over the eighteen months that she worked for the Freres. Anna's twenty-four stories follow. The literary English of the stories has nothing in common with the curated 'broken English' of 'The Narrator's Narrative'. The irony may be explained by the method through which the stories were transcribed: as Mary heard each story, she took notes, then she wrote up the story and read it back to Anna to check that she had 'correctly given every detail'. So, we can, with some confidence, say that the diction of the twenty-four stories is Mary's/European and the characters and the plots are mostly Anna's. 'The Narrator's Narrative' presumably provides just that touch of colloquial flavour, while the stories, with Anna's presence dissolved, satiate the narrative tastes of Victorian audiences. I realised that Anna's 'broken English' was in fact an accomplished act of translation. If Anna narrated these stories in English, it meant that she had translated a cultural world into an alien language system and renegotiated her cultural fluency for Mary's benefit. The book concludes with 'Notes' and a 'Glossary'. In two longish 'Notes', Bartle Frere raves about the heroism of British troops in the battle of Khadki ('Kirkee') and defends the economic policies of his government, riling against Anna's criticisms which she has expressed in 'The Narrator's Narrative'. Mary's single 'Note' is a translated text of two of Anna's songs. Finally, the 'Notes on the Fairy Legends' are glosses – sanctimonious micro-sociologies – by Bartle Frere on six of the stories and by Mary Frere on one story. Twenty Indian words form the 'Glossary' that closes the book. Five full-page, hand-drawn illustrations, one of which is a portrait of Anna Liberata de Souza, are interspersed.

As I browsed through the stories in the book, I remember being struck by the (curiously transliterated) phrase *'mera baap re'* (my dear father) and the name *'Guzra Bai'* (garland lady). I imagined how Anna might have told the stories at least partly in Marathi, the language of my childhood. The spell of *Old Deccan Days* gradually drew me to the Oriental and India Office Collection at the British Library in London. There, I found the hand-written manuscript of *Old Deccan Days* and letters between Mary Frere and her publisher John Murray. At the John Murray Archive (now held at the National Library of Scotland in Edinburgh), I found a trove of correspondence between the Frere family and Murray. I began to unfold the map of the making of *Old Deccan Days*.

The letters tell us how, in early March 1867, after thirty-three years in India, Bartle Frere returned to England for good. Mary brought back with her a nearly completed manuscript of *Old Deccan Days*. Anna's stories, which she had heard from her mother and her grandmother, travelled across the Arabian Sea, curved around the Cape of Good Hope, sailed up the Atlantic, and came to be fitted to a new prosperous life as a book commercially published on London's Albemarle Street. A few months after they had arrived in London, Bartle Frere seems to have written to the publisher John Murray with a query about publishing his daughter's manuscript. Murray accepted. A partnership of the prominent was sealed. Frere's stock was high; he was considered a formidable statesman of the British colonial government.

The publishing of *Old Deccan Days* quickly became a robust family venture for the Freres. The archivist of the Murray archive in London told me, 'In fact it seems the whole Frere family was writing to Murray and they appeared to be great friends'. As I went through the letters, which spanned the four editions of the book, a universe of negotiations and discussions about topics from pictures to profits emerged.

Old Deccan Days became a runaway success in England. It went through four editions after its debut in 1868, was presented to Queen Victoria, and raked in substantial royalty for the Freres. In my earlier writing on this collection, I appreciated its pioneering method. It had contextualised Anna with an autobiographical narration (story-collections of that time referred to storytellers as 'told by the boy who sold eggs' or 'the garrulous old woman' and so on). Although I had some caveats, I appreciated the play of voices in the collection that allows us to see the micro-politics of interactions.

In 2016, however, I stumbled on a passage in a nineteenth-century memoir that dramatically altered my view, forcing me to revisit my earlier assessment. *Recollections of a Happy Life* (1894) by Marianne North, a British traveller and botanical painter, is about her adventures in India and Sri Lanka. A paragraph casually says that in 1878, ten years after *Old Deccan Days* was published, she ran into Anna in one of the bungalows of

Government House, Bombay. At that time, Anna was working for the family of Richard Temple, the governor of Bombay.

The old ayah Miss Bartle Frere has made famous as the storyteller in her *Tales of Old Deccan Days* sat on the doorstep. People there said, the old lady was quite guiltless of any of the stories imputed to her; that the only thing she was famed for was idleness and a habit of getting drunk on Sundays, when she said: 'I Christian woman; I go to church'. But Sir Richard Temple promised the Freres to keep her, and he did. I liked the old lady, as she never worried me by putting things tidy, but sat picturesquely on the doorstep and told me of the wonderful things she had seen. She tried to persuade me to take her on my next travels with me: a female John! bottle and all!

The denigrating remarks jolted me. Had I, in my earlier writing on *Old Deccan Days*, been excessively impressed by Mary Frere's authorial generosity? Had I been wrong in seeing Anna Liberata de Souza through the eyes of a reading practice that is unaccustomed to admitting people like her as anything other than subaltern? Even if such a reading practice were to recognise Anna as a speaking subaltern subject, it would still allow us to see her only as an especially articulate servant whose life story provides nothing more than a rich social context for the audiences who read the stories she told. Two questions surfaced. First, did Anna mean anything more to Mary than an old storytelling ayah, a source of unmined Indian lore? It is true that Anna's stories enchanted Mary, dispersed the loneliness of a rugged journey, and challenged prevailing negative portrayals of India in England. Yet, had I under-read the condescension that breaks through in the prefatory material? For instance, Mary says that she provides explanations for things in the stories that could be rationally explained, but for things that are irrational, Anna is 'the sole authority'. When Anna translates *'Seventee Bai'* as 'Daisy Lady' (to help Mary understand *shevanti*, chrysanthemum, in the language Mary knows best), Mary comments that no botanist 'would acknowledge the plant under that name', and when Anna describes a place called *'Agra Brum'* as the 'City of Akbar', Mary says, 'no such province appears in any ordinary Gazetteer'. (Anna must have meant Agra Bhum, the land [bhumi] of Agra, where Akbar's tomb lies.) Second, had I underestimated the extent of Anna's disquiet about the writing down of oral stories? While Mary Frere appeals to record stories

like these lest they be lost, Anna believes the integrity of the oral telling is
ruined. She complains:

> It is true there are books with some stories something like these, but they
> always put them down wrong. Sometimes, when I cannot remember a bit of a
> story, I ask some one about it; then they say, "There is a story of that name in
> my book. I don't know it, but I'll read." Then they read it to me, but it is all
> wrong, so that I get quite cross, and make them shut up the book.

I began to see that Anna's upset with textualisation, like a rebel thread that
unravels an entire sweater, was a critique of the project of colonial
modernity itself—its education, economics, and its promise of progress.

I retraced my steps in the archive, confronting once again the infamous
limitations of colonial records: photographs, travelogues, fiction, minutes,
reports, and surveys materialise the coloniser's person and policy in
manifold ways, while the experiences of the politically-colonised are
subject to recovery and recoverability, a process frequently needing the
midwifery of special disciplines.

In this process, I noticed that across thirty years of correspondence
between the Frere family and John Murray the publisher, there are precisely
two references to Anna. In the first, Mary asks Murray whether it would be
better to use a photograph of Anna or a sketch of her made by Katie, Mary's
sister. In the second, Mary refers to Anna's death in Ganeshkhind in a side
note. In a larger discussion about what additional information should go
into the fourth edition, Mary Frere writes to Murray, 'I could add a word
or two if wished about my dear old ayah's death—but that would not be
necessary but could come into a later edition'.

The manuscript of *Old Deccan Days* presents its own complications as a
colonial record. While the stories in the manuscript are lightly edited –
recall that Anna's voice recedes in them – 'The Narrator's Narrative' is
heavily edited. It explicitly displays Mary's stitching together of
discontinuous snippets that were gathered across eighteen months into a
linear narrative. Numerous numbered hash marks designate blocks of text
that are assembled into the chronologically ordered narrative of Anna's life
that appears in the book. Perhaps all chronologies intrinsically, inescapably
have a fictive quality to them. Yet when the past is remembered disjointedly
over time in the form of musings or as responses to contexts and questions,

the sense of the person that emerges is different from the sense that comes from the tighter logic of a chronologically ordered story. Mary's seamless composition renders Anna as someone who once had a happy childhood of 'plenty' but had become a hapless ayah, dependent on the goodwill of English Christians.

I began to re-engage the same archives, the same book, with a different instinct, more attuned to an ethics of recognition and acknowledgment. Re-reading the elided material in Mary's handwritten manuscript helped me punctuate the record differently. As I began to disrupt the chronology with new pauses, the narrative acquired alternative meanings and affect that come from intuition, what the French phenomenologist Henri Bergson in *The Creative Mind* (1946) calls the 'receding and vanishing image which haunts [the mind] unperceived...in order to furnish "explanation"'. If Kant had insisted that the intellect is the fountain of all knowing, Bergson argued that 'intellection' gives us insight into physical operations, but it is intuition that takes us to the 'inwardness of life'. Intuition is sympathetic. It helps me see, for instance, the many shades of orange between red and yellow and thereby sense the spectrum of possibilities of colour. The result of interpreting through intuition is a sense reading, a term I adapt from Michael Polanyi. Polanyi's theory of meaning proceeds on sense giving and sense reading: Sense giving is the search for the words that will express the meaning I want to convey. Sense reading (akin to figuring out what that strange shape in the garden at night could be) is the striving to understand a text from 'an inkling of a meaning' in it.

My sense reading reveals an Anna who is robustly independent and audacious. Even under the surface of the only text available to us on her life, a colonial text, Anna's sovereignty shimmers. Anna shows that life, with all its comeuppances and happenstances, could still be lived fully and happily, without either the largesse of colonialism or its opportunities for labour. Colonial modernity turns out to be a ruse. Christianity too, Anna shows, could still be salvific for her, but without its exerting a dominant control over the everyday arts of a plural religious imagination. A sense reading reveals an Anna to whom dignity and belonging mattered more than increased colonial wages. This Anna is ultimately sovereign because her speaking ability is indestructible and empowers her to critique and defy, and to create and dream. Even when Marianne North ran into her a decade after the book had found lucrative shores, the much older Anna was just as keen as before to narrate her stories and travel to new places.

Slippages in the archive let us glimpse this other Anna. For instance, among the manuscript materials in the British Library is a note by Mary Frere that describes how Anna narrated her stories: as if she was in a trance, as if she was visualising and imaginatively re-living the story that she was recounting. But, like most readers, if we did not have access to this earlier appreciative, poetic description, we would only have the 1881 edition in which Mary describes Anna's narration as an effort of a sluggish memory. As she narrates, the published book tells us, she stares vacantly into the distance to avoid being distracted by interruptions. Anna is now part of common trope of the dull-witted Anglo-Indian ayah. But the same 1881 edition allows us to counter this view. In 'The Narrator's Narrative', Anna tells Mary that her mother lived to be ninety, that Anna was seven when she got a pet dog, eleven when her grandmother died, twelve when she got married, and twenty when she was widowed. Oddly, when Anna says her grandmother was 109 years old when she died, Mary strikes out the 109 in the manuscript and changes it to "about a hundred" for the final edition. We can conclude that Anna's memory is in fact lucid.

Thus, a sense reading leads to new questions; it demands that we pause longer at certain moments in Anna's life to imagine and connect to the events in her life. What was Anna's sense of herself? Certainly not as the proverbial ayah, the much needed but strategically distrusted figure of the Anglo-Indian household. She sees herself instead as resembling her grandmother after whom she is named: a physically strong and good-looking woman who had a capacious memory and a vast repertoire of stories, resilient in the face of hardship, and an inventive caretaker of her grandchildren. Anna's portrait in the book drawn by Mary's sister Katie shows her with youthful features and jet-black hair (of which Anna is rather proud). She sees herself in her outspoken and hardworking mother. And she recognises herself in her father and brothers' conviction that 'that girl can do anything!' If she had been a man, she tells Mary, 'I might now be a Fouzdar' (a commander in the Mughal army or a chief of police in British India). An everyday education forms Anna's 'world-ing' – on clear wintry nights when the sky is starlit, her grandmother teaches her about constellations; at a wayside shrine of a Hindu deity, she learns to stop and pray, surprising Bartle Frere that a Christian would do this; through stories of extraordinary lands and creatures, hours in the sun taming pets, visits to the bazaar with her mother, she learns to observe, to say 'maybe', and to engage with possibility. As I reflect on how my grandmother and my mother have shaped my own clay, I can intuit how resemblances, inheritances and dreams have powerfully fashioned Anna's self-understanding.

A sense reading takes me to Anna the prescient critic of colonial modernity. She is aware that colonialism had broken – or profoundly twisted – the links between occupation, flourishing, and happiness, and spends a 'great deal' of money to send her son to school. 'Now I'm grown up I'll get a clerk's place', he assures her, exposing a brazenly utilitarian curriculum designed to oil the human wheels of the colonial machinery. The school would probably have been some version of the Anglo-vernacular school – where a largely European curriculum was taught in both English and Indian languages to Indians. Yet, far from being lured into the hollow of colonial progress, Anna tells Mary 'my grandfather couldn't write, and my father couldn't write, and they did very well'. They had provided 'plenty comfort' for their families and ensured happy childhoods for their children. About herself, she adds, 'I know your language. What use? To blow the fire? I only a miserable woman, fit to go to cook-room and cook the dinner.' Her words throw me back to the stifling dungeon-like kitchen and pantry of the bungalow I grew up in, but I now hear the bold voices of 'miserable women' exposing the fictions of the British empire. The grand fiction, of course, was that empire would improve the natives' quality of life. Ironically, Government House had been built amidst the debris of Bombay's great financial crash of 1865, when inflation crippled the common person in India. On the veranda of Government House, Anna tells the governor's daughter that prior to the rule of the British, 'we were poor people, but living was cheap, and we had "plenty comfort"'. She compares the before and the after of British economic policies – the prices of oil, grains, sugar, meat, house rent, cloth, and various household commodities. 'This shows how much more money people need now than they did then,' she concludes. Bartle Frere bristles at Anna's trenchant assessment of the economy. He calls her remarks a 'specimen of a very widespread Indian popular delusion'. But Anna has struck at a fundamental self-justification of colonial rule.

A sense reading, finally, helps me fathom presence in absence. 'I have often been asked under what circumstances these stories were collected?' writes thirty-six-year-old Mary in the two-page preface to the third edition of 1881. As she describes the official tour through the Deccan during which the recording of Anna's stories was begun, we face a strange absence. Anna, present through descriptions of her mannerisms, is absent as a fellow-sojourner. How might we recover her as a sojourner?

From Mary's perspective, the infrastructure for the Deccan sojourn was well in place. A six-hundred-person crew – cooks, camel divers, elephant mahouts, horse grooms, tent pitchers, and so on – and a motley of animals supported the governor, his daughter, and a few British officers, on this journey.

She breathlessly absorbs sights and encounters, rehearsing the tropes of Orientalism that reproduce 'the East' as a site of seductive paradoxes – barbarism and civilisation, for example – and also marvels at the astonishing diversity of story and landscape. In Kolhapur, Mary meets the Rani in the palace. In Satara, she sees Shivaji's famous sword which the goddess Bhavani had given him; in Karad, the Buddhist caves; in Belgaum, the ruins of Jain temples; in Bijapur, the Pearl Mosque and the 'Soap-stone' Mosque; and the shrine with its three hairs of the Prophet Muhammad's beard. She visits the massive library whose contents her father had 'rescued' and relocated to the India Office Library in London. On the plains of Dharwad, she sees the Nawab's cheetahs hunting antelope. Anna's stories fit into this larger experience of exotic wonder.

'I chanced to be the only lady of the party,' Mary writes. 'Anna Liberata de Souza, my native ayah, went with me. As there was no other lady in the Camp, and I sometimes had no lady visitors for some days together, I was necessarily much alone.' Despite the predicament of them being the only two women in a camp of six hundred men, Anna could be only a necessary utility, not a companion. Mary was being imperceptibly groomed in the everyday praxis of empire. In imperial post-1857 India, vast privileges and protocols were at the disposal of the governor's daughter. Mary has learned to see herself as 'the only lady'. The Indian Uprising had been ruthlessly contained eight years before this journey (with her father playing a significant role in its suppression), and the avaricious British Crown had replaced the mercenary East India Company, whose sun had set in the east.

Mary evinces no curiosity about Anna's experiences during the journey, following the customary indifference that Anglo-Indian writings show toward domestic servants. But Anna becomes present if *we* draw on her narrative to punctuate Mary's telling and imagine some of her experiences during the journey. For instance, Mary tells us that when they reached the Krishna and Bhima Rivers, the sahibs and the memsahib crossed safely in wicker-basket boats, while the native men and animals either swam across or used open rafts. How did Anna, the only other woman in the retinue, ford river waters? Did the sight of the river remind her of her handsome son who had drowned in the Mula River near Poona just 'last year'? Sometime during the making of 'The Narrator's Narrative' she tells Mary, 'That was my great sad.' As they passed through Bijapur and Dharwad – places that are historically important to the Lingayat community to which Anna's family once belonged – did the sites somehow resonate for Anna? Kolhapur, where Mary recorded Anna's first story and later sent it on to her younger sister in England, would surely have viscerally reminded Anna of the terror of the 1857 Uprising, when she and her previous British employer had escaped in the middle of the night. She had fled with her two small children. Mary does not reproduce Anna's story about the Kolhapur escape in 'The Narrator's Narrative'. The allusion appears through Anna's remark, 'but I've told you before about all that'. This image of a widowed young mother, running with her children, scared for their lives, is the image that stays with me as I read 'Punchkin', the first story that Anna narrates. It is about a smart princess named Balna, who through a series of misfortunes is abducted from her room in the palace by an evil magician called Punchkin, who has turned her husband and his six brothers to stone. Punchkin separates Balna from her infant son and imprisons her for twelve years in a tower because she spurns him. When the son turns fourteen and learns of his history, he sets out in search of his parents and uncles. He finds his mother in the tower and rescues her and his family. It is a story of a mother who is reunited with her son. I am transported to 'The Narrator's Narrative', where Anna describes her son to Mary: 'he was such a beauty boy – tall, straight, handsome – and so clever…and he said to me, "Mammy, you've worked for us all your life. Now I'm grown up. I'll get a clerk's place and work for you. You shall work no more but live in my house".'

Mary tells her publisher John Murray that this story was the hardest to transcribe and write up because of the 'many repetitions' it contained. Did these repetitions occur because it was hard for Anna to narrate this story? Perhaps it echoed her own life. She says that after her son's death, she couldn't remember things as she used to do, 'all is muddled in my head, six and seven'. Wearied by the memory of self-altering loss but also enlivened by the magic of the stories she is telling, Anna reminds us that narration is in essence a fuzzy art, mingling real-life experiences with conjured enchantments. And narration is at the heart of history. Anna is deeply present during the Deccan journey, which in the final account would need to acknowledge that it was a journey that was experienced by two women, in vastly different ways.

A cobra twisted into an M appears on the outer cover of each of the four editions to signify it was Mary Frere's book. Yet if we 'sense read', we know that the collection is animated by Anna. Ultimately, we will have to contend with the irony that suffuses colonial-era texts. The record that smothers Anna in one part is the very record that allows us to discern her presence. If we follow that presence, Anna Liberata de Souza is the 'girl who could do anything'. It is not a small matter that when she was made an offer to relocate to England as an ayah, an offer that would have paid her almost twenty-five years' worth of her ayah's pay in India, she refused, honouring her better sense of belonging and dignity: '— "May be I shall make plenty money, but what good if all the little fishes eat my bones? I shall not rest with my old Father and Mother if I go"—so I told her I could not do it'.

Back at the Ouija board.

Over the course of writing my book, *The Audacious Raconteur*, a curiosity had turned into an obsession: Where had Anna been buried? In January 2018, I was in Guanajuato, Mexico when I got a call. It was my friend Trevor Martin from Pune. Although I had not been in touch with him for many years, I had turned to Trevor, a native Punekar and a former Jesuit priest, for help in tracing Anna's grave. I had shared Anna's story. 'I'd love to help,' he had said. Trevor now had a lead. Was this the piece of information for which I had looked for years? As with archival records, burial records and graves of Europeans had been very easy to find. Holkar Bridge, Khadki War Cemetery, more choices. New Poona Cemetery in the 1880s did not allow Indian Christians to be interred there, as per new burial laws, we learned. Although somebody had donated a plot of land for natives to be buried in Ganeshkhind, nobody in Pune seemed to know about it, but everybody I asked voluntarily visited sites and pored over records.

After much legwork, Trevor had learned that Catholics of Portuguese origin in colonial India had mostly been buried at the Church of the Immaculate Conception, commonly known as City Church. He was now calling to say he had found out that the church had scrupulously maintained burial records. He and a friend who had become interested were going to look at them. There was a chance that although she was not Portuguese, Anna as a Roman Catholic would have been buried there. Trevor sent me images of burial entries from around 1887. The entries were in exquisite calligraphic Portuguese on large, yellowed ledger pages. I do not know Portuguese, so each time I saw the name 'Anna' or 'de Souza', my heart raced. (These are common Portuguese names). At Duke University, where I teach, I studied these entries with a Brazilian colleague. Sadly, there was no entry for Anna. My brother, co-accomplice at Ouija board sessions in our childhood, put me in touch with Vincent Pinto, his friend from their Indian Air Force days. Vincent, a former intelligence officer who now lives in Pune, said, 'I'd love to be involved in such a historic search'.

Historic. My search, though still open, concludes for the moment with the realisation that the sense of Anna I have pursued is the very sense that has motivated others to help 'find' her. Like me, these persons, unconnected with my project, feel justice is served when we can grasp a sense of a person – belonging, perspectives, creativity, struggle – that is beyond what can be captured by a label or a category, and in so doing reimagine the past with more equity and dignity. Without my childhood beliefs, but with the intuitions, I am coming to believe that it is time to invite Anna Liberata de Souza's spirit, sovereign and audacious, to the Ouija board that, at the end of the day, history itself is.

ARTS AND LETTERS

DISPLACED HOMES

Ziauddin Sardar
Photographs by Iason Athanasiadis

An aged Syrian woman walks through the Zaatari refugee camp in Jordan, while a young boy carries bread to his family's trailer home. Another young boy with his father, from a community of internally displaced Pashtuns from southern Afghanistan, looks through a car windscreen refashioned as a mud hut dwelling in a camp close to the Afghan city of Herat. There is so much written on these displaced lives. The acute longing for home is starkly evident.

But what is 'home'? Is it something more than just an address, just the building where we reside, just the valley that is 'ours', just the country where we were born and live? We speak of 'home is where the heart is', of making 'a house a home'. What precisely do we mean? In exploring the associations of such commonplace expressions, we begin to wrestle with what is displaced by dislocation and what is invested in making relocation a new home. We live in a world where displacement and relocation are on the increase. Refugees and asylum seekers running from war and persecution – from Syria and Afghanistan, Myanmar and Ethiopia, and now Ukraine. Environmental refugees escaping extreme weather events. Young Africans and Asians forced to leave their homes in search of employment in a hostile Europe, risking their life and limbs in hazardous journeys. Are we all becoming homeless persons or is the drive to make our living space home too strong? And what are the implications for society when fewer and fewer people are rooted to the soil of their origins? If we live in a country dominated by displaced homes what becomes of the sense of community and cohesion and how are we to bind people together in shared concerns? In short, how do we 'live together', we who come from so many diverse continents and nations, who occupy this space called Earth?

Ask the Palestinian refugees in camps, the asylum seekers crossing the English Channel in dangerously precarious boats, the Rohingyas in insanitary camps in Bangladesh, the persecuted Uyghurs in Turkey, and the Ukrainians in Poland and Hungary. Or the Afghan migrant at Pedion tou Areos (Champ-de-Mars), sleeping on mother earth, after arriving overnight in Athens from the island of the eastern Aegean Sea.

They will tell you that they desire nothing more than to return to their home – if only home was more accommodating, a place of liberty rather than oppression, poverty, persecution, war and death. Home is our beginning, a place of origin, the starting point of an identity. Yet place of birth does not necessarily equate with 'home'. Home is the place where the people we are related to by birth reside, and that is much more than an accident of birth. Home is a place of belonging but much more than belonging to a physical location. And yet the place itself, the spot of the map – *that* valley, village, town – where we begin our terrestrial existence is not a matter of indifference. Place of birth and home are complex distinctions within the shifting patterns of complicated lives and displaced homes.

How complex? Think of an example such as Rudyard Kipling. Born in India where he lived for his first five years, educated in England and then returning to India, where his parents still resided, he worked as a journalist for a mere seven years before returning to England never again to visit India. Kipling's place of birth was no incidental fact of his life. India was the bedrock on which his reputation as a writer is established, an identification inseparable from his creative output and achievement. And yet, never was there a more English Englishman, a man whose identity was more shaped by a historic sense of Englishness, which became the subject of his later literary output. Kipling belongs to India in a most particular way, and despite it all Kipling was never in any recognisable sense Indian. He is quintessentially displaced in the public mind, if not his own. Displaced too are all those people rotting in the port city of Calais, the asylum seeker who cannot pass through the channel marked 'EU citizens'; or, even, the one left for all others. They too are quintessentially Syrian, Afghan, Ethiopian; and their identity is also shaped by their historic experience. But unlike Kipling, they can, and some will, become the citizens of their displaced homes somewhere. And like Kipling, they are unlikely to abandon the sense of their original 'home' even when they have settled at 'home away from home'.

The associations of home are all about origin and identity, beginning and belonging that are lasting, enduring through generations. It is an attachment to place that is emotive but consists of far more than love of landscape, ecology and habitat. Home is the receptacle of history, a formation of life and living within a culture that is itself shaped by a particular land, the people who have lived on that land and how they have refined their way of life. Home is the comfort of normality, the place where we learn and develop our normative ideas of what it is to be human, to be part of the associations of human existence: family, neighbourhood, community, clan, tribe, nation, Europe, Africa, Asia. Home is the hook attaching us to past, present and future. Home is the concept through which we identify ourselves and relate our individuality to people beyond ourselves. If this had not been true in the past, for the generations that went before our existence, it is almost impossible to imagine how the sociability of homo sapiens, the social animal, could exist.

Times change. But the world does not begin afresh for each new generation. We are born and grow in a family that is our home. But the very nature of our family life is shaped by home-grown identities that are cultural and historical. Culture is the sum total of our learned behaviour. Culture is expressed through the language we learn, the habits and customs we acquire. Culture fashions our history and is simultaneously the birthright and legacy we inherit. The historic experience of our culture shapes our outlook on the events of today and our aspirations and vision of the future. Part of the essence of cultural identity is a common mind, a shared repository of ideas.

There is a sense in which the concept of home denies that humanity was ever a wanderer. Home is about stasis, the isolation and exclusiveness of an identity that belongs only to defined and bounded groups of people born, raised and spending their lives in one place, one culture as one people entire and of themselves. And yet it is unlikely any such people exist anywhere on this earth, or have ever so existed for time out of mind. The reality is human history is a tale of displaced homes, of human movement of mutual influence and diffusion created by the simple fact people have never stayed still. Muslim civilisation itself emerged out of displaced homes: the migration of the Prophet from Mecca, where persecution was the norm, to Medina where liberty was discovered; and the foundations of a civilisation was laid. Humanity has been a wandering, moving, shifting and changing entity throughout history. Yet that is not the image of history we cherish. Our concept of home eradicates much of the reality that was and is human life. Home is an excluding idea, an idea of place and belonging that divides and differentiates us from them.

But it need not be so. Home can be and is the positive and negative pole by which we navigate the best and worst of human identity. At best, home inculcates a sense of identity so secure it has place and space to recognise, respect and extend toleration to everyone, but especially people who do not share our identity. At worst, home is the sense of identity that makes us suspicious, fearful and innately antithetical to anyone who is not just like us. And home is the continuum between these alternate poles of being.

The yearning for home is, not surprisingly, encrusted with ideas of sacredness, a spiritual attachment to place, to people and to history that can elevate human understanding of self and others, or be distorted into hatred of others. The monotheistic religions all teach and encourage the sacredness of home. Ultimately, they teach it is God who is humanity's true home, and our homing instinct and its cultural expressions are the reflections and signs that lead or should lead to a better appreciation of the divine. Yet, down the ages such expansive ideas that should inspire toleration of others have been resolved into the dictates of God on my side – but not on anyone else's. This is, of course, equally true of other notions such as 'my nation right or wrong', or 'my territory, my place' that has no place for others of different faith, culture and ethnicity. Displacement of the meaning of home can be as pernicious a condition as physical displacement from a terrestrial home. But displacement can also be enticed with false promises of rewards – with devastating consequences, as the victims of a new slave trade, the trade in sex trafficking that now plagues Europe, demonstrates. Displacement can be a shroud behind which unspeakable acts of inhumanity are committed.

Our sense of home, of belonging, may be where we all begin but the imperatives of making a living or the consequence of events can have a great bearing on where we actually spend the rest of our days. We go out in search for employment, education, or a better life or simply for a more peaceful existence. New opportunities, new discoveries, ecological changes wrought by nature or human activity, shifts of power and disagreements within and between cultures, peoples and nations that are the rumours of wars and effects of wars, have all made displacement a permanent feature of human existence. By choice and the exigencies of circumstance people have always sought new homes. But in our times, the opportunity to make new homes is limited to a particular category of people. Perhaps it was always the case. But it is so self-evident today.

How do people cope with displacement? How shall we count the innumerable ways in which it works on people and their sense of identity? How do displaced people survive? How does the young woman looking out of her bombed house, in the southern Lebanese village of Aita al-Shaab, the scene of intense battles between the Lebanese Hezbollah and the Israeli army, make sense of her displaced life? When the dust settles, I suppose, the displaced must make a home just like those comfortably settled in their homes.

At best, displacement is the positive agent of constructive change, the introduction of impetus and ideas that enables new developments to emerge. Displacement can bring in its wake the gradual diffusion from which synthesis can be fashioned. People taking new industries, new technologies and ideas to the place where they settle have founded new developments, promoted the wellbeing and enrichment of the places where they settled. Synthesis can be seamless, it can look and feel like the inevitable development of what was and forget what it owes to what has been introduced from outside, brought in by displacement. At worst, displacement can produce the penetrative oppression of one people overwriting the existence, identity and home of another. The colonial imperialist imperative has been at work down the millennia of human history. Indeed, archaeologists long conceived of human history as total eradication of one group of people by displaced incomers. Displacement is defined by the sense of home the traveller and settler take with them, the scale and numbers in which they move and how they set about the business of remaking their displaced homes wherever they come to rest.

Home and displacement are architects that between them have made human history and continue to construct the world in which we live. Yet we harbour very different attitudes to these concepts. What is warm, consoling and comforting about home is vaunted while we look with disfavour on the rupture and challenges that always accompany displacement. How can displaced persons fit into a new location, a new culture, a new nation? They make their adjustment by and through the sense of home they bring with them. It is the human impulse to make a house a home that travels with the displaced. Home is so embedded in our sense of self that the most natural consequence of displacement is to seek out, reconstruct in a new place, elements of familiarity and recreate the means to perform the customs and rituals of one's cultural identity in a new land. The history of the world is replete with positive and negative examples of how the homing instinct has operated in the process of relocation.

So, it is incumbent on us to remember that the history of the European peoples begins with the recreation of displaced homes. The Franks, Huns, Alans, Goths the peoples who became the Europeans all were displaced out of Asia in historic times and through relocation and synthesis fashioned modern national identities, even as they overwrote, included or superseded earlier identities home-grown in Europe. European history also demonstrates how rapidly displaced homes become the only home of relocated peoples. Jutes, Angles and Saxons made their way as displaced people from Northern Europe to Britain and there founded a new identity, a new home-grown sense of being Anglo Saxon. Other groups from Northern Europe settled in France to become Normans. When the Norman William the Conqueror sallied across the English Channel two identities, from common stock, forged in displaced homes came into direct conflict – and together have fused into the history of Britain.

European nations know a great deal about displaced homes. The modern history of the world has been shaped by the displaced home Europeans carved out for themselves across the globe. The colonial mindset, the expatriate way of life, is an archetype of the displaced home. Colonists took their culture and way of life with them and recreated it, as well as they could and such amendments as were acceptable to them, wherever they went. The history of Europe has many negative lessons of what can be wrought by displaced homes, of the tensions and injustices that can be created in the power relations produced by the displacement and relocation of people. And yet, examined in a different light Europe has a wealth of experience on which to draw to find the positive, accommodating and creative possibilities of displaced homes being built within its bounds.

Home tugs at all our heart strings that make us human. Yet, if the tug of home is also an intimation of the divine in each and every one of us, then it is a call to something much greater and beyond ourselves. We have the choice to look and think of home in ways that enable cohesion, acceptance, mutual respect, toleration and synthesis between the multiple or plural ideas of home that exist in today's world. We also face the challenge of withstanding the growing sense of displacement that is the consequence of an ever more mobile population. More and more people are faced with the task of making private displaced homes for themselves in faceless cities where all sense of neighbourhood and community has evaporated.

We have much to consider when we think of home. A young, internally-displaced Afghan boy laughs as he makes himself at home in an abandoned bus in the outskirts of Kabul, Afghanistan. Another boy runs in front of the ruins of Darulaman Palace in Kabul, home of the deposed and displaced Afghan king, Muhammad Zahir Shah.

What being at home or in a displaced home actually means is not self-evident and given. It is a consciousness, a moral challenge we have no choice other than to construct.

FLOWERING SKY

Arif Ay
Translated by Mevlut Ceylan

Arif Ay's first book bears the title *Hira*. The title is significant; hira is the name of the cave where the Prophet Muhammad first received revelation. Ay sees the poetic role as closely paralleling the prophetic: both prophet and poet are seers. This essentially religious vision of the poet's place in society pervades all his work and helps explain the unpoetic title of his second collection: *Dosyalar* (dossiers). A dossier is a file the secret police keep on a person, particularly if he is a dissident. Ay dissents from the received view of Turkish history as imparted by state organs and institutions; he views with dismay the collapse of national institutions following the First World War, when they were replaced with institutions on the western model. In his verse he laments the passing of a culture and its replacement with a wasteland of the spirit.

Ay was born in 1953 in Nigde, central Anatolia. He read Turkish Literature and Islamic Theology at Ankara University, and worked as a civil servant before accepting a post as a lecturer in the Department of Turkish Language and Literature in the Faculty of Science and Letters at Kırıkkale University. Ay, who has published nine collections of poetry, has a wide appeal for the youth who flock to his readings in Ankara. The secret of his attraction lies not only in his scorn for hypocrisy (as seen in 'Ramp') but in the directness of his voice, sometimes compared to a clenched fist in its relentless ambiguity.

He writes in *vers libre* which became fashionable in Turkey from the 1940s onward, using modern methods to indite modernism. His most recent collection *Candles of Poetry* uses the same metric form as the previous collections. Critics hailed it as his most mature work, establishing him as a major figure amongst contemporary poets.

Ay cries aloud, and his tone is often bitter. He is particularly scathing of
the cash nexus, with its all-pervasive materialism, which he sees as having
sapped the moral values underpinning the Turkish spirit. A nation cut off
from its spiritual roots (the forgotten alphabet refers to Arabic, the
language of the Qur'an) ultimately faces extinction, this long sleep which
the somnolent system state education anticipates:

> sleep, sleep, go to bed and sleep
> that's what they taught you
> on your first day at school.

'Time', a haiku, expresses the poet's sense of futility. Another poem in
haiku tradition, 'Horses', conveys with epigrammatic pithiness a meaning
not immediately apparent to a non-Turk. The Turks were a race of hardy
horsemen out of Central Asia: the horse is a symbol of what they were
when they formed the vanguard of Islam. Such a horse, divinely appointed
or assigned, is riderless because he is the vehicle of faith itself, of the
supernatural truth of Islam. Horses amount to a repetitive, almost
obsessive image. In 'Ostlers' the nostalgia for a remote Turko-Islamic past
causes the poet to imagine himself dead:

> like a flowering sky
> the night rises over my skull.

His poetry is affirmative as well as destructive. And 'Labour', with its
echoes of Horace, replaces the Latin poet's faith in the poetic faculty with
a religious faith in the eternal edifice of supernatural, religious truth. In
the Qur'an the believer is referred to as a labourer, who labours in the
garden of the Lord:

> Their Lord has answered them: 'I will not allow the deeds of any one of
> you to be lost, whether you are male or female, each is like the other. I
> will certainly wipe out the bad deeds of those who emigrated and were
> driven out of their homes, who suffered for My cause, who fought and
> were killed. I will certainly admit them to Gardens graced with
> flowering streams, as a reward from God: the best reward is with God.'
> (3:195)

Ay's popularity also rests in part on his skill in love poetry. 'Asking' is an example of this genre, showing another side of Ay's inspiration. A gentler mood suffuses his verse at these moments.

River

I am a thundering river
in the lands of darkness

with a single stroke
I wrench the sleep
from the eyes of night

Poems of Destruction (fragment)

I would like to know you, sir
put aside your mask
all frogs have a night of their own
my absence and my voice have a night of their own
find me a place to leave my voice

What is it that whittles mankind away, sir
silence or speech
how do men multiply, sir
let us find a place to dump the speeches

In the sitting rooms of all houses
there is now a bright hungry guillotine
all sewers are open to us sir
everything flows towards heaviest indifference
forget about the one that doesn't flow, sir

you always stay put
like an antiquated port from times well past
where fishes of unknowable age swim in moonlight
you are an antiquated mister, sir

I am falling apart in the darkness
find me a place to leave my silence
a shining ship of death on a sorry wharf
we are truly romantic executioners, aren't we sir?

Ostlers

sometimes I can be divided into three or five
sometimes into infinity
I don't know if you've been told
but I am a docile stable-boy
looking after horses

the horses are long dead
the ostlers long gone
a broken currycomb scratched into tombstones

like a flowering sky
the night rises over my skull

Looking at Istanbul

This is Istanbul in the sun
When you look at her
She is standing on guard
And resists your attacks.

These are the minarets
That convey news
From heaven to earth
And from earth to heaven.

When a generous heart
Looks with love,
Doors open to the sea
And streets mirror the morning.

Only with love does she come to you,
When you turn your eyes,
This is Istanbul.

Torment

a desk has teeth to bite a man
dead paper and lively pen
do not make neighbourly sense
the child starts being a little book
and then grows into a fire

words roam and roam around
hurt and godless
man is a lost item of furniture
alive with worms

night is a tight knot
haunting our rooms
everything bites everything else
sleep is held at bay

Love

are those who love
and those who are loved

bruised and mangled
over there as well

are the middayshadows
long over there as well

Birds

to tell us the time
birds flap their wings
by our window

birds are the pendulum of the sky
their inexhaustible passion
winds up the clock

they carry our houses to the sky
they are the crew of heaven
they pull us out
from our darkness

Guerrilla

to the oppressed and to those who
suffer with them and fight at their side

the stars are fading away
how deep is your countenance
our heart is a wasteland
the walls of the world are collapsing

here the sun is so fresh today
the roads flanked by cypresses
the guerrilla is out there
thousands of suns in his eyes

come, move on
remember stars fade and shine
we march with the Book in our hands
when the trees cover
the face of the guerrilla
like a night bird

before the pitiless gun
he turns, and turns
and falls in spirals
once more
the honour of the earth is shattered

A Traveller in Enlightenment

my friend I am a passenger of love
distance is the measure of stars
closeness is the measure of my love
as bright and as dark
as the stars
I am a passenger of enlightenment

Dull

where the sun's heat boils in the sand
you can see me gathering the dark and gleaming
snake skins
with my hand I scoop your voice
I shed my skin like a shirt
where the sun casts a spearing shadow

Past-Participle

it is not in vain
that time stands still
that clocks err

Doomsday

mind you, time's carrionbird,
be off with your galleons
my heart walks before me
on its way to the Day of Judgment

Ramp

look the liars are passing, I can tell by their hats
they do not like the sun
their shadows are longer than themselves
they greet prostitution they fornicate with money
and then go on pilgrimages with saintly beards,
songs of usury

poet, tell me what kind of poem is this?
must you reel off unsettling dreams
must you upset this moonlight
how quickly you've forgotten your alphabet
sleep, sleep, go to bed and sleep
that's what they taught you
on your first day at school

Voice

the mountains facing me
are all rubies
oh holy Jacob
where are the sheep

Sand

there
the simple
the universal
building

Asking

what time is it I asked
the wind was still
I looked into your eyes
the sea had receded

what time is it I asked
the sun was just rising
I waved to the birds
there were smiles in their eyes

what time is it I asked
the night was new
make the night long I said
rippling tides echoed through the length
    of her eyes

Here

the wind blows quietly
a tile falls into the garden
the sun looks at my hand
a rain drop falls in my tea
a cloud like a ship slowly
draws up to my table
hand in hand we climb up
to the deck of the evening

here are the stars we say
we repeat the names of flowers
later as though nothing has happened
you feed the chickens first thing in the morning

Carnations

Like two people meeting for the first time
Carnations came between us
Like their scents and voices
Like their faces and hands
Carnations came between us

Parting moved in between us
Then sorrow and hunger
Darkness fell
You said something impossible
And it became possible
Everything happened at once
Carnations came between us

Guest

There's the steep road
Who is leading that caravan?
There's something inside us that grows
People should understand
That the squares are always filthy
And filth flows
The day is a ball of steel
Without love and affection
Children grow

Neither scales nor cranes
Can match a heart's endurance
Wastelands will be salty
Decay and rot shall end

Time

A dry sea
Caught
When I throw my fishing rod
Into the day

Labour

Neither cement
Nor steel
Are stronger
Then the wall built

Sky

Where are those deep heavens?
We had in the villages
Why, why do we not have them
In the cities?

Horses

Whilst the sun rises
Those wise horses
Carry the skies
On their backs

Parting

The dreams are loaded with laments
And the flowers blossom early in an Andalusian morning
From Merve the beloved comes to the shore
The Tigris flows by the evening tales
The beauty of Istanbul, perhaps, is a childish beauty

But the children live a thousand Badr wars in their hearts
Istanbul's face is scratched and the cut goes deep
Alas, henna is the colour of the sea
Dripping from the hands of mothers
As Andalusia ages she smells of iodine
Now, our love is warmer than our hatred

I am the child wearing the face of St.Sophia, the orphan
Oh heart, a thorny rose in my handkerchief
Thousands of voices have divided our voices

Those who silenced our voice
Have died one by one

This is the endless struggle
Of my heart
Dear heart you're warm!

What Time

And what era
There's no repeat of loves and roses
Your face is an illusion in the mirror of innocence
In the wild waters of time in which I am shattered
Ebb and flow of time and fire are the same
A rose of wind, a shadow of cloud
The yellow leaves, death and cries
Tell me, what time and what era
And when

Requiem

Someone somewhere
Someone in our very soul
As he faces the firing squads
Our blood is the fire that flows
Jerusalem is the name of the blazing sea
Part of me throbs
Wherever I am
Standing as a nightguard

My love is forlorn
Jerusalem is as strong as mountains
Its honour stands still and larger than life
Like a huge mountain
The children speak to the mountain
They talk about the honour
Wherever I am
Standing as a nightguard

Even if sorrow hits a thousand times
It grows
Water increases
Children grow green
Jerusalem grows
Wherever I am
Standing as a nightguard

POEM(S)

Adrianne Kalfopoulou

In shā' Allāh

He will go with a new name, passport, discover a hired parent at the port.
Europe's borders closed, so illegal journeys will begin anew at the port.

I'm called by my passport name, buy groceries, cook the food I bring home.
Vitamins and toothpaste, I say to a boy who asks me to get him shoes at the port.

An Afghan girl grabs my hand, points to a rotting tooth, repeats *me! me! me!*
Her brother has soccer cards, 30 euros, dreams himself a goalie at the port.

If you're Syrian you'll have less trouble getting papers, otherwise sell jewelry,
bribe your way, bargain for a stolen cell phone, be sure not to get stuck at the port.

In the middle of the night, I wake thinking I forgot to say *Take water with you.*
Ali says *thank you*, his English polite, his manners promise safe passage at the port.

Boats appear, more disappear, sunk with people who sold all they had for some luck.
Smugglers are on the lookout, they know opportunity and smell profit at the port.
God be with you, Judi says, holding her hand to her heart. *In shā' Allāh* Azize says.
We pray *Allāh* is welcoming, a father who won't abandon his children at the port.

Are You Dressed for a Party?

The end of the road is a beautiful mirage,

Fady Joudah, 'Atlas'

He was waiting for me at the metro stop

Above ground

Alizera

As I waited for him   more than I can now say   how

My life   so different from his

Felt bereft

Ali, a poet   writes continuously   *I have not written a poem in*

a long while I say   it embarrasses me to say this   Then

Ali thanks me and I begin to weep   *for what are you thanking me?*

    we had had a few meals together   texted messages

Over a period of months when he would tell me what he was cooking

I would say something like   *Sunday! I'll finally read something*

This to someone whose every day is a day inside

Days   he texts me   *I read & read because there is nothing else*

in days of unemployed waiting when he quotes lines of Szymborska to me

And finally described the trip

Over the mountains between Iran and Turkey where there is a plain
border guards

More than 500 of us
and the smugglers
perched in three places
we had minutes to make it
across
and the guards
passing
were always looking

I am trying to say goodbye when

He says *you are*   *too much* and I'm not sure how to understand this

But he is thanking me   when I say *nothing* meaning

It was nothing

This is *too much* in the *never enough*   of getting Ali into an English class

meeting up a few times   some readings we did

Ali reading poems in Persian, teaching me a few words

Arouz   *thank you*   *merci*   I learn his family ate watermelon during

Yalda the winter solstice

I tell him *I'm lost* he says *how can anyone not be*

Now that he's received his papers, he'll go to the Netherlands

He's never been on a plane though he crossed the plain

In shoes like these he tells me and I look at the black shine of the gleaming patent leather and look up from my salad thinking there's a strand of hair in my mouth as I'm eating and have not removed the hair from my mouth, but do and say *no*, and he nods *yes* and describes the *Afghan friends* who lifted him from under his arms to carry him, that he had *a candle* he was carrying and traded it for *a cup of water*, that *saved me*

I listen eating, or rather not eating

When Ali tells me he won't have any of my wine

Beer maybe?

He shakes his head, says he used to make his own alcohol

In Iran

He saw me carrying groceries   he'd just gotten out of his English class

I was not well   Ali crossed the street, took my bags

Holding them the way he held the umbrella after we'd had a meal as it started to rain

  and asked *do you have a bathtub*

suggesting I *put on some music*

Very loud   lay in the bath   Forget everything

Instead, I surfed the net and thought of the night Ali sent a text with pictures of welts on his back

He told me what he cooked for dinner   he was *sore*

I asked why

some boys he said   *they were so young, how sad*

These boys

He was not going to tell me
He was going to tell me
He felt sorry for whoever they were
He was *very sorry for this*   *don't they have hopes?*
He wants to know why this happens
He didn't fight back
He let them hit him   until they left

No, he was not packed yet, but knew he was going to wear what he was
wearing this evening, as we talked   the same patent-leather shoes   *I was
like this then   when I was crossing over the plain, the smugglers asked me Where are
you going dressed this way? Are you going to a party?*

You are I say, and Ali nods, and I give him

A black moleskin notebook

I thought might be useful

FIVE POEMS

Tawfiq Zayyad
Translated by Adia Bamia

I Shake Your Hands

I implore you,
I shake your hands,
I kiss the ground on which you tread,
And I say: I will redeem you.
I offer you my eyesight,
The warmth of my heart I give you.
The tragedy I endure is my share of your plight.
I appeal to you,
I shake your hands.
I did not disparage my homeland,
Neither did I yield.
I confronted my gaolers, alone, naked, and barefoot.
My hand was bleeding,
Yet, I did not give up.
I maintained the grass over my forefathers' tombs.
I implore you; I shake your hands!

Evening Chat in Prison

I remember, I do,
The Damoon, its bitter nights and its barbed wires,
Justice hanging on the fence, and
The moon crucified
On the steel window.

I remember plantations of red freckles
On the face of the pesky gaoler.

I remember, I do,
When we chatted in the dark night,
In the dusty Damoon cell.
We would sigh as we listened to a love story,
We would threaten when we heard the story of a theft,
But we cheered when a rebellious people achieved freedom.

***

Oh, my people,
Oh, sticks of incense,
You are dearer to me than my own life.
We keep the promise.
We endure life in a prison cell,
The ties of injustice and the prison bars,
If we endure hunger and deprivations,
It is to undo the shackles of the crucified moon,
To give you back your usurped rights,
To recuperate the future from the darkness of greed,
Lest it be bought and sold!
Lest the boat remains without sails.

A Letter Sent Through the Mandelbaum Gate

Beloved mother!
I send you two hundred kisses,
From our house on top of the hill,
From the vegan tree, the rose tree, and the Indian jasmine,
From the joyful ground tickled by animal feed,
From the setting for the olives and the buttress,
From the fasting stove, the sticks, and the pot,
From a grapevine that fills the basket every summer
From a Damascene mulberry tree, white and ailing,
From a premonition wondering when the night would end.

***

Mother, you are the most beautiful in the whole wide world,
You are the eyeball I adore, oh my heart!
To me, yearning is like a rose kept alive with my love.
Mother …
How are you doing?! The heart is far away.
How is the black tent, the friends?
Tell me, by God, have you withered away as we did, wishing
    to be close to you?
We send you greetings, green like the grass.
The longing bird offers them to the flock,
He asks the stars about you, hoping for an answer
Asking about the first step on the road!
Our news, you ask? There is plenty to say, they break my
        heart:
Abu Salah lost his eyesight from grief,
Fakhri's mother, passed away grieving over Fakhri
The brunettes of the village have gone grey waiting.
The spring dried up and stopped flowing.
Our land is slipping away under the cover of darkness.
All that is left mother, is boredom and rocks.
But we resist, throughout the years, like iron,
How couldn't we not,
When the pride of the eagle is in our blood.

***

Your son is not alone any more, an only child since his birth.
I married the neighbour's daughter, sometime ago.
She is my support in a life filled with hardships.
If you see her you would say, 'she is the mint of the village'.
My apologies for failing to invite you on my wedding day,
I did not invite you because the road is blocked.

***

Mother, you have become a grandmother,
I have now from your flesh and mine, a rose,
A naughty three years old, like a monkey.
I called her Fahda, she is so sweet.
She asks me every morning, 'Where is my grandmother?!'
She loves Fairuz;
Her favourite song is *The Return*.

We Are Here to Stay

We are like a multitude of impossibilities
In Led, Ramleh and Galilea.
Here we will stay, a weight on your heart,
Like a wall.
In your throats,
We are like a piece of glass, like a prickly pear.
And in your eyes,
We are a fire storm.
We are here to stay, like a wall over your chests.
We clean the dishes in bars
We fill the glasses of the masters,
We sweep the floors in the black kitchens,
To provide for our children,
Ripped from within your blue jaws
Here we will stay, over your chests, like a wall,
We endure hunger and thirst; we are defiant.
We recite poetry,
We fill the angry streets with demonstrations,
We fill the prisons with pride.
We make children, one revolted generation after another,
Like a multitude of impossibilities,
In Led, Ramleh and Galilea.
We are here to stay,
So, drink the sea.
We protect the shade of the fig and olive trees,
We implant ideas like yeast in the dough,

Our nerves are cold like ice
While hell's fire burns in our hearts.
We press the rocks to quench our thirst,
We eat dirt when we are hungry, but we won't leave!
We generously give our precious blood, generously,
        generously!
Here is our past, our present and our future.

***

We are like a multitude of impossibilities,
In Led, Ramleh and Galilea.
We hold fast to your origins,
Our roots are deep down in the ground.
It would be better for the oppressor to revise his accounts,
Before the thread comes undone.
For every action, read,
What is written in the book!

The Convergence of Roads

I came from a city hanging on a cross
I carry its greetings made of burning letters,
I carried them from my beloved homeland,
From the fugitives in the mountains and the valleys,
From those whose backs are ripped
With the whips of slavery

***

From our mothers wrapped in black,
From the eyes of the children,
From a jasmine tree that climbed on our fence,
Teasing the light of the day,
Smiling for the sun and blooming.

I carried it from my beloved homeland,
Hidden in my burning wound.
I freed it like a happy butterfly
In your vast horizon,
Oh Moscow,
Where all roads meet.

REVIEWS

SCRIPT FOR A BETTER FUTURE

Shanon Shah

'I'm surprised you still want an iced black Americano,' said the barista, not unkindly.

I was looking for a place to catch up with a friend who was visiting me in London from Malaysia and thought, why not meet at this delightful café near Borough Market? It's a stone's throw from the shared office space I had started working from and was a recent discovery for me. Iced black coffee became my medicine of choice during the scorching summer months, and the barista knew it. But today was a rainy, grey autumn day, she said, a portent of winter – why was I not transitioning to hot coffee?

'I'm in denial,' I joked. 'As far as I'm concerned, we're still in British Summer Time, and in my mind it's only *early* autumn. Possibly still late summer.'

She laughed and nodded. 'I like how you think,' she said. 'And this weekend it's going to be a wonderful sunny 20°C.'

'That's lovely, but also a little bit scary,' I confessed. 'The weather we've had this year is just not normal.'

I don't know what I was expecting in response. But certainly not what she – a young, articulate, hipster southern European (judging by her accent) – came up with: 'Oh, well, I think all of this is just part of our natural planetary cycle – everything is OK.'

Probably what made matters worse was the woman who was eavesdropping and decided to interrupt us. Also, southern European, again judging by her accent, and wearing an off-putting goofy smile, she said to me, 'Don't be such a doom-monger.'

I said, 'We've had record-breaking temperatures and drought this summer in the UK, complete with wildfires and 3,000 excess deaths – how is this normal?'

'Well, the summer wasn't nearly as bad as you say, and every tiny bit we are doing makes a huge difference for the better,' said European Pollyanna, the disturbing smile never leaving her lips.

I started shaking my head, maybe a bit too vehemently.

The barista said, in an effort at faltering diplomacy, 'I'm not getting into this.'

The scene where Jennifer Lawrence berates the climate-sceptic newscasters in the black comedy *Don't Look Up* flashed through my head. 'Oh my God,' I thought, 'I need to pull myself together.'

'I'm not getting into this either,' I finally managed to reply, still a tad defensively.

'Here's your iced Americano,' said the barista with a forced smile. 'Thanks so very much,' I said with an equally forced smile. Mad European Pollyanna then ambushed the barista and said, 'It's so lovely to hear you speak so much sense!'

Perhaps if it was another day, I would have reacted differently. But this was the day that Liz Truss, the UK prime minister, resigned after only forty-four days in power, unable to outlast the shelf-life of a lettuce. It was also the day Malaysia's Election Commission announced that polling day for the country's snap elections would be held on 19 November 2022 – during flood season. I had spent the morning attending online meetings and briefings and reading about climate-related developments in the leadup to COP27, the upcoming UN climate talks in Egypt.

Anwar Ibrahim, *SCRIPT for a Better Malaysia: An Empowering Vision and Policy Framework for Action*, Institut Darul Ehsan, Shah Alam, 2022.

The West African country Chad had just declared a national emergency because of flooding affecting one million people. There was also a rising death toll in the southeast of Australia because of extreme flooding. Barely weeks before, Hurricanes Ian and Julia unleashed catastrophic damage in the Caribbean and Central and North America. And just weeks before *that*, a third of Pakistan was submerged underwater, with a fifth of its entire population displaced, due to record-breaking floods. Experts agreed that Pakistan's floods were made much worse by climate change. And, even though it contributes less than one percent of global carbon emissions, Pakistan had to bear the burden of up to $40 billion in damages, not to mention thousands of lives lost.

We hardly heard about the Pakistan floods in the UK because the news back in September was saturated with the national period of mourning following the death of Queen Elizabeth II. It seemed as though the British public was more outraged by TV personalities jumping the queue for the lying-in-state than the colossal destruction of an impoverished member state of the Commonwealth – a grouping which the Queen, we were reminded repeatedly by the BBC, cared for deeply.

In late 2021 and early 2022, Malaysia, too, experienced catastrophic flooding. Not at the same scale as Pakistan, or the Caribbean, or Chad, but shocking enough by Malaysian standards. The floods affected eight out of Malaysia's thirteen states and three federal territories, and more than 70,000 people lost their homes. Damages amounted to more than $1.3 billion. The floods were probably made worse by climate change, but political corruption, mismanagement, and maladministration also contributed to the woefully inadequate prevention, warning and relief efforts.

Public anger exploded and the hashtag #KerajaanPembunuh (Killer Government) went viral on Twitter. In fact, what would have been inspiring, if the situation was not so mortifying, was the civilian relief efforts that sprang up in the face of government incompetence. Against this backdrop, government spokespersons from the Malaysian Islamic Party, PAS, insisted that the floods were an 'act of God'.

This, I wanted to tell the barista, is the day I am having. This is the context in which my motherland, Malaysia, is going to the polls just so that a corrupt regime can return to power. And this, I wanted to continue, is the kind of stuff the British political establishment consistently blocks in international climate negotiations – additional and adequate money to help the communities that have done the least to cause climate change but are suffering its worst impacts. And, I wanted to carry on, even though I am livid about all the injustices that plague my two homelands now – Malaysia and Britain – I am actually not without hope. Which brings me to *SCRIPT for a Better Malaysia* – the latest policy framework by Malaysian opposition leader Anwar Ibrahim.

It is not in my habit to read political documents. I'm part of a generation of Malaysians that grew up during the golden age of Southeast Asia's dictators and charismatic authoritarian leaders. We had Prime Minister Mahathir Mohamad in Malaysia, of course, but there was also Indonesia's Suharto, Singapore's Lee Kuan Yew, and Ferdinand Marcos of the Philippines. These strongmen claimed success for turning their young post-independent nation-states into economic powerhouses – even in primary school, I was flushed with pride when Malaysia, too, became an 'Asian Tiger cub'. At the same time, they crushed all dissent and disagreement and – with the exception of Singapore's Lee – created environments in which corruption could flourish.

Political and economic scandals proliferated when I was growing up in the 1980s and 1990s under Mahathir's ruling coalition, Barisan Nasional (the National Front). But my own awakening was triggered in 1998 when, in the middle of the Asian political and economic crisis, Mahathir sacked and then jailed Anwar, his Deputy Prime Minister, for sham allegations of corruption and sodomy.

This was the crisis that birthed my real learning about human rights (and its violations), judicial independence (and its corruption), parliamentary democracy (and the myriad ways it can be undermined), and the politics of Islam (from its liberationist strands to its debased and draconian aspects). I went on to become deeply involved in movements for social change in Malaysia, especially in the leadup to the historic 2008 elections which severely undermined the Barisan Nasional's decades-long dominance. Ten years later, when I had already relocated to the UK, Malaysian voters created history by booting out what had become a gargantuanly corrupt Barisan Nasional regime in what can only be described as a David-and-Goliath election. But the new coalition government, called Pakatan Harapan (the Alliance of Hope), only lasted twenty-two months. It was brought down through a series of backdoor defections on the eve of the Covid-19 lockdowns of 2020.

The years since then have become a political blur, not least because of pandemic-related complications. Mahathir and Anwar, who had a much-publicised rapprochement in the leadup to the 2018 polls, fell out yet again. Meanwhile, another despot, former Prime Minister Najib Razak and his wife, Rosmah Mansor, were finally convicted for the eyewatering amounts of money they stole from Malaysians during Najib's administration. Najib was sent to jail with a twelve-year sentence.

The political scene is more fragmented than it has ever been and, by most predictions, Anwar leads an opposition bloc with only a slim chance of electoral success. Even with Najib in jail, it seems Malaysians are poised to see the return (and revenge) of Barisan Nasional. This is why I was exhausted before I even started Anwar's new offering.

But something shifted when I started skimming its first few pages.

The volume opens with a heartfelt paragraph – Anwar addresses (Malaysian) readers directly, empathising with our 'growing cynicism and loss of faith in politicians and, more tragically, in each other'. This is eloquent enough, but more jaded readers might say, 'So show us what you got then?'

This is where the second line of the second paragraph goes deeper: 'From passively accepting the notion that "things change", we now need to enthusiastically "change things".' This declaration of agency – of Anwar as a politician, of the reader as an individual or as a group, and of any and everyone who cares about Malaysia – frames the rest of the manuscript.

The Introduction straddles an acknowledgement of the many failures in recent Malaysian history whilst offering a big vision of a better future we can still build:

> ...SCRIPT is neither a philosophical dream nor an unrealistic ideal. It is a recognition that business-as-usual cannot continue. Moreover, it is a system of guidance, a torch in a dark place. And for us to take that first step – for these words to move from this page into the preferred futures we seek – one crucial element must ignite the touchpaper. That lynchpin is trust.

How does SCRIPT tackle this question of trust, among other elements? And why 'SCRIPT', anyway?

'SCRIPT' is simultaneously the manuscript's structure and its purpose. Above the introduction, we are given some possible definitions of the word (emphasis in original):

> Script /skrɪpt/ noun. 1. handwriting as distinct from print; written characters. 2. type imitating handwriting. 3. an alphabet or system of writing. 4. the test of a play, film or broadcast. 5. an examinee's set of written answers. 6. Law. an original document as distinct from a copy. 7. Psychology. the social role or behaviour appropriate to particular situations that a person absorbs through

cultural influences and association with others. *8. a holistic vision and policy framework for a viable, dynamic and inclusive Malaysian future.*

Developing from this eighth definition, Anwar's vision is to 'build a sustainable and prosperous Malaysia based on care and compassion, mutual respect, innovation, and trust, where inclusiveness and equality is embraced by the whole nation – ultimately a just Malaysian society'. This is where SCRIPT as an acronym becomes a structuring device for the text's narrative, standing for 'Sustainability, Care and Compassion, Respect, Innovation, Prosperity, Trust – key terms for shaping and building a thriving, dynamic future for Malaysia'.

The bulk of the document consists of individual chapters dedicated to each term – or 'driver', as Anwar also refers to them – in the SCRIPT acronym. Each driver is assessed in relation to its conventional definition, which Anwar transforms into 'our definition', followed by a statement of vision, the driver's target population/areas, and its policy imperatives.

What sets this framework apart from many similar-sounding approaches is the devotion that is then paid to analysing possible futures (in the plural), picking apart potential areas of 'complexity', 'contradictions', 'chaos', 'simultaneity', and 'futures/change'. These headings draw upon the work of Ziauddin Sardar, the editor of *Critical Muslim* as well as Director of the Centre for Postnormal Policy and Futures Studies which, along with Institut Darul Ehsan, co-published SCRIPT. These futures-oriented insights then feed into a methodology for 'monitoring' and engaging with or creating 'enabling institutions'.

The chapters on each SCRIPT driver are followed by two chapters that employ the same analytical framework – 'SCRIPT for a Post-Covid Malaysia' and 'SCRIPT for Navigating Cost of Living'. Anwar ends by providing his priority policies 'for a better Malaysia' and closes with an Epilogue.

The forward-looking nature of Anwar's thoughts do not negate or ignore the rich and complex history of Malaysia. Given his past experiences in Islamic social movements, there is explicit inspiration from the Qur'an and the hadith (traditions of the Prophet Muhammad). There are also framing quotes from Muslim scholars and activists, including the ninth century Persian scholar Ibn Majah, the fourteenth century Egyptian historian

Shihāb al-Dīn al-Nuwayrī, and contemporary Malaysians such as Nik Abdul Aziz Nik Mat, the former PAS spiritual leader.

These Islamically inspired insights are complemented by quotations and observations from thinkers and activists of other backgrounds. I was particularly pleased to see references to the renowned sociologist Syed Hussein Alatas, and veteran social justice activists Anwar Fazal and Anne Munro-Kua. Anwar also pays tribute to his avowedly secular comrades in Malaysian politics, including Lim Kit Siang (former opposition leader from the Democratic Action Party), and shares other insights from Confucius, Virgil, and the Indian Dalit reformer Bhim Rao Ambedkar.

This intellectual and spiritual sophistication is matched by concrete and progressive calls under each SCRIPT driver. Under 'Sustainability', Anwar writes that we have to 'abolish tax concessions and incentives that allow businesses and enterprises to pursue unsustainable goals and practices that show ill regard for human dignity or the natural world'. I fervently hope that this translates into urgent and ambitious steps to end deforestation and stop the extraction and burning of fossil fuels. 'Care and Compassion' calls for debt forgiveness (including for student loans), a living wage, and protections for refugees and migrants, including dedicated financial assistance and better legal safeguards. And under this driver, Anwar makes a simple yet remarkable pledge: 'we will abolish capital punishment in Malaysia'. This is huge, especially when so many ultranationalists from the United Malays National Organisation (UMNO), the senior party in Barisan Nasional, and ideologues from PAS remain fans of the death penalty.

'Respect' calls for a 'national human rights audit' and 'repealing of draconic and disrespectful laws and applications of laws with special regard to racial, religious, gender, and lifestyle inequalities'. 'Innovation' is not merely about creating fancy technologies and gadgets – it's about harnessing technology and new thinking to forge better welfare and wellbeing infrastructures for urban and rural populations. 'Prosperity' insists that Malaysia needs to abandon a 'model of justice as retribution' and move towards a 'model of justice as shared prosperity'. This may sound abstract but, again, it is notable, given that the idea of 'justice' held by ideologues from UMNO and PAS is largely based on violent and punitive interpretations of secular and Islamic legislation. Finally, 'Trust' reaffirms the need for independent institutions and oversight mechanisms that ensure 'equality under the rule of law'.

Elsewhere, there's a promise to launch a 'Royal Commission of Inquiry into the Covid-19 Pandemic'. There's recognition of a 'mental health pandemic', with the promise to secure separate funding for the establishment of a Malaysian Institute of Mental Health. In relation to the cost-of-living crisis, there is clear and explicit criticism of neoliberal capitalism as the main culprit and a promise to implement 'humane economics'. Anwar even promises to initiate a Green New Deal. And he is already taking steps in this direction as current Opposition Leader. According to the independent environmental journalism outfit Macaranga, he has called for the formation of a Parliamentary Select Committee on the climate emergency.

As I read through SCRIPT, I anticipated some criticisms that could be made, especially from certain liberal and secularist perspectives. For example, secular-liberal Western commentators might demand more explicit positions on gender equality or lesbian, gay, bisexual, transgender, queer, and intersex (LGBTQI) inclusion. Or for an unequivocal condemnation of 'Islamism', 'radicalism', or 'extremism'. In some ways, these are the easiest criticisms to deal with. Because from these perspectives, gender, sexuality, and Islam(ism) are often weaponised to reproduce tired stereotypes about the 'clash of civilisations' between a supposedly monolithic Islam and a supposedly monolithic West. The vision of human rights, equality, justice, wellbeing, and sustainability that Anwar lays out is actually bigger and more nuanced. Besides, in several parts of SCRIPT, there are concrete calls to address certain gender-related policy areas, such as stronger laws against sexual harassment and better implementation.

Perhaps more serious might be questions from Orang Asli and Orang Asal (Indigenous) communities, especially from Sabah and Sarawak in Borneo, about where they fit in Anwar's SCRIPT. These are, after all, communities that have been historically ignored, silenced, and manipulated by Barisan Nasional and PAS-controlled federal and state legislatures. Again, while this aspect of national self-determination is not systematically addressed, neither is it completely absent. SCRIPT does contain brief, open-ended mentions of how Peninsula Malaysia, Sabah, and Sarawak might negotiate their relationship. There is also recognition of the historic

ways in which Orang Asli and Orang Asal have been exploited and
impoverished by successive political administrations.

In some ways, SCRIPT reminded me of the South American concept of
Vivir Bien or *Buen Vivir* that inspired a new cohort of social movements at
the turn of the twenty-first century. According to the Bolivian social and
environmental justice advocate Pablo Solón, *Vivir Bien* emerged as a
response to the 'devastating impact of neoliberalism' and US imperialism
in South America as well as the 'failure of Soviet socialism'. It draws from
the wisdom and practices of the indigenous communities of the Andes and
their struggles for justice and self-determination. Solón proposes that *Vivir
Bien* contains five interconnected elements.

The first is that it is based on the vision of 'the whole', or the *Pacha*. The
monotheistic Islamic wisdom that Anwar imbues SCRIPT with might at
first appear at odds with First Nations wisdom. But, actually, the holistic
worldview in SCRIPT resonates with the notion of the *Pacha* as including
'humans, animals, and plants' as well as 'the world above...inhabited by
the sun, the moon, and the stars, and the world below...where the dead
and the spirits live'.

SCRIPT's emphasis on care and compassion, respect, and trust reminds
me of *Vivir Bien*'s second principle, which Solón summarises as 'coexisting
in multipolarity'. This means that an 'individual is a person only in as much
as he or she works for the common good of his or her community'. And
without community 'there is no individual and without singular beings
there is no community'.

The third element of *Vivir Bien* – 'the pursuit of equilibrium' – is the one
that appears most explicitly in SCRIPT. Anwar even uses the word
'equilibrium' and its Malay translation, *keseimbangan*, similarly to Solón, for
whom it represents 'a harmony not only between human beings but also
between humans and nature, between the material and the spiritual,
between knowledge and wisdom, between diverse cultures and between
different identities and realities'. This is connected to *Vivir Bien*'s fourth
element which also animates SCRIPT – the 'complementarity of diverse
subjects'. By this, Solón means that we must embrace 'differences as part
of a whole' as opposed to the neoliberal capitalist logic of competition,
scarcity, and exploitation in the pursuit of 'growth'.

Finally, *Vivir Bien*'s fifth element, 'decolonization', calls for 'rejecting an unjust *status quo* and recovering our capacity to look deeply so as not to be trapped by colonial categories that limit our imagination'. This aspect is present throughout SCRIPT, too, albeit more indirectly.

Solón does have a warning. *Vivir Bien* is not merely a democratic reform project for a self-contained nation-state. It will fail if applied only within the borders of a single country that is still enmeshed within 'a global economy that is capitalist, productivist, extractivist, patriarchal, and anthropocentric'. *Vivir Bien* has also become appropriated by corporate giants who praise and promote it in ways that are very different from the way that Solón articulates it.

It bears reflecting on how to avoid SCRIPT from suffering the same fate. It is therefore apposite to revive the thinking of another decolonial scholar whose legacy is evident in SCRIPT – the Malaysian sociologist Syed Hussein Alatas (1928-2007). I have already written in *Critical Muslim 41: Bodies* about the relevance of Alatas's legacy in efforts to address the climate crisis through his classic work, *The Myth of the Lazy Native*. It is therefore inspiring to see that Alatas's scholarly work on corruption has also informed SCRIPT. Given the scale of the damage caused by the Najib administration's corruption – as well as the political ecosystem that enabled it – it is worth revisiting the quote from Alatas highlighted by Anwar:

> In a corrupt society, corruption enters into our lives at frequent intervals and at several intersections. The child is already exposed to its damaging effects while in primary school. Corruption becomes part of the visible scenery. An entire generation of children growing up in its shadow. What this would do to the personality of the individual is certainly something to worry about.

In other words, corruption is not merely about the moral failing of certain leaders and individuals. Alatas is referring here to a society-wide 'tidal corruption' that infects us all externally and internally. This is corruption that is normalised as a social practice which, in many formerly colonised nation-states, has grown to become an industry in its own right.

It is worth dwelling on some key aspects of Alatas's thinking on corruption before returning to SCRIPT. First, there is the fairly straightforward definition of corruption – 'the abuse of trust in the interest of personal and private gain'. Ironically, it is the very straightforwardness of this definition that causes complications. Its common-sense simplicity has enabled some heinously corrupt dictators – from Suharto in Indonesia and Zia-ul-Haq in Pakistan – to claim that *they* were anti-corruption crusaders. In fact, Malaysia's Mahathir Mohamad was extremely popular in the early days of his premiership in the 1980s because he, too, promised to weed out corruption.

The paradox of corruption flourishing under these purported anti-corruption advocates is partly explicable through another key insight from Alatas. According to him, corruption has existed in all societies historically but all societies have always had people of conscience struggling against it – often risking their own lives and livelihoods. But corruption manifested in different ways in different contexts. For instance, corruption in the colonial era took particular forms in Dutch-controlled Indonesia compared to British-controlled Malaya, and so on. The events of the Second World War, however, catalysed corruption in most colonies in unprecedented ways. The swift wave of post-war decolonisation then created an 'outburst' of corruption in the newly independent regimes because of a variety of factors. These include the continuity and growth of wartime corrupt practices, the creation of new and independent state administrative systems that were easily hijacked by corrupt postcolonial elites, and the inexperience of newly independent leaders in democratic nation-building.

More perniciously, there was also the often invisible 'manipulation and intrigues of foreign financial and business powers through means of corruption'. Nowhere do we see this more clearly now than the role of fossil fuel and agribusiness giants in blocking international negotiations to end the climate crisis. There is, on one hand, the brazen and shameless corruption typified by rampant deforestation, land grabs, and wholesale murder of indigenous and poorer communities in places such as the Amazon. But, on the other hand, there is the less visible role of the fossil fuel lobby in influencing the (lack of) decision-making on the environment and human rights by lawmakers in liberal democracies such as the US, the UK, and the European Union.

Whilst Anwar's SCRIPT does contain frank criticisms of corruption in Malaysia and proposes much-needed solutions, I wonder if it is fully realistic about the systemic origins, nature, and scale of the problem.

Could it be even bolder in addressing the concerns from Alatas and Solón about capitalism and colonialism? And, anticipating what will probably be a recurring question from Anwar's critics, why should we trust his *SCRIPT for a Better Malaysia?*

These are questions to which Anwar does have an answer. He writes: 'trust being more than a one-way street, will require your participation and suggestions or ideas to take us from this starting line presented here towards the better Malaysian future we envision'. Anwar reassures the reader: 'The framework put forward here is not the final word; this document is an amalgam of living and ongoing policies, subject to revision and continual reiteration, as things change and as we change things.'

Reflecting on these passages, I understand the reasons for my near-tirade at the climate-denying Pollyannas in the café near Borough Market. Because I am not a doom-monger. I am actually a hopeful person. But my hope is not founded upon fantasies that allow us to surrender our agency and believe that everything will be just fine if we all 'do our tiny bit'.

Perhaps the Brazilian educationalist Paolo Freire expresses it best in his *Pedagogy of Hope*, written amid the endemic corruption that stifled his country's democratic transition in the 1980s and 1990s. It is not, he said, that he lacked empathy with feelings of hopelessness at the dire situation facing so many Brazilians at the time. But, to Freire (and it is worth quoting him at length):

> Hope is an ontological need. Hopelessness is but hope that has lost its bearings, and becomes a distortion of that ontological need. When it becomes a program, hopelessness paralyzes us, immobilizes us. We succumb to fatalism, and then it becomes impossible to muster the strength we absolutely need for a fierce struggle that will re-create the world. I am hopeful, not out of mere stubbornness, but out of an existential, concrete imperative. I do not mean that, because I am hopeful, I attribute to this hope of mine the power to transform reality all by itself, so that I set out for the fray without taking account of concrete, material data, declaring, 'My hope is enough!' No, my hope is necessary, but it's not enough. Alone, it does not win. But without it, my struggle will be weak and wobbly. We need critical hope the way a fish needs unpolluted water.

How profound that Freire should use the analogy of a fish in unpolluted water to explain his position on hope. And how significant that Anwar Ibrahim should try to transform the hopelessness of Malaysians into hope by starting off his vision with 'Sustainability'. On some level, this is not exactly new for Malaysia. Like many other formerly colonised nations, Malaysia says, and commits to, all the right things on the global stage in regard to sustainable development and the environment. And, like so many of these nation-states, the actual implementation of sustainable policies is frequently wanting. Often, there is brazen hypocrisy. As we saw in the aftermath of the floods of 2021-22, citizens and residents are paying the price for the current Malaysian government's systemic negligence and violation of social and environmental justice. But SCRIPT lays out the ways to correct this situation, internally and nationally, whilst keeping an eye on the need for regional, international, and global cooperation. It is a work in progress that provides a template for active, critical hope.

Maybe one way to approach *SCRIPT for a Better Malaysia* is through the analogy of theatre. To produce a play, one often needs a script. That script could be the work of an individual playwright or it could be devised by a team of performers through improvisation. But the written text of the script is not the play. The beginnings of the play emerge when it finds a director and actors who can breathe life into the written text. The play also needs stage managers, lighting, costume and sound designers, and, most importantly, an audience to experience it and respond to it when it is performed. Without these constituent elements, we do not have a play, we only have a text that has the potential to become a play.

The play simply cannot exist without constructive criticism and collaboration. And it certainly cannot exist if its creators do not release it and offer it to an audience who can engage with it and shape it for their own purposes. The best plays enable both makers and audiences not only to enjoy themselves, but to transform their hearts, minds, relationships, and worlds.

SCRIPT is a play waiting to be produced and performed. And it eagerly awaits an audience to appreciate it, implement it, and transform it for present and future generations to enjoy.

WOMAD RETURNS

James Brooks

Womad is not having a mid-life crisis, but maybe it should. After two years of Covid-induced hibernation, the World of Music, Arts and Dance festival returned to the grounds of Charlton Park in Wiltshire, England in the summer of 2021 celebrating its fortieth year. Yet rather than follow the lead of the archetypal insecure suburban dad crossing the threshold into middle-age by acquiring an interest in contemporary sounds, the festival line-up was dominated by pop styles and performers decades past their commercial heyday. Of the six headliners for the festival's three main days, three were over sixty years old – Angélique Kidjo, Wayne Coyne (frontman of The Flaming Lips), and Gilberto Gil – and none were under thirty. This can hardly be explained as Womad having a nostalgia blow-out for its big birthday year when 2019's headliners offered a similar demographic. And noting it is not to belittle the considerable talents of such 'heritage acts' nor those working in genres that have fallen out of favour in a fickle music industry, especially at Womad, which specialises in traditional and neglected styles. It's more that when you run a festival that trades in sounds from outside the hegemonic Anglo-American rock-and-pop landscape and two genres – afrobeats and K-pop – break through that hegemony spectacularly yet feature nowhere in your line-up, I'd say you've missed a trick to rejuvenate your ageing audience. Instead, Womad 2022 (28-31 July) stuck resolutely to a programming logic set by the parameters of the hazy and problematic 'world music' category of the eighties which admits, for example, afropop from that decade, but not today. The festival pulled off its return to Charlton Park with aplomb, and yet I still longed to witness it figuratively slapping the latest Blackpink or Burna Boy on the car stereo, like a suburban dad desperate for relevance, more than once during the weekend.

I'm getting this criticism out of the way early partially because such thoughts were never far from my mind at Womad 2022, and partially because I care about this annual jamboree. Womad was a personal high point of four of the previous five summers prior to the pandemic (I couldn't make it in 2019). It's hard to overstate, as mainstream UK culture becomes ever more homogenised, unadventurous, and conformist, just how vivifying a weekend spent engaging with culture from other lineages can be. Encounters can border on the transcendental. Arriving cold and miserable to the waterlogged main field in 2015, I sheltered from the drizzle in the first tent I saw. Within a few minutes Mahotella Queens, a South African all-female trio who trace their roots back to 1960s Johannesburg, had struck up their first song. I don't speak Zulu, but their summery township pop, sung in sublime harmony and backed by shimmering guitar, communicated faith, fortitude and joy beyond words. For one glorious hour it was as if a ray of African sunshine had broken through the grey English skies to light the stage and warm my soul. Much of the time I was watching through tears.

This time round, I think I'm in store for another of those precious moments about half an hour after setting foot on a much warmer and sunnier main field. Rizwan-Muazzam Qawwals, led by two nephews of the great Nusrat Fateh Ali Khan, are on the main stage. Their uncle's performance at the festival in 1985, finally released on record in 2019, is the stuff of Womad legend, having catalysed Nusrat's renown, and that of qawwali more widely, in the UK. Like their uncle back then, Rizwan and Muazzam Mujahid Ali Khan opened with 'Allah Hoo Allah Hoo'. I am sure I'm not alone in being unable to hear that song without hearing the voice of the 'King of Kings of Qawwali' in my head (in my case from a 1993 recording that introduced me to qawwali). No performer will come off favourably in comparison. This time the contrast was not helped by a rushed feel to the performance and Rizwan suffering a slight tightness of voice when attacking the most expressive passages. A Friday early-afternoon audience in milling-around mode was also not advantageous. Yet gradually performers and audience began to relax. Just as their uncle had in 1985, Rizwan and Muazzam followed the opening *hamd* (song in praise of Allah) with a *manqabat* (in praise of Ali or one of the Sufi saints) rather than the more usual *na'at* (in praise of the Prophet). Nusrat's 1985 Womad *manqabat* had been 'Haq Ali Ali', his own composition, and the brothers similarly presented one of their own works. Perhaps keen not to lose the growing connection to the audience, Rizwan led this one with renewed vigour, and as he launched into a series of ascending scales I felt a lump growing in my throat. Closing my eyes, I let the music work its magic and... my phone rang. Ramy Essam, the Egyptian singer-songwriter and activist whose hastily composed song 'Irhal' became the anthem of the 2011 revolution, had agreed to a short interview. About that, more later.

Back in the big blue Siam Tent, where I'd caught Mahotella Queens years before, I was gifted a personal discovery of the kind that Womad is so good at granting. The six musicians of Mazaher – four women and two men – filed unselfconsciously out across the stage dressed in variously decorated or undecorated djellabas. Four carried *mazhars* (large frame-drums) while one elderly woman sat with a *doholla* (a bass drum similar to a djembe) on her lap. A woman wearing an ornately decorated black sequinned djellaba and dark lipstick moved to the front of the stage, eyed the audience amicably but commandingly and began a slow, beguiling melody in a restrained yet powerful voice with an immediately hypnotic quality. The *mazhars* and *doholla* started up, beating a polyrhythm that I couldn't pick and the players sang in chorus. This mesmerising performance continued unhurried in this manner for four or five minutes when the rhythm gained in pace, complexity and volume, before collapsing in on itself.

Mazaher is Egypt's last ensemble to perform zār, the name given to a diversity of linked musical ritual healing or exorcism practices originating in the Horn of Africa. Zār came to Egypt in the nineteenth century, and has acquired various elements on its way, with parts originating in Sufi, mystic Christian and pagan traditions. The overall framework is Islamic, but the practice's diverse origins, its foregrounding of women and its flouting of the prohibition on contact with the world of *djinni* (spirits) means it has become marginalised and demonised as conservative currents in Egypt have risen to prominence. Zār ritual gatherings may last for days and involve long inductions of a trance state but even in the severely truncated form of a one-hour festival set, and in no small part thanks to the authoritative stage presence of Umm Sameh, the chieftess, Mazaher's performance is wholly captivating.

By the time I arrive at the red tent on the other side of the field, South Africa's Bantu Continua Uhuru Consciousness (BCUC) are midway through their set and have brought the crowd to a rolling boil. Stripped to the waist and glowing with sweat, frontman Jovi Nkose is offering praise to his ancestors atop a bubbling soup of bass and percussion. BCUC's music, widely praised in the music press, is redolent of Miles Davis' mid-seventies fusion excursions but with all instrumentation beyond the rhythm section stripped out and replaced with sung, chanted or spoken vocals. It's a heady concoction, especially if you're in the middle of the dancing throng, yet, to me, sounds hemmed in by its limited harmonic palette. BCUC's music is propulsive but, to paraphrase the title of a famous Davis fusion album, can often sound as if stuck on the corner, unable to take the turning it needs.

The same could be said of Electric Jalaba, a collaboration between Moroccan gnawa *maalem* (master musician) Simo Lagnawi and a British backing group featuring four brothers. Live, this is not a wholly successful fusion. Gnawa music works its magic (in its traditional form it is the main component in healing rituals, as with zār) through subtle manipulations of rhythm and melody from a harmonically stable base. Electric Jalaba's inflexible rock-based backing forbids such exploration. The result is, to European ears, an exotic yet rigid riff-rock that refuses to change key. I find myself unable to get lost in the groove, and quickly bored by it.

Olcay Bayır's set is more intriguing. Born in Gaziantep in southern Turkey close to the Syrian border, Bayır grew up in a Kurdish Alevi family. She came to London at the age of 16 before studying music with the aim of becoming a classical soprano. Instead, her interest in musical traditions of the culturally diverse Anatolia where she was raised came to the fore. Driven by a belief that, to quote a 2020 interview, 'culture – more than religion or nationality – provides identity' her choice of material is driven by a focus on 'traditions and regions, rather than specific religions and nations'. The seamlessness with which her set progressed despite songs being sung in four or five different languages, is testament to her approach. Bayır's voice, too, is delightful, even if her otherwise excellent band can sound a little reserved. One of the wonders of Anatolian music to outsiders is how danceable it is, despite its odd (to outsiders) meters. For example, set highlight 'Dolama Dolamayı', a Turkish folk song, alternates measures of 5/8 and 6/8. I would have loved for Bayır's band, maybe even Bayır herself, to encourage more bodily engagement with these rhythms beyond a gentle swaying or tapping of feet.

She may belong to that trio of headlining over-sixties, but restricted movement is not a problem for Angélique Kidjo. Her voice is as strong and fine as ever, but it's her dancing that draws some of the biggest cheers during her set, which was promised as an homage of Talking Heads' influential 1980 *Remain in Light* album. In the event, it starts out that way, with high-voltage readings of 'Born Under Punches' and 'Crosseyed and Painless', but soon pulls from her own back catalogue. Songs from her eighties and nineties heyday – like 'Agolo' and 'Afrika', on which she is briefly joined by Womad's founder, Peter Gabriel, in gratingly off-key style – gain the warmest reception. Bar Gabriel's vocals, everything is performed with gusto but it's nonetheless an exercise in nostalgia right down to the naïve 'one world' messaging beloved of humanitarian charity concerts from Live Aid to Live 8 (at which Kidjo performed). At the end, Kidjo delivers a bizarre but rollicking reading of 'Once in a Lifetime' which transforms a song wracked by the deep existential despair of modernity into a fanfare for resilience and endurance. I'm fifty-fifty as to whether she murdered the song or gave it new life. Maybe both.

Saturday, for me, was all about Bab L'Bluz. The Moroccan-French band's first appearance at Womad was at a midday workshop in one of the smaller tents. I half-expect to see them bleary-eyed and sullen for such an early call – they self-describe as a *rock* band, after all – but no, they're all smiles, clearly overjoyed to be playing their music to such a receptive audience. They'd had a long wait to do so. Bab L'Bluz's debut album, *Nayda!*, released on Gabriel's Real World Records imprint, was released in June 2020. For obvious reasons they'd been unable to tour behind it for two frustrating years. Their workshop was great fun, introducing us to the varied components of their sound. Gnawa features prominently, but is only one element in a mix which also includes other North African blues styles, Moroccan chaabi (popular folk music), and, yes, psychedelic rock. But there's nothing forced about Bab L'Bluz's sound. This is a band that's absorbed and integrated its influences into its own unique style. Their choice of lead instrument is also a novelty; lead singer Yousra Mansour plays the *awicha*, a smaller version of the *guembri*, tuned an octave higher and normally used as a teaching tool for the larger instrument. Mansour's *awicha* is backed by her bandmate Brice Bottin's *guembri* which then performs the role normally allocated to the bass guitar in a typical rock

band. The rhythm is handled with supple but propulsive power by Hafid
Zouaoui on drums and Jérôme Bartolomé on *qraqeb* (heavy iron castanets),
other percussion and occasionally flute.

What sets Bab L'Bluz apart from most other bands operating in the fusion
space is Mansour and Bottin's songwriting talent. *Nayda!* is an excellent
record because it features ten memorable songs rather than just
explorations of grooves. Its production, again by Mansour and Bottin, is
tasteful, holding the psychedelic influences mostly in check and giving only
a hint, on the barrelling 'El Gamra', of what kind of animal Bab L'Bluz are
live. In short, they rock. At their performance later that afternoon, every
song is imbued with muscular, overdriven force, and while this may obscure
some of the album's subtler moments, the loss is, I'm sure, not felt by
anyone in attendance. We're all too absorbed in the driving rhythms and
fleet-fingered solos of Bab L'Bluz in full flow. Mansour has spoken of her
love of Jimi Hendrix in interviews and there's something of Hendrix's
bluesy fire in her playing. Whether they push at that door and become more
expansive on their next record or rather double-down on the songwriting
remains to be seen but I can't wait to learn where this band goes next.

Between Bab L'Bluz's two appearances I catch a performance and
workshop by Elaya Soroor and Kefaya: an Afghan singer backed by a
UK-based band trading in a highly musically literate version of fusion (that
is, not just drones, spacey beats and runs up and down the double-
harmonic scale). Soroor is an artist who has been on quite a journey. She
was born in Iran to a family of Afghan refugees from the Hezara ethnic
minority who returned shortly after the fall of the Taliban. Success on the
TV talent show Afghan Star brought her to public attention both welcome
and less so. She was forced to flee – first to India, where she studied Indian
classical singing, and eventually the UK. Her album with Kefaya, *Songs of
our Mothers*, presents ten Afghan folk songs traditionally performed by
women, in a variety of arrangements. As with Bab L'Bluz, although to a
lesser extent, Soroor's selections acquire a rocky heft live. Album and
concert opener 'Jama Narenji' – a folk song from Herat celebrating
resistance to oppression – has the driving desert blues feel consistent with
the Moroccan band's output. Other set highlights include 'Charsi' – a
playful song of seduction where the object of affection is a macho weed-
smoker – and a masterclass of high-wire metric modulation from guest

tabla-player Gurdain Singh Rayatt. Soroor's emotions grew as she sang these songs from her homeland. Towards the end she cried out to the audience: 'Stop the genocide of the Hezara people!'

I hoped that Soroor would speak more about the Hezara – the third-largest ethnic group in Afghanistan – their history, and their current situation during the workshop, but this wasn't to be. The questions from Darren Ferguson, chief executive of a charity in Northern Ireland, who has worked with Afghan musicians, were mostly prompts for expatiations on the theme of How Bad the Taliban Really Are. Understandably, Soroor obliged but still managed to shade Ferguson's black-and-white depictions of modern Afghan society with a little grey. In response to Ferguson's mention of the Taliban banning music, Soroor noted that the Taliban have their own music which is performed and circulates freely. There was scant opportunity to hear the broader context explaining Afghanistan's desperate state today and, in fact, Soroor's desire to rescue traditionally female folk songs from oblivion. The *Songs of our Mothers* liner notes make this clearer: 'The US and Western-backed regimes that came to dominate Afghanistan in the latter part of the twentieth century created a climate of heightened patriarchal oppression and persecution of women.'

Ferguson's imposition of a certain pro-western narrative chimed uncomfortably with the attitude of a presenter I'd seen earlier at the Taste the World stage, where artists prepare and discuss cuisine from their places and cultures of origin. The artists in this case were Les Amazones d'Afrique, a female west African supergroup signed to Real World Records. When some members of the group arrived five minutes late to proceedings, the presenter, a white man in late middle-age, twice made a comment about 'running on African time' with the air of being an old Africa hand and thus accustomed to such ways. I asked a Kenyan friend who'd joined me at Womad if I was being too unforgiving of a bad joke in finding his comments patronising, but no, she was irked too.

Both incidents can be read as lingering signs of a certain kind of 'benevolent' neo-colonial attitude at Womad – where global-south artists are celebrated, but only on white, western terms. This would have been normal – and normalised – at Womad's inception forty years' ago but, thanks to the efforts of global-south and diaspora activists, it plays pretty poorly now. Again, a little mid-life reckoning could do Womad the world of good. More prosaically, just have fewer white, middle-aged, middle-class men presenting and/or running the show.

Sunday began with another exercise in afropop nostalgia, this time delivered with less brio than Kidjo achieved. Kanda Bongo Man has been serving up his brand of soukous – the fast-paced dance music that grew out of Congolese rumba in the seventies – largely unchanged for over forty years. As a singer working within a genre that leans heavily on prolonged instrumental passages for dancing, Kanda originally triumphed because of a crack backing band, redoubtable charisma and a live show that pulled out all the stops. Today, all three are diminished. To watch Kanda execute basic dance steps in a style typical of the portly sixty-seven-year-old he is while his band endlessly retraces the same three-chord guitar figure is to wonder with increasing regret what exciting, contemporary act, full of the energy of rising Africa, you might be missing out on.

As it happens, the act I next see evoke something like the opposite energy to that and sing of an Africa left behind. They take turns performing solo but Soubi (Athoumane Soubira) and M'madi (M'madi Djibaba) are billed collectively as Comorian. The name comes from their homeland, the Comoros, an archipelago in the Indian Ocean situated midway between the northern tips of Mozambique and Madagascar. Soubi, who is in his late sixties, is first to perform, walking out on stage in a shirt and dark trousers, somewhat incongruously carrying a dusty-looking *gabusi* (long-necked lute). Perched on a stool, he plays a rapid-fire but simple repeated figure. The *gabusi* is not a loud instrument and its muted notes die quickly. Over this, Soubi sings a plaintive melody in Comorian, a language that nobody in the audience likely understands but which transports us all to the imagined shores where it is spoken. M'madi, who is ten years younger and wearing traditional dress and sandals, takes over after a couple of songs. He plays a battered red *ndzendze* – an eight-string box-zither strung and played on both sides which is slightly louder than the *gabusi* but, because it's fretless, harmonically very restricted. M'madi's singing is deeper and more forceful than Soubi's and he is a more elaborate performer. His songs incorporate sudden expressiveness, mouth percussion and occasionally extended sequences of play-acting. At the end of one song he appears to be miming painful death from convulsions.

It's hard to know what to make of this. Is M'madi's outlandish style idiosyncratic or does it belong to a wider tradition? What is the usual setting for such music? How grounded in established Comorian song forms are these compositions? We're never directed towards the answers. The brief introductory presentation by Ian Brennan, an author and music producer who travels the world in search of underrepresented musical styles and who brought Comorian to play at Womad, focuses on the epic administrative battle necessary to secure a UK visa. Why go through all that only to have the music remain a mystery to all who see it performed? The liner notes to Comorian's *We Are An Island, But We're Not Alone*, the album that Brennan recorded while in the archipelago, offer little help and instead fetishise Comoros' poverty. 'There is a trash-filled beach meters past the Presidential Palace,' we are told, while the cover shows M'madi in the back seat of a burnt-out wreck of a car. Once again, we witness the imposition of a particular narrative at the expense of greater understanding of global-south musicians' art. In fact, this is not Soubi and M'madi's first European performance, something you feel nobody involved would be keen to admit. A websearch reveals they were (are?) part of a trio with Eliasse Ben Joma, a guitarist and singer from the nearby French-owned island Mayotte, called Elisouma. They toured Europe in 2013. YouTube clips catch them playing together in a more upbeat, accessible, and polished style than practiced here, a style that doesn't indulge western audiences' *nostalgie de la boue* so effectively.

After Comorian I catch the opening fifteen minutes' of Al Qasar's set; their Arab psych-rock competent enough but not quite as compelling as I needed, after three days of Womad, to overcome a fast-advancing case of festival-fatigue. Later, Dudu Tassa and the Kuwaitis offer a more potent remedy. Since releasing his first album in 1992 when he was fifteen, Tassa has become a mainstay of the Israeli pop-rock circuit. Over the last decade he has garnered international attention thanks to his work resurrecting the music of Saleh and Daoud Al-Kuwaiti – respectively his great-uncle and grandfather. The Al-Kuwaiti brothers were among the most famous and respected musicians in Iraq and Kuwait in the early twentieth century. They were a vital influence on the development of the Iraqi maqam style and composed for musical luminaries from beyond Iraq including Mohammed Abdel Wahab and Umm Kalthoum. They were also Jews (of

Iraqi and Yemeni descent), which was widely known and accepted during their careers and even for twenty or so years after the creation of Israel irrevocably soured Arab-Jewish relations. But later nationalist movements in Iraq, in particular the Ba'ath party, were not so well-disposed and the Kuwaitis' names began to disappear from the airwaves, before their songs did too. After he came to power in 1979, Saddam Hussein hoped to erase the last evidence of the Al-Kuwaitis' existence from record by having their names expunged from the Iraqi national archives. Their back catalogue was reclassified as anonymous 'folk melodies'.

Tassa's quest to resuscitate his forebears' legacy first gained public exposure in 2011 with the release of the first of three albums to date presenting the Al-Kuwaitis' songs in updated musical settings. Tassa arranges his relatives' repertoire sensitively, respectfully, but never with overbearing reverence. Mostly his arrangements work brilliantly. Both on record and live 'Wen Raich Wen' is a highlight, reimagined by Tassa as a gorgeous floating lament redolent of Radiohead (with whom Tassa has worked) whose first section seems inconceivable as a tune from early twentieth century Iraq. But my favourite moments during his set came in the sections of interplay between the old – via samples or string backing from cello and *qanun* (a large, flat zither) – and the new. This worked joyously on 'Walla Ajabni Jamalak', the Al-Kuwaitis' first composition, which opened with sampled maqam strings, settled into reggae-accented pop-rock buoying an unmistakably Arabic melody, before closing with a bouncy pizzicato section. Somewhat incredibly, it never sounded contrived.

And so, finally, to Ramy Essam, who was cruelly scheduled for something like the festival's graveyard slot: eleven o'clock at night on the smaller, less prestigious of the main field's two open air stages. Essam had stayed onsite all weekend. On Friday, before I put in the interview request at the media desk, I'd noticed him ambling around in front of the main stage. I didn't approach him at the time because he had such... bearing. It was a hot day and Essam, a tall, well-built man, had stripped to the waist and was running a hand through his mop of loosely curled black hair. He didn't look like a protest singer, or even a rock musician, so much as a model. Certainly, *a star*. Not the kind of person you'd just tap on the shoulder and start asking questions of. And yet, as I discover when I interview him, he's completely unassuming. Mentioning that I'm familiar with his backstory, I say what an honour it is to meet him and he seems genuinely taken aback. After some chat about his formative musical influences – grunge, nu-metal, hip-hop, but also the rhythms and quarter-tone melodies of Egyptian legends Sheikh Imam and Sayed Darwish – we discuss the current condition of his home country. Essam knows that, from the vantage point of 2022, the revolution failed miserably: 'The economy is the worst, freedom of expression is the worst; there is no stability, no security. People don't feel safe. Everything just went to the extreme. It's like the last era of Mubarak [the president ousted in the 2011 revolution] but times ten.' Yet he is not someone easily given to despair – 'I'm a very optimistic person. I was born like that. It's my software.' – and says the revolution 'planted seeds inside each one of us, and especially the next generation'. That is where Essam's hope for an Egyptian future not dominated by military dictatorship or autocracy lies: 'there is something special about this generation [of teenagers]. They are much harder to brainwash.'

Essam, an engineering student of twenty-three when the revolution began, has lived in exile in Sweden and Finland since 2014. He was arrested and tortured during the revolution and found his situation barely improved when the Muslim Brotherhood came to power. In late 2013 his songs were banned, and he was forbidden from performing publicly. He has since forged a highly atypical music career, writing and recording protest songs in a unique style that combines the American and Egyptian influences he mentioned, for an avid Egyptian fanbase. The YouTube video for his restrained acoustic song of homesickness 'Lessa Bahinlha', which ends with the couplet 'I'm like a fish caught on a rod / Whose life ends outside of the water', was rewarded with over eighteen million views. His live shows, meanwhile, are for western festival audiences who don't understand the lyrics, or probably care much about his struggle.

This is the first factor that produces a highly surreal vibe for Essam's show that night – his performance is for an absent audience. (Literally, for the first few songs; the field takes a while to fill up.) What is this man doing, throwing himself about the stage, pouring his sorrow and anger into songs whose meaning is indecipherable to British festivalgoers at a Wiltshire stately home? It's hard to say. The second factor is that, even though he is a genuine exiled revolutionary, he looks and acts nothing like what you might expect of such a person. Rather, with his good looks, muscular physique, and choice of outfit – spotless, very nineties dungarees and, again, no t-shirt – he's the perfect Disney teen-movie version of a rebel rock star. There's nothing remotely threatening about him; he is, in fact, disarmingly kind and gentle. Most musicians will voice their appreciation of the technical crew before the end of their set, a few will mention a name or two – Essam thanks them all by first name and last name, checking a piece of paper on the floor where he's noted all that down.

But despite these amusing incongruities, over the course of an hour, Essam's set blossoms into a fantastically enjoyable rock show. He starts to talk about the meaning and context of each song, and is always at his most engaging when reminiscing about the revolution. This was the case a few hours earlier, during a discussion session when he spoke these remarkable words:

> If you see any revolution that you can relate to on any matter, just fucking go. Don't think. It's one of the best things ever that you can feel. To feel the power of being part of a mass of people is amazing, I wish that every human being can feel that, can taste it. If I could go back in time a million times, I would do. Even if the revolution didn't succeed. Yes, whatever happened to me and my friends and how hard it is now, this is still the most beautiful thing that happened to us.

He ends his set with a John Lennon cover, a song about defying society's expectations. Coming from Essam's mouth, though, it acquires a different meaning. 'I don't wanna be a soldier, mama, I don't wanna die,' he cries at the end of each verse, and you sense he's lying. That's exactly what he wants; to be back in Tahrir Square, fighting to the last. In his heart, you just know it, he already is.

GRANADA, THEN AND NOW

Medina Tenour Whiteman

For locals, Granada might mean 40-plus centigrade summers and snow-huddled winters, mopeds zipping around narrow alleys, plaza nightlife, Corpus Christi and Semana Santa, flamenco and reggaeton, traffic and smog, graffiti, foreign students, and the notoriously grumpy temperament of its denizens, the untranslatably rude '*malafollá*'. But for tourists, Granada is all about the Alhambra. Perched on the natural lookout of the Sabika hill, its reddish rammed earth walls are at once magnificent and shy. Swathed in cypress forest, it conceals luscious interior gardens, shady patios, and languid pools, intricate cupolas of *muqarnas* and walls geometrically enhanced with *zillij* mosaics. While the Alhambra has become one of Spain's most-visited tourist sites, as Helen Rodgers and Stephen Cavendish show in *City of Illusions: A History of Granada*, this palace complex has undergone many a rewriting of Granada's history – partly through an Orientalist lens that exoticises its Moorish heritage, so often mis-portrayed. Over the course of a millennium, as leadership changed hands and the population evolved, the idea of Granada has been transformed many times over: from a Neolithic habitation to a Roman settlement, an ancient Jewish town, a medieval Muslim capital, a Christian city scrabbling for authenticity, a key site in the struggle between Republican and Nationalist forces, to a modern city whose most lucrative export is arguably the Islamic culture it once trampled. In 2019, over three million tourists visited the Alhambra complex, drawn not only by its stunning beauty, but also by the mythos of its former Moorish splendour. The irony that this is the city where Islamic rule in Spain came to an end, indeed housing the remains of its conquerors, King Ferdinand and Queen Isabella, is not lost on the reader.

The book's chapters encapsulate the sequence of Granada's historical periods, beginning with the Introduction and Early History. The authors' opening gambit reveals a lot about a Christian city so desperate to establish a pre-Islamic origin story that it forged Roman artefacts in the eighteenth century. Recent archaeological findings reveal there *was* in fact an important Roman settlement here, where the Fourth Synod was held; Granada's secretive nature begins to be revealed. *City of Illusions* goes on to cover the Zirid Dynasty, the first Islamic leadership of the city-state; the tumultuous Almoravids and the Almohads; and, finally, the Nasrids – a period so noteworthy it's covered in three chapters, the Founding of a Dynasty, Splendour and Decline, and Reconquista. These reflect the development of much of the city, some of it – such as sections of Zirid walls and gates – still extant.

Many events of this period stand out as examples not only of cultural sophistication, but also of the cynicism of political rivals. Petty kings allied themselves with Christian forces against fellow Muslims; there was even a complex war with the Marinids in North Africa, who also had designs on the remains of Al-Andalus. Infighting was gruesome and rife. The founder of the Nasrid dynasty was probably poisoned by his own son, who was likewise ousted and later drowned by his half-brother, whose overthrow was in turn orchestrated by his half-sister. She egged on her son to storm the fortress in the Alhambra, but he was also murdered by a cousin. The penultimate emir Muley Hacén, in a fit of rage, had his own son beheaded. Dysfunctional families of the 2020s have nothing on the Nasrids.

But the grandeur of Nasrid Granada steals our admiration. Several of the more despotic rulers of this dynasty made great strides in developing the Alhambra palaces, adding poetry to the walls, patios with pools, gates and towers, and fostering a court full of scholars. The city, too, was flourishing. Gardens throughout the emirate meant that even the poor ate well, and provided silk, sugar, and dried fruit for export. Granada's burgeoning economy, bolstered by waves of Muslim immigrants fleeing Christian conquests, bankrolled the monarchs' penchant for intellectual pursuits such as astronomy. Yet it was the ceaseless treachery of the Nasrids' ruling elite that eventually cost the Muslims of Spain their autonomy. Ferdinand and Isabella laid siege to the city in 1491, and after months of starvation, desperately calling on North Africa and the Ottoman Empire, who refused to offer help, Granada surrendered to Ferdinand and Isabella, on 2 January 1492.

The book then takes us through some of the most painfully gripping episodes of Granada's history. These relate the story of the Mudéjars – Muslims who were allowed to remain after the so-called Reconquest – and the Moriscos ('little Moors'), those who were obliged to convert to Catholicism but were regarded, in most cases with good reason, as secret Muslims. The initially placatory attitude of the new Catholic monarchs towards the Muslim inhabitants of Granada soon gave way to harsh reprisals against the populace. Islam, Arabic, even bathing at home were all banned; many thousands of Arabic books were burned. Baptisms took place en masse. Moriscos were obliged to hire 'Old Christians' to certify that certain activities met Christian standards, putting them under crippling financial pressure. After some Moriscos began to rebel in the early sixteenth century, a group were taken captive and massacred. Not long after, all Morisco males aged from ten to sixty were rounded up from the Albaicin, their hands tied, and marched out of the city through the Puerta de Elvira which their own ancestors had built.

Helen Rodgers & Steven Cavendish, *City of Illusions: A History of Granada*, Hurst Publishers, London, 2021.

This was the beginning of the ethnic cleansing project – one of the most systematic in European history – that the new Christian monarchs of Spain decided was necessary to purge Granada of its heathen Muslim character. But its nadir would come in 1570, after the crushing of the second Alpujarra Rebellion, when Phillip II ordered the expulsion of all Moriscos from the former Emirate of Granada. The authors write: 'these banishments took place during a bitter winter…Thousands of men, women, and children died of exposure, disease and exhaustion. Some were robbed and murdered by the guards who escorted them; others were kidnapped and sold into slavery.'

These refugees were often unwelcome wherever they fled, their clothing, speech, and cooking habits markedly different even from other Mudéjars, who had become more culturally Castilian. They had to be registered with local authorities and were prohibited from returning to Granada on pain of death. By this point, the Muslim reader is surely sensing many resonances with our own time. The surveillance of Muslims in a majority non-Muslim state; refugees whose religion and culture are deemed foreign and undesirable; a persecuted Muslim population calling vainly on fellow Muslims for help. We might well think of Palestine, Kashmir, the Uyghur people, or Syrians and Afghans fleeing violence. Still bent on dealing with the 'Morisco problem' once and for all, in the early seventeenth century, Phillip III ordered the expulsion of all Moriscos from Spain, totalling some 200,000 to 300,000. These had to leave all their wealth, and even young children, behind. Many died en route.

In the following chapter, A Very Christian City, we see how Granada's new leadership tried to rebuild the city in their own image. While converting mosques into churches and building monasteries, even founding the University of Granada to train preachers to convert recalcitrant Moriscos, this process benefited from the lucky discovery of several lead tablets in the caves of what is now Sacromonte. According to Old Latin inscriptions on these tablets, two men of Arab origin were baptised by Christ himself and arrived in pre-Islamic Granada together with Spain's patron, Saint James the Greater, where they celebrated the first mass in Europe. To bring even greater prestige to Catholic Granada, the brothers were burned to death for their faith by the Romans, and the charred remains of bodies were found in a nearby cave. The Christians of Granada were overjoyed, finally able to claim the city as their own. A local historian wrote up a revised history of the city, claiming that its Islamic past was a mere blip in this ancient Christian settlement's history. For Moriscos, this offered definitive proof that one could be a genuine Christian and also an Arab. In 1682, though, the lead tablets were declared by papal bull to be – at the risk of sounding blasphemous – a load of bull. The offenders were thought to have been the translators themselves, who were of Morisco descent – a heartrending indicator of their desire to be accepted and live without persecution.

Christian Granada became known for several important Christian figures, including Saint John of the Cross, who wrote one of his best-loved poems, The Dark Night of the Soul, while staying in the Monasterio de los Mártires in Granada. The Arabist Asín Palacios would later point out connections between St John's writings and those of Ibn Arabi, as well as between the Sufi tradition and that of eastern Christian ascetics. It begs the question: who is distinct from whom? By this time, European and

American visitors had already begun to spin a romantic tale of faded Moorish glory, of crumbling monuments largely ignored between a myopic elite and the grinding poverty of the masses. However, their depictions of the city, in paint or words, reinvented it to a large extent through the lens of Orientalist fantasy.

In the early nineteenth century, Granada's attachments to these elements of its heritage would be reinvigorated...by the French. Chapter 10 discusses the little-discussed Napoleonic period. Ironically, given France's current stance toward Muslims, at the time there was a growing interest in the Moors – at least, from the other end of an Orientalising telescope. The brief period of French occupation saw the first efforts to restore the by now dilapidated Alhambra to its former glory. However, General Sebastiani's troops being garrisoned at the Alhambra did as much damage as he had repaired, burning wooden doors and religious artefacts to stay warm, and damaging fortifications in the Alhambra and across the city.

Once the Spanish monarchs were restored to the throne, they were keen to put this unfortunate episode of secularism behind them and instigated a return to religious absolutism. This Catholic zeal was not shared across the board, with working classes in Granada – who mainly lived in the overcrowded, underdeveloped Albaicin – furious that their needs were being subjugated to the whims of clergy and nobles. The seeds were sown for the terrible events of the Civil War a few decades later. Meanwhile, the vestiges of Granada's Islamic past would prove hard to shift because of the thrall it had on the European imagination. 'Visitors from northern European countries and America ... came to see the Moorish influence of the past—the mystique of the Orient so tragically destroyed, as they saw it, three centuries before...' In Dreams of the Past, Visions of the Future, we meet a few of the Romantic writers and artists who felt the call of Granada's Moorish aura, as well as its Gypsy heritage – again, packaged to be more consumable by tourists – and set up studios in Granada's seemingly more authentic districts, the Albaicin and Sacromonte. One of these was Gabriel Garcia Lorca, who appears in the following chapter, Creation and Destruction. This renowned, Granada-born poet and playwright lambasted the ostentatious Holy Week processions, part of the re-Christianising fever, writing: 'and don't profane the Alhambra, which isn't and never will be Christian.' Lorca would later be executed by the extreme-right Falangists who were soon to seize power.

The chapter Civil War and Dictatorship explains how the new Falangist leader, Francisco Franco, used Granada's historical position to leverage his own propaganda: 'Nationalists had likened their fight against the left to the Reconquista against the Moors', portraying Republicans as violent barbarians in state-controlled newspapers and radio. Yet Franco's own political power was established through staggering acts of carnage. Women and children fleeing the Albaicin, where most of the working-class resistance lived and fought, were taken to concentration camps. Between 4,000 and 5,000 Republican fighters were shot against a wall in the cemetery, their bodies thrown into mass graves. The *Esquadra Negra* pulled suspected Republicans from their houses at midnight to send them to the same fate, and even dragged sympathisers from hospitals to be executed in the street.

Once again, the Albaicin was a hotbed of resistance against an oppressive regime. The district was systematically (re-)Christianised, restoring damaged churches and re-erecting crosses to expunge the Marxist horror. Obsessed with an idealised traditional Spain, Franco also encouraged the beautification of the Albaicin, into the pretty, whitewashed streets with floral windowsills that we know today – paid for not by the State, but by the already starving residents. Despite some legendary efforts, for example by the swashbuckling Quero brothers, to keep up the fight against totalitarianism, eventually Granada sank into a begrudging acceptance of its fate. More pressing than the reds to the administration was now the impending reality of modernity, and the introduction of the motorcar. Large parts of the city, whose narrow alleys were part of the Islamic genius for keeping pathways cool, were demolished in order to make way for wide, northern European style boulevards. Massive urban sprawl accompanied a boom in tourism, which Granada's city hall really started to capitalise on after Franco's death in 1975.

In Granada Today, the authors bring us up to date while posing important questions about how the city relates to its Muslim past, as well as the Gitano (Gypsy) presence it has consistently repressed. While the descendants of Jews expelled from Spain in 1492 have been offered the right to return and citizenship, the same offer has not been extended to the descendants of expelled Moriscos. There are even protests now against the appropriateness of celebrating the *Día de la Toma,* the day Islamic Granada fell. As a Muslim, Granada is a complex place to be. There are all the Muslim clichés, of kebab restaurants and souvenir shops selling belly-dancing attire and Moroccan slippers, people willing to write your name in Arabic calligraphy on a street corner, or the unamplified sound of a muezzin calling the faithful to prayer beside a crowded tourist spot. Above all, Granada inhabits our imagination as the last bastion of Islam in Western Europe. It's not only longed-for as a geographical location but as a personal state, of authenticity, of being both Western and Muslim without contradiction.

I have often wondered why Granada exerts this almost mythic attraction. It is like so much of Islamic history, bittersweet for its admixture of the lofty and the lamentable. The old city seems to have a character of its own, at times smouldering, magical and romantic, at other times tempestuous, insolent, traumatised. It conceals many wounds, manifesting as the piercing howl of *cante hondo* at midnight, or the startling discovery of Muslim skeletons buried inside old houses or unearthed on building sites.

Granada is iconic, not only of the triumph of Christianity over Islam in Europe, but also of the persistence of Moorish influence here, even if it be in warped ways. For a millennium, the city has been a fulcrum in the balance – often delicate, sometimes violent – between Islam and Christianity as religious, cultural, and political forces vying for supremacy, and later, between far-right Nationalism and Marxist-inspired Republicanism. That Granada's Moriscos concealed their true selves behind a Castilian Christian facade may well, as the authors suggest, have bequeathed to Granada a sense of illusion, touching on the contemporary nerve of identity performance and optics. Centuries later, Republicans would find themselves having to conceal their political leanings in an atmosphere of brutal fascist repression.

If anything was lacking from *City of Illusions,* I felt it was a fuller discussion of who the Moors really were. The authors mention how contemporary DNA testing in Spain finds little evidence of North African genes, supposedly proof of the efficiency of these expulsions. However, this rests on the fallacy that the Moors were of entirely Arab or North African ancestry. The slow adoption of Islam throughout Al-Andalus incorporated converts of numerous ethnic backgrounds, including Slavic,

Visigothic, Jewish, and Iberian Celt, not to mention migrants from Persia, Yemen, and beyond.

Unfortunately, this idea supports the racist narrative, so prevalent in Spain today, that the Moors were a foreign Arab faction rightfully expelled from Spain by the Reconquest – a term that did not gain currency until centuries after the fact, as part of the narrative-building of a unified Christian Spain, cleansed of foreign blood. The Moriscos had to pay extortionate rates to travel into exile; for a largely agricultural population, how many could have managed it? Although history books rarely agree on figures, there is contemporary research suggesting that as many as 40 percent of Moriscos remained, and another 10 percent, finding it impossible to integrate anywhere else, returned.

History generally, frustratingly, tells only the masculine side of the story. One tantalising exception in *City of Illusions* is a Moorish woman healer who went to the Alhambra to cure, of all people, Cardinal Cisneros. Another is that of Mariana Pineda, whose memory is restored as a courageous resistance fighter who helped her cousin escape prison and conveyed messages for the liberal cause – and all this as a widow of eighteen with two children.

The authors of *City of Illusions* trace shapes on an alluded-to map, of forbidding city walls and periodic expansions, as well as the phases of the Alhambra's development, grounding the abstraction of history in something tangible. The reader is empowered to walk around the city in an amplified way, witnessing the city's past loom out of the veneer of the present. Sixteen sides of colour plates offer visual aids, in this eloquently written, encyclopaedically researched reference to Granada as the locus of several major periods of history, jointly European and Islamic. The reader comes to understand Granada as a perennial symbol for the struggle for Europe's 'hearts and minds', or perhaps simply the struggle to be true to oneself, free from illusions.

THE OTHER AFGHAN MUSICIANS

Susannah Tarbush

In 1973 a young British couple, Veronica Doubleday and her ethnomusicologist husband John Baily, arrived in the city of Herat, western Afghanistan, where Baily planned to spend a year researching the local music tradition. They returned to Herat in 1976 for a further year. In between these two full years of residence, they made a shorter visit to a city whose music, people, and ambience had captivated them.

During her first year in Herat, Doubleday lived as 'a lone woman in a public world of men' she recalls in her classic *Three Women of Herat*. Originally published in 1988, the book has been republished recently in an updated edition.

She sometimes visited male musicians or attended musical events with Baily and at home she helped him work on the transcription and translation of Herati songs, with the help of a local schoolteacher who also gave them lessons in Persian (the Afghan version of Persian, Dari, is spoken in Herat). Doubleday also began studying miniature painting with a Herati master in his studio. But she had limited interactions with women at that time. When she and Baily were invited to houses, she sat and ate with the men, 'nourished and refreshed by unseen hands. Trays of food were carried in by men and children; the women seated out of sight'. Sometimes she was taken to meet the women in their quarters. 'In this way I cut through the curtain of purdah, no longer an honorary male visitor. Nevertheless, I found these early encounters with the women exhausting and even humiliating, as I was inevitably bombarded with questions and exposed to a mixture of delight, admiration and ridicule.'

In 1976, before the beginning of her final year in Herat, Doubleday decided to withdraw from public life and to explore the world of Herati women, 'as by then I had become sufficiently attuned to make some close friendships'. Although men treated her with respect and courtesy, she began to feel self-conscious and out of place in their company. At the same time Doubleday had become increasingly interested in ethnomusicology and she realised she could make an invaluable contribution to Baily's work if she undertook a complementary study of women's music, which was completely inaccessible to him as a man. She found learning to perform Herati music enjoyable and challenging. She learned not only the style of singing but also to play the *daireh* – a frame drum similar to a tambourine, with bells and rings inside the frame, which is used to lay down rhythms for dancing or to accompany singing. 'Herati voice production is also very different from our own, with a strained nasal quality. The vocal line is free and ornamented and texts are improvised from a bank of well-known quatrains.'

As part of her efforts to enter the women's realm, Doubleday abandoned her study of miniature painting because it left her isolated at home or in the company of men in her teacher's studio. Instead, she took up embroidery, a women's art whose patterns were related to those in miniature painting. She realised that she needed to accept some of the limitations of purdah in order to penetrate the women's milieu. 'There was no point in feeling outraged by customs such as veiling, as this would have emphasised our differences rather than brought us closer.' She refused to go as far as wearing the all-enveloping *burqa* however. She had once tried on a *burqa* 'whose latticework window provided very limited vision and felt stifling'. Instead, she opted for an Iranian-style *chador* and had a seamstress make one from black Iranian cotton with a tiny flower print. 'The reaction among Herati women was unanimous: the veil looked beautiful and they were pleased that I had adopted their custom. They had not liked my Western clothes – the fur boots, thick jumpers and jeans that I had worn throughout the freezing winter.' However, she is ambivalent towards the veil. She writes: 'adopting the veil was a far bigger step than I ever imagined: it took me right inside Herati psychology and affected me deeply. Ironically this symbol of oppression had liberating aspects for me, since it minimised the differences between me and the Afghan people.' Wearing a veil in public also initiated an important and subtle change in her, 'cultivating an aura of modesty and self-containment. It masked my foreignness, enabling me to join many women's outings where I would otherwise have attracted undue attention, and it brought a welcome privacy. It was also fascinating and salutary to discover that being invisible is addictive.'

But she does not approve of the veil and sees it as a vehicle of oppression through which men assert their power over women. Strangely, wearing the veil and becoming like Herati women actually resulted in building her commitment to feminism.

Gradually Doubleday came to appreciate the strength and self-sufficiency of Herati women, and began to see how 'arrogant and ill-informed' the Western view of Muslim women is. 'The ill-assorted images of exploitation and oppression are in reality only half-truths, based upon facts that have been jumbled and poorly understood.'

Doubleday arrived back in Britain with an overwhelming amount of accumulated information in the form of detailed fieldwork notes, diaries, and musical recordings. She had originally planned to write generally about Herati women, but she eventually decided to shape the narrative around three particular friends who had played a vital role in her understanding and experience of Herat: Mariam, Mother of Nebi, and Shirin.

Veronica Doubleday, *ThreeWomen of Herat: Afghanistan, 1973-77*, Eland Publishing, London, 2022

Mariam was the daughter of hereditary musician Latif Khan, the authority on classical music in Herat. The majority of the city were Sunnis but there was also a strong minority of Shia Muslims who were affluent shop keepers, businessmen, or artisans. Latif Khan was in a sensitive position because he was both Shia and a musician; some mullahs taught that music was the work of the devil. Mariam introduced Doubleday to the social rules of family life, and the rituals and beliefs of Shia Islam. She saw Mariam as a steadying influence who helped her to understand how women functioned and exercised power within the community. She found the women of the family to be 'humorous, welcoming and affectionate'.

Mother of Nebi 'provided a darker attraction'. After a religious healer or Agha had cured a serious illness caused by spirit possession, she had become his disciple and practised as a diviner and helped women who came to her with problems. She 'lived in strict seclusion, and in her I saw how damaging the psychological effects of purdah could be on women'. In contrast to calm and cautious Mariam, Mother of Nabi was passionate, temperamental, and uncontrolled. 'What particularly drew me to her was her exuberance in performance, her creativity and her delight in music.' Though she was not an ideal teacher because her versions of songs varied from day to day, she excelled as a performer and was especially skilled in the art of improvising poetry, particularly the slow, highly ornamented style known as *charbeiti*.

Shirin was Doubleday's main music teacher. She came from a notorious clan of musicians known as the Minstrels who were rivals to Mariam's family, and who had made recordings at Radio Afghanistan. 'No Herati woman could have gone to her house for lessons: the Minstrels' work as entertainers at weddings so offended against the rules of propriety that they were regarded as loose women.' As Doubleday's music skills progressed, Shirin realised she could pass as a musician. Doubleday was eager, willing, and honoured to join the band and also acquired a new name. Shirin thought the name Veronica sounded weird and said 'I know: I'll call you Farahnaz! That's much prettier.' Some of Doubleday's friends in Herat were scandalised that she had joined Shirin's band, seeing it as a corruption of morals. She was particularly upset by a conversation with Latif Khan and Mariam, who tried to dissuade her from continuing in the band in order to safeguard her reputation, but she continued to perform.

Shirin's eldest daughter Gol Dasteh told her not to say she was from England: 'they'll all crowd round and bother you. Let's say you're from Iran'. On a few occasions Doubleday 'lied glibly, making up whatever story came into my head: my mother was kin to Shirin or I was from Kabul'. Doubleday remains highly appreciative of Shirin's role in her Afghan musical education.

She writes:

During our association I collected more than seventy songs and at least as many quatrains of poetry from Shirin, and I made recordings at weddings and at her house. Words on paper and sounds on tape, tangible gifts from her to me: songs expressing the different aspects of love – excitement, pain, wonder, sleeplessness, long: songs with humour, pathos or spirituality; lullabies for me to sing to my own baby.

When I sing my songs from Herat they evoke a different world of emotion, recalling the shining moon in a clear sky at night, the soft cooing of doves in a shrine courtyard, or the rare beauty of a dew-filled rose at dawn. I riffle through my book of songs and sigh: faith, longing, hardship – they seem so removed from the experience of British life.

This rich world of emotion was conveyed to a rapt audience at Eland's launch of *Three Women of Herat* in March, which took the form of an hour-long performance of Afghan music and song featuring Doubleday accompanied by Baily on rubab and dutar, and by Sulaiman Haqpana on tabla drums. The occasion was a double celebration, of the launch of the book and of Eland's fortieth anniversary.

Three Women of Herat was first published by Jonathan Cape in 1988 and republished by Tauris Parke paperbacks in 1999. It has received many plaudits. The novelist and Nobel laureate Doris Lessing said: 'I was fascinated by this story of ordinary life before the Russian invasion of Afghanistan. The three women are remarkable and unforgettable, and the story of how the author gained their friendship is like a novel.'

Prominent Pakistani journalist and author Ahmed Rashid found 'her understanding of "purdah" is certainly the most illuminating by any Western writer for a long time.'

Eland's republication of *Three Women of Herat* could hardly have been more timely, coming seven months after the UK and US withdrawal from Afghanistan, the overthrow of the government and the takeover by the Taliban. After the dashing of early hopes that this second period of Taliban rule would be less severe than the first, the Taliban have again banned music and musicians, smashing musical instruments, and have imposed severe restrictions on women and girls. Many musicians have left the country and those who remain fear for their safety. The new edition of *Three Women of Herat* includes a fresh Afterword outlining events in the years since the book first appeared. In writing the book Doubleday had taken care to disguise the identities of its characters, in keeping with the practice of anthropology, so as to avoid the betrayal of trust.

In her Afterword Doubleday reveals that Shirin was in fact the well-known singer Zainab Herawi ('Zainab from Herat'), now long dead. The new edition contains for the first time a selection of delightful photographs taken by Doubleday in Herat, some of which show Mariam, Mother of Nebi, or Shirin in musical settings or with young children.

When Doubleday and Baily lived in Herat the political situation was relatively stable. 'Afghan people look back on the mid-1970s as a golden age. But its peace was soon to be shattered,' notes Doubleday. The bloody communist coup of April 1978 precipitated Afghanistan's slide into a long, bitter struggle between opposing political forces. 'Now, almost half a century on, Afghanistan is still a conflict zone, trapped in an impossibly complex web of political intrigue, corruption, violence and poverty. Millions of Afghans have left their country, many more have been internally displaced and I cannot keep count of the enormous loss of Afghan lives.'

By 1985 many Afghans had become refugees in various countries and Baily went to Peshawar to make an ethnographic documentary film on refugees there. By chance he met Amir, a musician from Zeinab's household, who became the subject of Baily's award-winning film *Amir: An Afghan refugee musician's life in Peshawar, Pakistan*. Doubleday accompanied Baily to Peshawar. 'I felt compelled to follow him, but dreaded what I would find, and it did not take me long to realise that the refugee women were suffering far more than the men.' The men had choices but 'women had no options. They were trapped at home with harrowing memories and the psychological pain of dislocation and isolation, impotent to act against the powerful forces that had transformed their lives'. Through an audiocassette sent later by Amir, Doubleday learned of Zainab's death. 'All he said was that before she died, she had been paralysed for some time – a tragic end to her hard life.'

By 1994, the Russians had left Afghanistan and, despite heavy fighting in Kabul, Herat was an oasis of relative calm and stability. Doubleday seized the chance to visit the city for the first time in sixteen years, travelling on a UN plane from Pakistan. In Herat she was reunited with Mariam, who 'humorously resumed her role of teacher, informant and special friend'. Mother of Nebi was still living in her old house. Although she still saw her Agha, people rarely came to her for divinations. 'Overall I felt that she was psychologically stronger and I also noticed that Father of Nebi had grown into a gentle character.' Doubleday went with a heavy heart to Zainab's old house, where her eldest son Yaqub lived. When Yaqub introduced his wife, he firmly told Doubleday 'she's not working as a musician. My mother did that work, but it's a bad profession. In any case, female musicians are not allowed to go to weddings now.' Doubleday gave Yaqub a copy of *Three Women of Herat* saying it was a gift in memory of

Zainab. After scanning it Yaqub complained: 'why is there no photograph of my mother? You must publish her picture! Now that she has died it could not be sinful to show her face!' Doubleday also gave copies of *Three Women of Herat* to Mariam and Mother of Nebi. 'I felt a little uneasy, doubting that they would like to be linked with the Minstrel women, but they did not complain. Mariam was gratified that her part of my book was the thickest of the three.'

There are now two separate Persian translations of Doubleday's book, and a Persian language publication recently published coverage on Zainab's career and Doubleday's involvement with her.

Things became much darker in Herat in the six years after the Taliban captured Herat in 1995. Every so often men would be forced to fill the football stadiums to witness executions, or the burning of musical instruments, audiocassettes, and videocassettes. Many professional musicians migrated to Iran, but a few continued to operate on a secretive, underground basis – including some of the Minstrel women. After the overthrow of the Taliban in 2001 the Afghan situation eased somewhat and in 2004 Baily and Doubleday visited Kabul, and manged to get to Herat for four days. 'Contrary to persistent rumours that women musicians were not allowed to work, three female Minstrel bands had formed. As in the old days they were playing at women's wedding parties but none of Zainab's daughters was involved.' In 2014, Doubleday and Baily were invited to spend two weeks in Kabul as teachers and performers of Afghan music at the Afghanistan National Institute of Music (ANIM), a remarkable co-educational school founded in 2010 by Afghan-Australian ethnomusicologist Ahmad Naser Sarmast. But it was too dangerous to consider making a side trip to Herat. Following the Taliban takeover in August 2022, many pupils of ANIM managed to escape the country and have been given sanctuary in Portugal. An international organisation has been set up called the Campaign to Protect Afghanistan's Musicians, and Doubleday and Baily are doing all they can to help Afghan musicians and promote Afghan music.

In an interview with BBC Radio 3 last October, Doubleday said: 'The situation is really tragic, the people in charge have a very hardline attitude towards music and so the future looks extremely bleak. I do feel very strongly that we have a great responsibility for the world to understand Afghan music.'

ET CETERA

ON COPYCATS

Youshaa Patel

I was eating a *chapli* kebab burger at a restaurant in Damascus in 2007, when I had a chance encounter with an angry young man. Walking briskly past my outdoor table, he overheard my friend and me speaking English and abruptly turned around to ask where we were from. 'America,' we replied. 'I just made *hijra* from the UK,' he proudly announced. Donning a white kufi and carrying a large backpack, the 21-year-old Brit of South Asian origin had just arrived at this ancient crossroads of Arab-Muslim civilisation. Curious, I asked him what he was fleeing from. He told us that he had traveled alone, financed the trip himself by working odd jobs, and detested infidel '*kuffar*'. He took pains to explain why Islam mandated that he flee his home country of Great Britain. Put simply, Muslims should not live among unbelievers. 'We can't even imitate them,' he exclaimed.

The young man was alluding to the famous hadith of the Prophet narrated on the authority of the Companion Ibn Umar: 'Whoever imitates a people becomes one of them.' Although the hadith may be read as a neutral observation about how imitation defines group belonging, most Sunni scholars across time and place read it as a morally-charged admonition *against* emulating non-Muslims, especially Jews and Christians. The Prophet, in other words, was defining the line between *us* and *them*. Over time, the key Arabic term in the hadith, *tashabbuh*, came to signal this forbidden type of imitation. How and why this reading transformed into a religious obligation for Muslims to be different was the subject of my PhD dissertation—and why I was visiting Damascus, where a key unpublished manuscript on the subject was held.

I do not mean to draw a straight line between Islamic scripture and the young man's decision to emigrate from Britain. What experiences led to his hostility towards unbelievers never entered our brief conversation that day, and I never saw him again. How people come to believe in the truth of an idea is too complex for me to claim that it originated with Islam; religion may simply be a pretext. The polyvalence and ambiguity of Islamic scripture and tradition resist sweeping generalisations.

But the encounter with the young man confirmed that my historical research was relevant to Muslim lives today. Not limited to fundamentalists and extremists, a broad spectrum of believers, including 'moderate' Sufi Shaykhs, hold the conviction that Muslim have no business imitating unbelievers. In modern times, many thinkers have decried the tendency for Muslims to ape the 'West.' They have lashed out at the *umma* for being copycats in everything from wearing brimmed hats and bowties to celebrating Valentine's Day and Christmas. Many Muslims living under colonial rule adapted the Prophet's mantra against imitation into a slogan of anti-colonial resistance. The Iranian intellectual Jalal Al-e Ahmad dubbed Muslim adoration for all things European a plague, *Gharbzadeghi*, translated variously into English as Westoxification or Occidentosis.

Consider Ayad Akhtar's Pulitzer Prize-winning play, *Disgraced*. It is a tragedy centered on the character of Amir Kapoor, a Pakistani Muslim immigrant, whose personal and professional life fall apart in post-9/11 America. We first meet Amir, happily married, about to become a partner at his New York law firm, but helplessly watch his American dream become a nightmare, as he loses both his job and his wife by the end of the play. Amir's teenage nephew, Abe, follows a similar fate. Modeling himself on Amir's example, Abe works hard to fit into mainstream American culture. He dresses like everyone else and changes his birth name, 'Hussein' to 'Abe Jensen'. But Abe's efforts to belong end in failure when a barista at Starbucks mistakes him for an extremist and calls the FBI to take him in for interrogation—and potentially deportation. By the final scene, Abe has reclaimed his original name, Hussein, and wears a kufi, a visible token of his turn to religion. When I first watched the climactic scene where Abe's resentment and despair boil over into a diatribe against Western civilisation, I could not help but see the young British man I met in Damascus:

Abe: The Prophet wouldn't be trying to be like one of them. He didn't conquer the world by copying other people. He made the world copy him.

Amir. Conquer the world?

Abe: That's what they've done. They've conquered the world. We're gonna get it back. For three hundred years they've been taking our land, drawing new borders, replacing our laws, making us want to be like them. Marry their women. They disgraced us. They disgraced us. And then they pretend they don't understand the rage we've got!

Disgraced and humiliated, Abe turns to the Prophet for a solution. He concludes that the way for him to restore his self-respect is not to copy others, but to be *different*. This may even mean returning to Pakistan. 'Maybe we never should've left.'

In the narratives of Abe and the young man, I saw something of my own struggle to belong. Born in Edinburgh, Scotland, to parents of Indian heritage, I learned very early that I was not like everyone else. I was five years old when Ms. McGowan placed me—the only student of colour and only Muslim in my primary one class—at a table alone, set apart from all the other white children who sat together in reading groups. I was sad and hurt. Why did Ms. McGowan put me in a group all by myself I complained to my mother? When she confronted the school administration, they did nothing. With my classmates, I didn't fare much better. I didn't understand why Ewan told me, 'You have honey in your socks' while the other white children laughed. I only knew that his insult made me feel different since no one else had honey in their socks. The incident with Ms. McGowan marked a tipping point for my family who made the decision to emigrate from Edinburgh to New Jersey in 1982.

Human beings are social animals. Centuries before Charles Caleb Colton coined the famous saying 'Imitation is the greatest [form] of flattery,' Ibn Khaldun observed that imitation is borne of admiration. The role models we emulate shape who we become. Children imitate their parents. Students imitate their teachers. Believers imitate their prophets. How would late capitalist societies survive if big corporations did not pay celebrities and athletes millions to influence the masses to buy their products? When the Prophet Muhammad counseled his followers to beware of who they imitate, he was reminding them to choose their role models wisely.

The truth is that many of us don't think much about who we emulate. Operating beneath the surface of our psyches, we are often unaware that many of our everyday acts are copied from others. In the Qur'an, God criticises unbelievers for blindly 'following their ancestors'. The subtext is that they are being irrational—that the stubborn insistence on being chained to tradition is borne of willful ignorance, or *jahiliyya*. 'Do you not reflect?' God rhetorically asks. But the unbelievers refuse this call to enlightenment. One millennium later, the Qur'an's critique of blind conformity was echoed by German philosopher Immanuel Kant, who proclaimed that 'Genius is the opposite of imitation.' In Kant's view, slavishly following tradition opposed the spirit of the European Enlightenment, which was the free spirit of rational inquiry.

We have inherited Kant's disdain of imitation, itself a product of Western modernity's replacement of God with the human—the individual—as the centre of the universe. Imitation within this emerging secular cosmology opposes reason, originality, innovation, and authenticity—values most modernists hold sacred. Today, we punish plagiarisers as cheaters. We urge children to become good leaders before becoming good followers. Big corporations and egocentric professors boast of their innovation, not imitation. What explains this 'unilateral swerve away from anything that could be called mimicry, imitation, or mimesis,' as the philosopher Rene Girard puts it? We run away from imitation, he wrote, because it brazenly exposes 'all that transforms us into herds'. Who wants to be a lowly sheep?

We tend to view imitations as inferior. When reading a translation, we often say, pessimistically, that 'Something is lost in translation'. We do not ask, 'What is gained in translation?'— even though a translation takes on new meanings when transported to new languages and cultures. This insight begs the broader question: is a copy *always* inferior to the original? No, not always. Consider Fyodor Doestoevksy's early novella, *The Double*. The story's protagonist, Golyadkin, is a civil servant filled with social anxiety. Urged by his doctor to go out and make friends, one day he encounters his likeness, his double. 'This was a different Mr. Golyadkin, quite different but at the same time identical with the first.' Is this 'Golyadkin Jr.' a real person or a hallucination of 'Golyadkin Sr.'? As the story progresses, we learn that the copy of Golyadkin is a better version of the original Golyadkin at functioning within society. In fact, Golyadkin Sr. becomes so tortured by his double's superiority that he experiences a mental breakdown and is taken to an asylum.

It is useful to think of imitations as adaptations that build on what came before it. Most premodern Muslim sages were unashamed of cutting and pasting ideas from earlier authorities, often without attribution or citation. For them, tradition was a palimpsest that submerged the individual *nafs*, the ego-self, in the immense ocean of wisdom contained in the past. Demonstrating that the *salaf*, the First Muslims, upheld a specific view or performed a specific practice carried far more weight than a single independent thinker concocting something novel, claiming that he knew best. Such hubris was portrayed as a symptom of pride and arrogance, vices that disqualified one from being a model of piety and wisdom.

This outlook helped institute *taqlid*, the practice of deferring independent reasoning to past authorities, within the elaborate architecture of Islamic law. But, as many students of Islam know, *taqlid* has been a flashpoint dividing Muslim reformists from traditionalists for centuries. Reformists see *taqlid* as a form of ignorance that stifles independent thought, creativity, and reason in Islam—noting its uncanny resemblance to the blind imitation of unbelievers criticised in the Qur'an. Muslim traditionalists see *taqlid* as a useful form of imitation that ensures consistency, stability, and standards of excellence in Islamic scholarship. *Taqlid*, in this view, is a *form of reason* that prevents intellectual anarchy. Consistent with this outlook, the Catholic philosopher, Alasdair McIntyre, argued that what we call *tradition* is comprised of arguments—rational debates and discussions—extended over time. Tradition, then, is embedded in reason. We must recall that the Qur'an does not uniformly reject tradition, singling out loyal adherence to the Prophet Muhammad's conduct (*ittiba' al-sunna*) as a path to salvation. The Qur'an suggests that this virtuous form of imitation is rational, unlike the deplorable form of imitation rooted in unbelief.

Is *tashabbuh*, then, a form of imitation borne of ignorance or enlightenment? The short answer is that it depends. The term's lexical field spans a broad range of interrelated concepts, including imitation, simulation, resemblance, assimilation, mimesis, and mimicry. Most

YOUSHAA PATEL

fundamentally, *tashabbuh* expresses a relationship between self and other. However, this relationship is characterised by ambiguity, as indicated by the series of related Arabic terms that share its triliteral root, which include doubt (*shibha*), uncertainty (*shubha*), confusion (*tashbīh*), comparison (*tashbīh*), and fool's gold (*shabaha*). They suggest that imitation contains within it the potential to deceive. And in the textual context of the hadith, 'Whoever imitates a people becomes one of them,' *tashabbuh* is an act that blurs, and even erases, the line between self and other.

However, the Prophet's pithy but potent statement is a warning only if we perceive the Other ('them') as dangerous, inferior, and radically different. Through this lens of hostility towards the Other, imitation is construed as reprehensible or forbidden. Although Muslim perceptions of outsiders across history were diverse and dynamic, and far from uniform, most Muslim jurists adopted this reading of the hadith, embedding the concept of *tashabbuh* in a logic of exclusion. They attached a stigma to the act of copying non-Muslims, casting a dim outlook over the Other that sharpened the line between believers and unbelievers. Only the ignorant and unruly become copycats.

But to be fair to the jurists, most did not mandate that Muslims shun emulating non-Muslims altogether. They realised that to be a copycat is to be human. They also recognised that the Prophet Muhammad did not envision a society in which Muslims and non-Muslims inhabited entirely separate worlds. He willingly adopted many practices that were common to Arab Jews and Christians because he wanted to *connect* his *umma* to the society and culture around them. A close study of the Prophet's *sunna* shows that he and his followers gradually set themselves apart in ways that were small, not grandiose and spectacular. In fact, it was because their lifeways shared so much in common with their neighbours that those small differences mattered. Whether it entailed styling beards and turbans a specific way, or praying with one's shoes in the mosque (a practice now rarely observed), the Prophet strategically selected certain practices that visibly set apart Muslims from the crowd, but nonetheless allowed them to remain connected to mainstream society. The Prophet, in other words, assumed Muslims would be interacting and engaging non-Muslims every day, just like he did. The invitation to be different, then, was not a call to run away or to obliterate the Other; it was a call to solidarity. This is not a farfetched interpretation. By dubbing Jews and Christians 'People of the Book (*ahl al-kitab*),' the Qur'an reminds us of the enduring connection Muslims have with their rival faith communities through God.

With the objective of strengthening Muslim social and spiritual connections, other Muslim thinkers—mainly Sufis—adopted less hostile and more inclusionary readings of the hadith that portrayed the Other in a more favourable light. The object of emulation, in this case, was not the non-Muslim Other, but a Sufi master, prophet, or other moral exemplar. When visiting a Sufi master in Aleppo, I was taught the following couplet: 'If you cannot be like them, then imitate (*tashabbahu*) them. For imitating the virtuous is success.' This versified gloss on the hadith urges novices to seek out and emulate moral exemplars as a path to spiritual transformation (or, put more crudely, fake it till you make it). The Ottoman Sufi-jurist, Najm al-din al-Ghazzi, encouraged believers to look beyond the human world and emulate animals like the noble eagle to become soaring minarets of piety and virtue. According to these Sufis, becoming a copycat is the way to piety and enlightenment. It is thus not entirely true that imitation 'is all that transforms us into herds' since self-cultivation is a creative act.

Can we draw inspiration from these inclusive readings of the hadith to extend its reach to non-Muslims? I think so. One way to institute a different reading of the hadith is to see beyond confessional lines and be mindful of the divine breath that inheres in *all humans*. This certainly merits our esteem, as the Qur'an reminds us: 'We have honoured the children of Adam.' When we see the shared humanity that connects 'us' to 'them' the Prophet's statement becomes an exhortation to emulate what is best in others. In fact, because imitation is an index of admiration and affection for others, it may even be read as an exhortation to '*love* thy neighbour'.

We may think of the Prophet's statement as a mirror that reflects how we see the world and our place in it. How we perceive our relationship to the Other, how we imagine our social entanglements, determines what we hear the Prophet say. Those besieged by inner-demons may hear the Prophet telling them to shun those who are different, while those who have resolved to 'respond in the best way' may hear the Prophet urging them to expand the circle of belonging. So let us pause for a moment, take a deep breath, and reflect on the Prophet's words. What do you hear?

THE QUEEN
AND TEN HISTORICAL OTHERS

While the death of Queen Elizabeth II marked the end of a historical era, much has also been written about the swathes of people who mourned her on a very personal level and in their own unique ways. The period of national mourning in Britain was a modern-day religious spectacle, reminiscent of medieval rites of visitation for the Christian masses to grieve the deaths of popes. The queue for the Queen's lying-in-state is now legendary, even affecting the fortunes of celebrities. Football legend David Beckham enjoyed a boost in popularity for spending hours in line whilst ITV presenters Phillip Schofield and Holly Willoughby became tabloid hate figures overnight for allegedly jumping the sacred Queue.

Traditional media tributes to the Queen also sought to connect her personal qualities of public service, humility, humour and faith with her historical and symbolic role as the UK's monarch and other jurisdictions where she was head of state. The Queen, we were assured, reigned over a remarkably peaceful dissolution of the British Empire and its graceful transition into the Commonwealth which she personally held dear. The lack of blemish in her record was underscored by the fact that the violent Partition of India and Pakistan occurred before she ascended the throne.

This narrative was and is not without its detractors within and beyond the borders of the UK. After all, did Elizabeth II not begin her reign in 1952, the same year that the Mau Mau uprising in Kenya erupted? Was the violent British military campaign to suppress the revolt and the racist imperial propaganda that painted it as the work of savages merely an aberration in Lilibet's benevolent stewardship of the new Commonwealth of Nations?

To be fair, Queen Elizabeth II's role as head of state was largely ceremonial. It would be stretching it to suggest that she was responsible for the British imperial response to Mau Mau or that she could have done much to change it. It is not the Queen's personal legacy that is therefore the subject of this list. We are rather concerned with the ways in which dates, images, and events have been assembled by the British media and political establishment to present a nostalgic narrative of benign monarchy and imperialism. But for every archival morsel served, what were the historical 'others' that had to be consigned as political compost?

Our list retrieves ten historical others that have been suppressed in favour of more iconic representations of particular moments in history. We do not rank or rate these in order of importance. Rather, we construct but one possible snapshot of modern history as an example of a liberating counter-narrative of and for the dispossessed.

September 11

We begin with what must be *the* archetype of modern historical metonymy. We're not language snobs, so we'll spare you a pedantic definition of metonymy. But you get our drift – saying 'the bench' to refer to the judicial profession or 'dish' to refer not to the plate or bowl but to the food it contains. That sort of thing.

Similarly, September 11 – also styled 9/11, betraying its US-centric vantage point – now conjures images of Islamist terrorists crashing aeroplanes into the World Trade Centre in New York City in 2001. It's become shorthand for Samuel Huntington's infamous clash of civilisations thesis, with Islam cast as the violent 'other' to the West's values of liberalism, democracy and humanism.

But what about the other 9/11s? In 1999, this date saw mass civil disobedience against the World Trade Organisation (WTO) Ministerial Conference in Seattle, Washington. Tens of thousands of protesters opposed the injustices that they said were caused by neo-liberal capitalism and economic globalisation. The demonstrations escalated and spilled over the coming weeks, with the police and National Guard quelling them with pepper spray, tear gas and stun grenades.

More infamously, on 11 September 1973 the democratically elected Marxist president of Chile, Salvador Allende, was ousted and later died, perhaps by assassination, in a *coup d'état* backed by the US Central Intelligence Agency (CIA). Which brings us to the year...

1973

The year that Salvador Allende was assassinated was also the year of *Roe vs Wade*, the US Supreme Court's landmark ruling that the US Constitution conferred the right to have an abortion. This milestone in Western feminist activism was overturned in 2022 when the Supreme Court declared that the constitution did *not* recognise abortion as a right. The same year saw the build-up of the Watergate scandal that eventually led to President Richard Nixon's resignation in 1974.

But what was happening elsewhere in the world? Barely a month after Allende's death, the fourth Arab-Israeli War (also known as the October War, Ramadan War, or Yom Kippur War) erupted. In retaliation towards US support for Israel, the Arab members of the Organisation of Petroleum Exporting Countries (OPEC) embarked on an oil embargo which then triggered a global energy crisis.

South America and the Middle East were not the only regions to experience convulsions in which US interference played a key role. One little-known historical 'other' that exemplifies Uncle Sam's version of imperialism takes us back to the year when Allende was first elected, which was...

1970

A few months before Allende became president in November of this year, the Ohio National Guard shot and killed four unarmed students and wounded nine others at Kent State University, some forty miles south of Cleveland. The killings happened during a peace rally that opposed US involvement in the expansion of the Vietnam War into Cambodia. How perverse that these students were murdered for objecting to documented killings by US forces, such as the mass murder of South Vietnamese civilians in the Mỹ Lai massacre of 1968.

Meanwhile, the Nobel Peace Prize winner and civil rights activist Martin Luther King, Jr. was assassinated shortly after Mỹ Lai. By the time he died, King was courting controversy for refusing to rest on the laurels of the national civil rights movement. He had turned into a critic of US imperialism abroad, exemplified in the Vietnam War. In fact, the year before he died, King effectively recanted the ideals of his famous 'I Have a Dream Speech' in 1963, when he told the NBC network that his dream had 'turned into a nightmare'.

It is not that things were easy for King before he became an anti-war activist and a critic of imperialism. The struggle for civil rights within the US was no picnic either, which brings us to the year...

1963

We've already said that this was the year of Dr King's fabled 'I Have a Dream Speech', which he delivered in August. Back in April of the same year, King penned his famous Letter from Birmingham Jail, in which he laid out the rationale for non-violent civil disobedience, captured in the oft-quoted phrase 'injustice anywhere is a threat to justice everywhere'. Between King's incarceration and his iconic speech, another civil rights hero, Medgar Evers, was assassinated by a white supremacist in June.

It has become commonplace to wax lyrical about King, even in the UK, and to revere him as a modern-day prophet of peace and equality. It is not that King and many other civil rights activists were not remarkable moral leaders worthy of emulation. But putting disproportionate emphasis on the US civil rights movement downplays or even erases the struggles that were being fought contemporaneously elsewhere, including in the UK. After all, 1963 was also the year of the Bristol Bus Boycott against Bristol Omnibus Company for its refusal to employ Black or Asian bus crews.

This is the kind of detail that challenges the narrative of enlightened and orderly transition from Empire to Commonwealth under Elizabeth II's reign. If there was indeed a transition, it emerged out of deep struggle from grassroots communities, and was hardly bequeathed by a benevolent Crown and is far from complete.

Moreover, the situation in UK was no less perilous than it was in the US. A fortnight after King was assassinated in the US in 1968, the British Member of Parliament Enoch Powell delivered his famous 'Rivers of Blood' speech. It is hard to decide which was more disturbing – its content (in which Powell warned that white Britons would soon be subjugated and colonised by swarms of swarthy immigrants) or its ecstatic reception by a significant portion of the British public.

This racist and anti-immigrant baiting by right-wing politicians would only grow in the following years. A couple of decades after Powell's speech, Muslims (and Islam as a religion) became the new scapegoats in the British political landscape, which takes us to the year...

1989

Yes, this was the year the infamous *Satanic Verses* controversy, more popularly known in the UK as the Rushdie Affair, kicked off in earnest. From book-burnings in Bradford to the infamous fatwa against Salman Rushdie by Iran's Ayatollah Ruhollah Khomeini, this was the year of the global blockbuster hit *The News*, starring Islam. Another blockbuster released during this year was *The Fall of the Berlin Wall*. But over the ensuing decades, it is Islam and Muslims that have proven to be the more profitable franchise, spawning innumerable sequels, prequels, and spin-offs.

Some of these instalments have received mixed reviews. For example, there is little reflection in Western media circles about another monumental struggle that developed in 1989 – the First Palestinian Intifada, which was ignited in 1987 and lasted more than five years. Instead, the Palestinian liberation struggle inaugurated an enduring Western media obsession with 'Islamic' terrorists and suicide bombers. And this brings us to...

1999

This was a rare year in which the news headlines referred to fatal incidents of terrorism that did *not* involve Muslims, occurring in the same month on both sides of the Atlantic. The Columbine High School massacre on 20 April is probably the more well-known tragedy, where twelfth graders Eric Harris and Dylan Klebold murdered twelve students and one teacher in what, at the time, was the deadliest high school shooting in US history.

Lesser known and, if it is possible, more sinister were the London nail bombings which occurred over three consecutive weekends in the second half of the same month. David Copeland, a British Neo-Nazi militant, detonated home-made nail bombs in Brixton, Brick Lane and the Admiral Duncan Club in Soho, targeting black, Bengali and lesbian, gay, bisexual, transgender and queer (LGBTQ) communities. Overall, three people were killed and 140 were injured.

Copeland was motivated by a desire to start an apocalyptic race war, inspired by *The Turner Diaries*, a novel by the American Neo-Nazi and white supremacist William Luther Pierce III. The book, labelled by the US Federal Bureau of Investigation (FBI) as the 'bible of the racist right', was published in 1978, the year before...

1979

This was, of course, the year of the Iranian Revolution which deposed the Pahlavi dynasty and transformed Iran into an Islamic republic headed by Ayatollah Khomeini as its Supreme Leader. But whilst this Revolution became the enduring face of 'radical' Islam in the traditional Western media, another Islamic revolt during the same year has quietly disappeared under the historical radar. Because this same year, another Islamic monarchy was also under threat – Saudi Arabia.

On 20 November, a former soldier of the Saudi National Guard, Juhayman al-Otaybi, and his followers laid siege to the Grand Mosque of Mecca with the aim of overthrowing the House of Saud. In addition to his anti-monarchical stance, al-Otaybi also condemned the Saudi religious class, the *ulama*, for colluding with the corrupt Saudi monarchy. The siege lasted two weeks but, unlike the Iranian revolution, failed and al-Otaybi was publicly executed in Mecca the following year.

When juxtaposing the Iranian Revolution against the siege of Mecca, the line between terrorist and revolutionary becomes a bit murky. One leader who allegedly had no problem drawing this line was former UK Prime Minister Margaret Thatcher who, incidentally, came into power also in 1979.

Thatcher is infamously attributed with labelling Nelson Mandela's African National Congress a terrorist organisation. This is the same Nelson Mandela, joint winner of the 1993 Nobel Peace Prize (with FW de Klerk), who would go on to become the first president of post-apartheid South Africa in 1994, which was the year before...

1995

This was the year that Israeli Prime Minister Yitzhak Rabin was assassinated.

It was also the year of the Oklahoma City bombing (which claimed at least 168 lives and injured nearly 700 others), the Tokyo subway sarin attack (causing thirteen deaths, severely injuring fifty, and impairing more than 1,000 others), and the Srebrenica massacre (claiming more than 8,000 lives).

What do all these tragedies have in common? They were acts of terrorism or genocide that were *not* caused by Muslims. Sorry (not sorry) for belabouring the point.

For completeness, Rabin was assassinated by Yigal Amir (an Orthodox Mizrahi Jew), the Oklahoma bombing was masterminded and led by Timothy McVeigh (a Gulf War veteran and lapsed Roman Catholic), the Tokyo attack was masterminded by Shoko Asahara, founder of Aum Shinrikyo (a Japanese religious movement derived from Buddhism), and the Srebrenica massacre was masterminded by the Bosnian Serb convicted war criminal Ratko Mladić.

But now that we've established that Muslims do not have a monopoly on terrorism and other acts of mass public violence, it is time to address the elephant in the room. This brings us to the year…

2015

This year was bookended by horrific acts of terrorism that both happened in Paris, France. In January, two Islamist gunmen broke into the headquarters of the satirical weekly *Charlie Hebdo*, killing twelve people. In November, a fortnight before the historic UN climate change negotiations in the city, COP21, a series of coordinated Islamist terrorist attacks targeted different locations in Paris. The highest death toll occurred at Bataclan nightclub, which claimed at least 90 lives. Similar attacks happened the day before in Lebanon.

But while *Je suis Charlie* became a political slogan for secular liberals, yet another startling development escaped the attention of traditional Western commentators, especially in the UK – probably because it was a shameful aspect of British history.

After the Slavery Abolition Act of 1833, the British government agreed to pay £20 million in compensation – not to the people who were formerly enslaved but to 46,000 slave *owners*. And it was in 2015 that British taxpayers finally finished 'paying off' this debt which, according to the Bank of England's inflation calculator, would have been the equivalent of £2 billion in 2015.

Is it the fact that it took 182 years for the British state to give out reparations to these former slavers that is so galling? Or is it that, knowing this to be a fact, ex-colonial powers such as the UK still refuse to fork out even minimum amounts of aid for – not to mention cancel the 'debts' of – formerly colonised peoples around the world?

We don't have the answers. We'd rather end with an example that complicates our attempt to tell a singular story of history. And this brings us to the year…

1961

This was the year that, shortly after midnight on 13 August, post-war Berlin was divided between the West and the Soviet-controlled East.

This was also the year which launched the civil disobedience of the Freedom Riders – civil rights activists who rode interstate buses into the segregated South in the US. They were violently attacked by white mobs, including the Ku Klux Klan, often with the tacit approval of the police. Many were also arrested.

In 1961, South Africa became a republic and withdrew from the Commonwealth because of objections from other member states towards its policy of apartheid.

And this was also the year in which Queen Elizabeth II famously danced with Kwame Nkrumah, the first president and prime minister of Ghana. The Netflix series, *The Crown*, portrayed this incident as having major global implications, suggesting that the dance was instrumental in keeping Ghana within the grip of British control. Historians have argued that this is unlikely and that the truth is not so simple.

More plausible, however, is the idea that the Queen *did* care about the future of the Commonwealth, and that her embrace of an African leader on the dance floor was her personal way of giving the royal middle finger to the apartheid regime of South Africa.

CITATIONS

I, Historian by Iftikhar H. Malik

The Chinua Achebe quotation is from a 1994 interview with the Paris Review: https://www.npr.org/sections/thetwo-way/2013/03/22/1750 46327/chinua-achebe-and-the-bravery-of-lions; the quote from A. J. P. Taylor is from, *From Napoleon to Stalin,* quoted in E. H. Carr, *What Happened in History?* (London: 1987), p. 53.

The works mentioned in the article include: E. P. Thompson, *The Making of the English Working Class,* (London, 1966); Howard Zinn, *A People's History of the United States,* (New York, 1980); Victor Kiernan, *The Lords of Human Kind: European Attitudes to Other Cultures in the Imperial Age* (Edinburgh, 1969 (reprinted by Zed Books, 2015); Bartolome de las Casas, *History of the Indies* (New York, 1971); Primo Levi, *The Complete Works of Primo Levi* (New York, 2015); Frederick Douglass, *Narrative of the Life of Frederick Douglass: An American Slave.* (Oxford, 2009, reprint); Solomon Northrup, *Twelve Years a Slave* (London, 2012, reprint); Gretchen Gerzina, *Black England: A Georgian History* (London, 2022); Barrington Moore, *Social Origins of Dictatorship and Democracy: Lord and Peasant in the Making of the Modern World* (London, 1993, reprint): Tajul Islam Hashmi, *Pakistan as a Peasant Utopia: The Communalization of Class Politics in East Bengal, 1920–1947* (Denver, 1992)

My books include: Iftikhar H. Malik, *U.S.-South Asian Relations, 1784-1840: A Historical Perspective* (Islamabad, 1987); *U.S.-South Asian Relations: American Attitudes Toward Pakistan Movement* (Oxford, 1991; *State and Civil Society in Pakistan: Politics of Authority, Ideology and Ethnicity* (Oxford, 1997); and, *Islam, Nationalism and the West* (Oxford, 1999). On diasporic dynamics and tensions among Muslims within the West, see Iftikhar H. Malik, *Islam and Modernity: Muslim in Europe and the United States* (London, 2004); *Crescent between Cross and Star: Muslims and the West after 9/11* (Oxford, 2007); *The Silk Road and Beyond: Narratives of a Muslim Historian,* (Karachi/Oxford,

2020) and *Curating Lived Islam among Muslims: British Scholars, Sojourners and the Sleuths,* (London, 2021).

See also: Dane Kennedy, *Decolonisation: A Very Short Study* (Oxford, 2016); and Richard Evans, *In Defence of History,* (London, 1997).

Historical Beings by Ebrahim Moosa

The following citations were referenced in this article: Car, Edward Hallett. *What is History?* New York: Vintage, 1961; Collingwood, R.G. *Speculum Mentis or, the Map of Knowledge.* Kindle Edition: Read Books Ltd, 2011. As well as Collingwood's *The Idea of History.* Revised ed. Oxford & New York: Oxford University Press, 1994. 1946; Graeber, David, and David Wengrow. *The Dawn of Everything: A New History of Humanity.* New York: Farrar, Strauss & Giroux, 2021; Ibn Khaldūn, ʿAbd al-Raḥmān. *Muqaddimah Ibn Khaldūn.* Edited by Darwīsh al-Juwaydī. Ṣayda/Beirut: al-Maktaba al-ʿAṣrīya, 1460/2000; Iggers, Georg G. 'Historicism: The History and Meaning of the Term.' *Journal of the History of Ideas* 56, no. 1 (1995): 129; Irwin, Robert. *Ibn Khaldun: An Intellectual Biography.* [in English] Princeton & Oxford: Princeton University Press, 2018; Khaldūn, Ibn. *The Muqaddimah: An Introduction to History.* Translated by Franz Rosenthal. 3 vols. New York & Princeton, NJ: Bollingen Series XLIII Princeton University Press, 1980. 1958; Khalidi, Tarif. *Arabic Historical Thought in the Classical Period.* Cambridge: Cambridge University Press, 1994; Koselleck, Reinhart. *Sediments of Time: On Possible Histories.* Translated by Sean Franzel and Stefan-Ludwig Hoffmann. Stanford, Ca.: Stanford University Press, 2018; Landes, David S. 'What Room for Accident in History?: Explaining Big Changes by Small Events.' *The Economic History Review* 47, no. 4 (1994): 637-56; Pomeranz, Kenneth. *The Great Divergence: China, Europe, and the Making of the Modern World Economy.* Princeton, N.J.: Princeton University Press, 2000; and Schumpeter, Joseph A. *Capitalism, Socialism, and Democracy.* New York: Harper Perennial, 1975.

The History of History of Religions by Joshua S. Lupo

For a comprehensive review of the early field of comparative religion on which this summary draws, see Edward Sharpe, *Comparative Religion: A History*, 2nd ed. (La Salle, IL: Open Court, 1986).

In his article on Eliade and the history of religions Rudolph describes Eliade's notion of history of religions in similar terms. Where I part from Rudolph is in seeing the irony of telling the history of that which transcends history as more broadly endemic to the field. See K. Rudolph, 'Mircea Eliade and the History of Religions,' trans. By Gregory Alles, *Religions* 19 (1989): 101–27; Gerardus van der Leeuw, *Religion in Essence and Manifestation*, trans. J. E. Turner (Princeton, N. J.: Princeton University Press, 1986 [1933]), 655–57; Brian K. Pennington, *Was Hinduism Invented?: Britons, Indians, and the Colonial Construction of Religion* (Oxford: Oxford University Press, 2005).

I explore this connection in a forthcoming book project, *After Essentialism: A Critical Phenomenology for the Study of Religion.*

For a more in depth analysis of Eliade on history, see Rudolph, 'Mircea Eliade and the History of Religions.'; Mircea Eliade, *The Sacred and Profane: The Nature of Religion*, trans. William R. Transk (Orlando, FL: Harcourt, 1959 [1957]), 153; Rudolf Otto, *The Idea of the Holy: An Inquiry into the Non-rational Factor in the Idea of the Divine and its Relation to the Rational*, trans. John W. Harvey (Oxford: Oxford University Press, 1959 [1923]), 175; Tomoko Masuzawa, *The Invention of World Religions: Or, How European Universalism was Preserved in the Language of Pluralism* (Chicago: The University of Chicago Press, 2005).

For more on MacIntyre's anti-liberalism as the conceptual through line for his career, see Émile Perreau-Saussine, *Alasdair MacIntyre: An Intellectual Biography*, trans. Nathan J. Pinkoski (Notre Dame, IN: Notre Dame University Press, 2022); Talal Asad, 'The Idea of an Anthropology of Islam,' *Qui Parle* 17, no. 2 (Spring/Summer 2009): 1-30, at note 33; Saba

Mahmood, *The Politics of Piety: The Islamic Revival and the Feminist Subject* (Princeton, NJ: Princeton University Press, 2005), 115.

Emphasis mine. W. E. B. Dubois, *Black Reconstruction in America* (New York: The Free Press, 1998 [1935]), 722.

Past Futures of Islam by Robert Irwin

Lewis Namier on historians predicting the past is found in his *Conflicts: Studies in Contemporary History* (London, 1942) p.70. Muslim apocalypses (though mostly modern ones) are the subject of *Apocalypse in Islam* by Jean-Pierre Filiu, tr. M.B. DeBevoise (Berkeley and Los Angeles, 2011). William of Tripoli's reported prophecy in his *De Statu Saracenorum* in H. Prutz, *Kulturgeschichte der Kreuzzüge* (Berlin, 1883). The best translation and edition of Nostradamus is published by Penguin. *Nostradamus, The Prophecies*, tr. Rochard Sieburth, ed. Stéphane Gerson (New York, 2012). The Third Edition was used in reference to John L. Esposito's *The Islamic Threat: Myth or Reality?*, (Oxford University Press, 1999). For Browne on the menace of European interference, Robert Irwin, *For Lust of Knowing: The Orientalists and Their Enemies* (London, 2006) pp.204-7.

The New Iconoclasm by Jeremy Henzell-Thomas

Parts of this essay are an elaboration of my discussion about dominant narratives in my previous essay, 'Simple Stories, Complex Facts' in *Critical Muslim* 28, *Narratives,* 13-30, Oct-Dec 2018. I have also referred to my essay 'The Power of Education', *Critical Muslim* 14, *Power,* April-June 2015. On Francis Bacon's views on 'the idols of the human mind' I have referred to my keynote address 'The Power of the Word' at the Muslim Institute Annual Winter Gathering at Sarum College, Salisbury on 29 November, 2015.

On Women's History Month, see https://www.history.com/topics/holidays/womens-history-month. On the National Women's History Alliance (NWHA), see https://nationalwomenshistoryalliance.org/2022-theme/

On narrative fallacies, I have referred to Jack Goody, *The Theft of History* (Cambridge University Press, 2006) and *Renaissances: The One or the Many?* (Cambridge University Press, 2010; John Hobson, *The Eastern Origins of Western Civilisation* (Cambridge University Press, 2004); Jonathan Lyons, *The House of Wisdom: How the Arabs Transformed Western Civilisation* (Bloomsbury, 2009).

On the destruction or desecration of statues and monuments and the boycotting of historical sites as examples of the 'new iconoclasm', I have referred to Martin Farrer, 'Who was Edward Colston and why was his Bristol statue toppled?' *The Guardian,* 8/6/2020 https://www. theguardian.com/uk-news/2020/jun/08/who-was-edward-colston-and-why-was-his-bristol-statue-toppled-slave-trader-black-lives-matter-protests; Claire Schofield, 'Why was a Winston Churchill statue defaced? The life and views of the UK wartime PM as graffiti brands him "racist"'. *The Scotsman*, 8/6/2020 https://www.scotsman.com/ news/people/why-was-a-winston-churchill-statue-defaced-the-life-and-views-of-the-uk-wartime-pm-as-graffiti-brands-him-racist-2878135; Gino Spocchia, 'Fox News host complains Columbus is being "cancelled" by people marking Indigenous People's day', *The Independent*, 11/10/2021 https://www.independent.co.uk/news/world/americas/fox-news-indigenous-people-day-b1936345.html; 'Cecil Rhodes statue: Explanatory plaque placed at Oxford college', *BBC*, 12/10/2021 https://www.bbc. co.uk/news/uk-england-oxfordshire-58885181; Ruchira Sharma, 'National Trust finds 93 properties have slavery and colonialism links', *inews*, 22/9/2020 https://inews.co.uk/news/national-trust-properties-slavery-colonialism-links-full-list-houses-655683; Katelyn Beaty, 'Taj Mahal vandalized as Hindu nationalists dispute site's Muslim origins.' *Religion News* 19/6/2018 https://religionnews.com/2018/06/19/taj-mahal-vandalized-as-hindu-nationalists-dispute-sites-muslim-origins/; 'Priti Patel says toppling of Colston statue is "utterly disgraceful" - but Piers Morgan hits back.' *BristolLive*, 7/6/2020 https://www.bristolpost.co.uk/news/bristol-news/priti-patel-says-toppling-colston-4202300; Benjamin Kerstein, 'Neo-Totalitarianism and the Erasure of History'. *Quillette,* 26/6/60 https://quillette.com/2020/06/26/neo-totalitarianism-and-the-erasure-of-history/; Tim Lethaby, 'Link between Glastonbury Tor and slavery is revealed in National Trust report.' *Glastonbury Nub News*, 22/9/2020.https://glastonbury.nub.news/n/link-between-glastonbury -tor-and-slavery-is-revealed-in-national-trust-report

On 'cancel culture' I have referred to Brooke Kato, 'What is cancel culture? Everything to know about the toxic online trend.' *NewYork Post*, 31/8/2021 https://nypost.com/article/what-is-cancel-culture-breaking-down-the-toxic-online-trend/; Dino Sossi, 'Can we Cancel "Cancel Culture"?' *The Conversation*, 21/7/2021 https://theconversation.com/can-we-cancel-cancel-culture-164666; Lauren Williams, 'BBC slammed for making "woke cuts" on classic shows including Dad's Army and Steptoe', *Express*, 22/1/2022 https://www.express.co.uk/showbiz/tv-radio/1554179/ BBC-slammed-woke-cuts-editing-classic-shows-racial-slurs; 'JK Rowling house name dropped by Essex school over trans comments', BBC, 5/1/2022 https://www.bbc.co.uk/news/uk-england-essex-59880493.

Other sources referred to include Pankaj Mishra: 'After the Paris Attacks: It's Time for a New Enlightenment', *The Guardian*, 20/1/15; 'Indigenous Peoples', Amnesty International, 2022 https://www.amnesty.org/en/ what-we-do/indigenous-peoples/; Elisabetta Povoledo and Ian Austen, '"I Feel Shame and Pain": Pope Apologizes to Indigenous People of Canada.' *The NewYork Times*, 1/4/2022 https://www.nytimes.com/2022/04/01/ world/europe/pope-apology-indigenous-people-canada.html; Robert Trivers, *Deceit & Self-Deception: FoolingYourself the Better to Fool Others* (Allen Lane, London, 2011); Ziauddin Sardar, *Mecca:The Sacred City* (Bloomsbury, London, 2014); Martin Lings, *Muhammad* (Islamic texts Society, Cambridge, 1983), 302; Darío Fernández-Morera, 'The Myth of the Andalusian Paradise', *The Intercollegiate Review*, Fall 2006, 23–31; David Nirenberg, *Communities ofViolence: Persecution of Minorities in the Middle Ages* (Princeton University Press, 1996), 9; Hans Rosling, *Factfulness* (Sceptre, London, 2018); Thomas Merton, *Seeds,* selected and edited by Robert Inchausti (Shambhala Publications, Boston, MA, 2002), 131, originally published in *Contemplation in aWorld of Action* (Doubleday, Garden City, N.Y.,1971), 164.

Anticolonial Resistance in Morocco
by Abdelaziz El Amrani

The following was referenced in this article: Jamal Abun-Nasr's 'The Salafiyya Movement in Morocco: The Religious Bases of the Moroccan Nationalist Movement.' *St. Anthony's Papers* 16.3 (1963): 99-105; Allal Al-Fassi's *The Independence Movements in Arab North Africa*. Translated by H.z. Nuseibeh (American Council of Learned Societies, Washington DC, 1954); Sahar Bazzaz's 'Heresy and Politics in Nineteenth-Century Morocco.' *The Arab Studies Journal* 2.1 (2003): 67-86; Justin Beaumont and Klaus Elder's 'Introduction: Concepts, Processes, and Antagonisms of Postsecularity.' In: *The Routledge Handbook of Postsecularity*. Ed. Justin Beaumont (Routledge, London, 2019); Mohamed El Mansour's *The Power of Islam in Morocco: Historical and Anthropological Perspectives* (Routledge, London and New York, 2020); John P. Halstead's *Rebirth of a Nation: The Origins and Rise of Moroccan Nationalism, 1912-1944*. (Harvard University Press, Cambridge, 1969); Maxwell Kennel's *Postsecular History: Political Theology and the Politics of Time* (Palgrave McMillan, London, 2021); and David Motadel's 'Islam and the European Empires'. *The Historical Journal* 55.3 (2012): 831- 856.

Hamka's Reflections On Ignorance
by Khairudin Aljunied

In writing this article I have used the following works by Hamka: *Ayahku: Riwayat Hidup Dr. H. Abdul Karim Amrullah dan Perjuangan Agama di Sumatera*. Djakarta: Djajamurni, 1967; *Falsafah Hidup* (Jakarta: Republika Penerbit, 2015); *Lembaga Budi* (Jakarta: Republika Penerbit, 2016); *Tasawuf Modern* (Jakarta: Republika Penerbit, 2015); *Pandangan Hidup Muslim* (Jakarta: Bulan Bintang, 1992); *Bohong Di Dunia* (Jakarta: Gema Insani, 2017); *Pelajaran Agama Islam* (Kelantan, Malaysia: Pustaka Aman Press, 1967); *Tafsir Al-Azhar, Vol. 17* (Singapore: Pustaka Nasional, 1982); *Renungan Tasawuf* (Jakarta: Republika Penerbit, 2019); *Dari Hati Ke Hati* (Jakarta: Gema Insani, 2015); *Kenangan-Kenanganku Di Malaya* (Selangor: Jejak Tarbiah Publication, 2019); *Pelajaran Agama Islam* (Kelantan, Malaysia: Pustaka Aman Press, 1967); *Dari Lembah Cita-Cita* (Jakarta: Bulan Bintang, 1982);

Filsafat Ketuhanan (Jakarta: Gema Insani, 2017); and *Empat Bulan Di Amerika.Vol. 2* (Djakarta: Tintamas, 1954).

Other quoted works include M. Ashraf Adeel, *Epistemology of the Quran: Elements of a Virtue Approach to Knowledge and Understanding* (New York: Springer, 2019), 14; George Orwell, *Nineteen Eighty-Four* (Oxford: Oxford University Press, 2021), 167; Francis Bacon, *The New Organon* (Cambridge: Cambridge University Press, 2000), 74-75; Rumadi, *Islamic Post-Traditionalism in Indonesia* (Singapore: ISEAS Press, 2015), 61; Daniel R. DeNicola, *Understanding Ignorance: The Surprising Impact of What We Don't Know* (Cambridge, MA: MIT Press, 2017), 82; and Imran Ahsan Nyazee, *Theories of Islamic Law: The Methodologies of Ijtihad* (Kuala Lumpur: The Other Press, 2002), 287.

Also see James R. Rush's *Hamka's Great Story: A Master Writer's Vision of Islam for Modern Indonesia* (Madison, Wisconsin: University of Wisconsin Press, 2016).

Pakistan's Constitutional Turns by Raza Ali

For more on Pakistan's Constitution, see 'THE CONSTITUTION OF THE ISLAMIC REPUBLIC OF PAKISTAN'. *National Assembly of Pakistan*, 28 February 2012, https://na.gov.pk/uploads/documents/1333523681 _951.pdf. Accessed 16 October 2022. For more on Pakistan's political history, see 'Parliamentary History'. *National Assembly of Pakistan*, https://na.gov.pk/en/content.php?id=75. Accessed 16 October 2022.

The following were reference through this essay: Muhammad Ali Jinnah's first Presidential Address to the Constituent Assembly of Pakistan (August 11, 1947). http://www.columbia.edu/itc/mealac/pritchett/00islamlinks/txt_jinnah_assembly_1947.html; Orya Maqbool Jan, Hamare Quami Jhoot Bolne Wale. *Roznama Dunya*, 30 Dec, 2013. https://dunya.com.pk/index.php/author/orya-maqbool-jaan/2013-12-30/5529/16461313; A H Nayyar, Stop Distorting Jinnah's Words, *Express Tribune*, 13 Aug, 2013. https://tribune.com.pk/story/589785/stop-distorting-jinnahs-words; From The Past Pages Of Dawn: 1947: Seventy-five years ago: Attack on

CITATIONS

Delhi Dawn, Dawn. https://www.dawn.com/news/1711104/from-the-past-pages-of-dawn-1947-seventy-five-years-ago-attack-on-delhi-dawn; Jon Boone, Pakistan's independence celebrations omit Jinnah's words on tolerance, *The Guardian*, 14 Aug, 2012. https://www.theguardian.com/world/2012/aug/14/pakistan-independence-religious-intolerance-jinnah; Anita Joshua, AIR help sought on Jinnah's Secular state' speech, *The Hindu*, 3 Jun, 2012. https://www.thehindu.com/news/international/air-help-sought-on-jinnah-secular-state-speech/article3487079.ece; Fahad Husain, Presidential System?, *Dawn*, 22 Jan, 2022. https://www.dawn.com/news/1670861; CJP.org, Results filtered by years 2002-2016 https://cpj.org/data/killed/asia/pakistan/?status=Killed&motiveConfirmed%5B%5D=Confirmed&motiveUnconfirmed%5B%5D=Unconfirmed&type%5B%5D=Journalist&type%5B%5D=Media%20Worker&cc_fips%5B%5D=PK&start_year=2002&end_year=2016&group_by=location; Pakistan most dangerous country for journalists: UN, *Dawn*, 4th May, 2014. https://www.dawn.com/news/1104120; 'Extreme fear and self-censorship': media freedom under threat in Pakistan, *The Guardian*, 5 Nov, 2019. theguardian.com/world/2019/nov/05/extreme-fear-and-self-censorship-media-in-pakistan-under-attack; https://rsf.org/en/country/pakistan; Women journalists demand protection from 'vicious' social media attacks by 'people linked to govt', *Dawn*, 12 Aug, 2020. https://www.dawn.com/news/1574031/women-journalists-demand-protection-from-vicious-social-media-attacks-by-people-linked-to-govt; Pakistani Wife Embodies Cause of 'Disappeared', *New York Times*, 19 July, 2007. https://www.nytimes.com/2007/07/19/world/asia/19missing.html; Muslim Institute Sixth Annual Ibn Rushd Lecture by Mohammed Hanif: Hearts & Minds & Things That Are Not Terror. https://musliminstitute.org/events/muslim-institute-sixth-annual-ibn-rushd-lecture-mohammed-hanif-hearts-minds-things-are-not; Sabeen Mahmud, Pakistani rights activist, shot dead, *The Guardian*, 25 Apr, 2015. https://www.theguardian.com/world/2015/apr/25/sabeen-mehmud-pakistani-womens-rights-activist-shot-dead; Choudhury, G. W. 'Bangladesh: Why It Happened.' *International Affairs (Royal Institute of International Affairs*, 1972; Niazi, Zamir. *The Press in Chains*. Edited by Zubeida Mustafa, OUP Pakistan, 2010; Pardesi, Yasmeen Yousif. 'An Analysis of the Constitutional Crisis in Pakistan (1958–1969).' *Dialogue (Pakistan)*, vol. 7, no. 4, 2012;

Rahman, Fazlur. 'Islam and the Constitutional Problem of Pakistan. *Studia Islamica*, no. 32, 1970.

Memory Censored by Anna Gunin

To read more on the adage 'History is written by the victors' See 'The History of "History Is Written by the Victors"' by Matthew Phelan, *Slats*, 26 Nov 2019 https://slate.com/culture/2019/11/history-is-written-by-the-victors-quote-origin.html.

Vasily Grossman, translated by Robert Chandler, *Everything Flows* (NYRB Classics, 2009).

A. Anatoli (Kuznetsov), *Babi Yar: A document in the Form of a Novel* (Jonathan Cape, 1970); also see Wendy Morgan Lower's 'From Berlin to Babi Yar: The Nazi War Against the Jews, 1941-1944,' *Journal of Religion & Society* Volume 9 (2007)

Mikail Eldin, translated by Anna Gunin *The Sky Wept Fire: My Life as a Chechen Freedom Fighter* (Portobello Books, 2013).

Herstory and Feminist Erasures by Sunera Thobani

The following was referenced throughout this article: Amos, Valerie and Parmer, Pratibha. 1984. 'Challenging Imperial Feminism', *Feminist Review*. Vol. 17, Issue 1; Arat-Koc, S. 2002. 'Hot Potato: Imperial Wars or Benevolent Interventions? Reflections on Global Feminism Post September 11', *Atlantis*. 26 (2). 433-444; Bannerji, H. 1995. *Thinking Through: Essays on Feminism, Marxism and Anti-Racism*. Toronto: Women's Press; Barlas, A. 2002. *Believing Women in Islam*. Austin: University of Texas; Butler, Judith. 2004. *Precarious Life: The Powers of Mourning and Violence*. London: Verso; Chesler, Phyllis. 2003. *The New Anti-Semitism: The Current Crisis and What We Must Do About It*. San Francisco: Jossey-Bass; Chesler, Phyllis. 2010. 'Ban the Burqa? Argument in Favour', *Middle East Quarterly*. Fall. Vol. 17, Issue 4. 33-45; Crenshaw, Kimberley. 1991. 'Mapping the Margins:

Intersectionality, Identity Politics and Violence Against Women of Colour',
Stanford Law Review. Vol. 43, No. 6. pp. 1241-1299.

Davis, Angela. 1983. *Women, Race and Class*. New York: Random House;
Eisenstien, Zillah. 2004. *Against Empire: Feminisms, Racisms and the West*.
London: Zed Books; Eisenstein, Zillah. 2007. *Sexual Decoys: Gender, Race and
War in Imperial Democracy*. London: Zed Books; Harris, Cheryl. 1993.
'Whiteness as Property', *Harvard Law Review*. Vol. 106, Issue 8. pp.1709-
1791; Hill Collins, Patricia. 1990. *Black Feminist Thought*. New York:
Routledge; LaDuke, Winona. 1997. *Last Standing Woman*. Voyageur Press;
Lowe, Lisa. 1996. *Immigrant Acts: On Asian American Cultural Politics*. Durham:
Duke   University Press; Maracle, Lee. 1988. *I Am Woman: A Native
Perspective on Sociology and Feminism*. Vancouver: Press Gang Publishers;
Monture Angus, P. 1995. *Thunder In My Soul*. Halifax: Fernwood Press;
Perry, Loiuse. June 20, 2019. 'How a Feminist Prophet became an Apostate:
An Interview with Dr. Phyllis Chesler', *Quillette;* Pitts, Claudia. 2017.
'Phyllis Chesler: A life on Behalf of Women', *Women and Therapy*. Vol. 40,
Issue 3-4; Razack, S., M. Smith and S. Thobani (eds.). 2010. *States of Race:
Critical Race Feminism for the 21st Century*. Toronto: Between the Lines;
Shanahan, Noreen. Fall, 2009. 'Armstrong Continues Chronicles of
Afghanistan Women'. *Herizons*. p. 45; Stack, Liam. October 19, 2017.
'Burqa Bans: Which Countries Outlaw Face Coverings?', *The New York Times;*
Stolba, Carol. Winter, 2002. 'Feminists Go to War', *The Women's Quarterly*,
Independent Women's Forum; Torres, Lourdes, Chandra Mohanty and Ann
Russo (eds.). 1991. *Third World Women and the Politics of Feminism*. Indiana
University Press; Scott, Joan Wallach. 2007. *Politics of the Veil*. Princeton
University Press.

I have also relied on arguments made in my own previous work: Thobani,
Sunera, 2007. *Exalted Subjects: Studies in the Making of Race and Nation in
Canada*. Toronto: University of Toronto Press; Thobani, Sunera. 2007.
'White Wars: Western Feminism and the "War on Terror"', *Feminist Theory*.
pp. 169-185; Thobani, Sunera. 2020. *Contesting Islam, Constructing Race and
Sexuality: The Inordinate Desire of the West*. London: Bloomsbury Academic.

Museum Islam by Hassan Vawda

For more information see Jonathan Gornall, 'A British Museum Exhibition Challenges Misconceptions about "Islamic Art"', and visit *Arab News*, 2021 https://www.arabnews.com/node/1808206/art-culture; Hesse, Barnor, and S Sayyid, 'The 'War' Against Terrorism/The 'War' for Cynical Reason', *Ethnicities*, 2.2 (2002), 149–54; Jonathan Jones, 'Inspired by the East Review – a Glorious Show Boris Johnson Really Ought to See', *The Guardian*, 2019 https://www.theguardian.com/artanddesign/2019/oct/08/inspired-by-the-east-review-europes-glorious-fascination-with-islam; Yassir Morsi, 'Melbourne's Islamic Museum of Australia: The "White-Washed 'I'"' as an Apollonian Celebration of Liberal Myths', *Journal of Muslim Minority Affairs*, 35.2 (2015), 203–14 ; Raha Rafii, 'How the Contemporary Art World Repackages Orientalism', *Hyperallergic*, 2021 https://hyperallergic.com/author/raha-rafii/; Wendy M K Shaw, *What Is Islamic Art? Between Religion and Perception* (Cambridge; New York; Melbourne; Delhi: Cambridge : Polity, 2019); Eva-Maria Troelenberg, 'Regarding the Exhibition: The Munich Exhibition Masterpieces of Muhammadan Art (1910) and Its Scholarly Position', *Journal of Art Historiography*, 6, 2012, 1–34; R Ward, 'Islamism Is Not an Easy Matter', in A.W. Franks, *19th Century Collecting and the British Museum*, ed. by M. Caygill and J. Cherry (London: British Museum Press, 1997), pp. 272–85.

Remembering Kerbala by Masuma Rahim

The text of Fatima's speech after the land of Fadak was seized from her, can be seen here: https://archive.org/details/religiousauthori0000mava/mode/

The Arbaeen figure is based upon the official register of visitors, quoted in a statement from the Secretariat General of the A-l-Abbas Shrine, dated 17 September 2022: https://alkafeel.net/news/index?id=16372&lang=en A detailed description of the detention of my father by the regime in Iraq can be read in the August/September 2020 edition of *Prospect Magazine*.

Finding Anna by Leela Prasad

This essay is adapted and excerpted from Leela Prasad, *The Audacious Raconteur: Sovereignty and Storytelling in Colonial India* (Cornell University Press, Cornell, New York, 2020).

All quotations and paraphrased text from *Old Deccan Days* referenced in the essay are from Mary Frere, *Old Deccan Days; or, Hindoo Fairy Legends, Current in Southern India* (John Murray, London, 1898, reprinted 4th edition); Marianne North, *Recollections of a Happy Life* (Macmillan, London, 1894) pp. 72–73; Michael Polanyi, 'Sense-Giving and Sense-Reading', *Philosophy 42* (1967): 301–325; and Henri Bergson, *The Creative Mind*. Trans. Mabelle Andison (Philosophical Library, New York, 1946). P. 109.

Script for a better future by Shanon Shah

Disclosure: I am a registered Malaysian voter. I am not a member of the People's Justice Party (PKR), led by Anwar Ibrahim, or any other political party in Malaysia or the UK. Neither have I ever nor do I currently receive any financial payment or salary from Anwar or PKR or any other political party.

Anwar Ibrahim's *SCRIPT for a Better Malaysia: An Empowering Vision and Policy Framework for Action* can be freely downloaded at https://postnormaltim.es/script.

The information on the major floods discussed in this article are from Munir Ahmed, 'Pakistan: World Bank Estimates Floods Caused $40B in Damages', AP News, 19 October 2022. https://apnews.com/article/floods-pakistan-south-asia-islamabad-25ee9dc0ec7aee6f4f2ef7b55721 6ee7, BBC News, 'Malaysia: Death Toll Rises after Massive Floods', 21 December 2021, https://www.bbc.com/news/world-asia-59723341, Rashvinjeet S. Bedi, 'Malaysia Massive Floods Result in RM6.1 Billion Losses, Selangor Worst Hit', Channel News Asia, 28 January 2022, https://www.channelnewsasia.com/asia/malaysia-floods-2021-2022-losses-statistics-department-2465656, Mei Mei Chow, 'What It Takes to Manage Landslides'. Macaranga (blog), 24 December 2021, https://

www.macaranga.org/what-it-takes-to-manage-landslides/,   Agence
France-Presse, 'Malaysia's Worst Flooding in Years Leaves 30,000 People
Displaced', *The Guardian*, 19 December 2021, https://www.theguardian.
com/world/2021/dec/19/malaysias-worst-flooding-in-years-leaves-
30000-people-displaced, Ida Lim, 'Experts: Selangor Floods Show Failure
to Prevent a Repeat of Kelantan in 2014; Malaysia Needs Better Warning
Systems', *Malay Mail*, 22 December 2021, https://www.malaymail.com/
news/malaysia/2021/12/22/experts-selangor-floods-show-failure-to-
prevent-a-repeat-of-kelantan-in-201/2030182, Reuters, 'Chad Declares
State of Emergency as Floods Affect 1 Million People', 19 October 2022,
https://www.reuters.com/world/africa/chad-declares-state-emergency-
floods-affect-1-million-people-2022-10-19/, Amir Yusof, 'Malaysia's
"Once in 100 Years" Flood Exposes Reality of Climate Change, Better
Disaster Planning Needed: Experts', Channel News Asia, 21 December
2021, https://www.channelnewsasia.com/asia/malaysia-once-100-years
-flooding-climate-change-disaster-planning-2391316.

My discussion on *Vivir Bien* draws upon Pablo Solón's chapter 'Is *Vivir
Bien* Possible? Candid Thoughts about Systemic Alternatives', in *Climate
Futures: Reimagining Global Climate Justice*, edited by Kum-Kum Bhavnani,
John Foran, Priya A. Kurian, and Debashish Munshi, 253–62. London: Zed
Books, 2019.

The quotes from Syed Hussein Alatas are from his work, *The Problem of
Corruption*, Kuala Lumpur: The Other Press, 2015. The extended quote
from Paulo Freire is from *Pedagogy of Hope*, London: Bloomsbury, 2015.

Examples of the connection between corruption and climate change
were taken from Hugh McFaul, 'What's Corruption Got to Do with
Climate Change, and Why Should We Care?', https://www.open.edu/
openlearn/history-the-arts/history-the-arts/whats-corruption-got
-do-climate-change-and-why-should-we-care.

Womad Returns by James Brooks

More about Mazaher and zār can be found in 'My journey with the Zār
People and the Mazāher Ensemble', Ahmed El Maghraby, translated by
Muna El Shorbagi, in liner notes of Mazaher's album *Zār* (ajabu! records,
2020) and 'Spiritual Harmony', Louis Pattison, *TheWire*, November 2021.

Olcay Bayır quote from 'Quick Questions: Olcay Bayir' interview for Turner Sims Southampton, available at https://bit.ly/3MgMCEg. Quote from liner notes to Kefaya and Elaha Soroor's album *Songs of our Mothers* (Bella Union, 2019). Ian Brennan quote from liner notes to Comorian's *We Are An Island, But We're Not Alone* (Glitterbeat, 2021). The YouTube video of Elisouma performing on their 2013 European tour can be found at https://bit.ly/3MfZFpJ, and that for Ramy Essam's 'Lessa Bahinlha', with lyrics by Karim Magdy, at https://bit.ly/3EktjrY.

CONTRIBUTORS

Raza Ali is a London-based disenchanted Pakistani activist (not an Imran Khan fan) ● **Khairudin Aljunied** is an Associate Professor at the Faculty of Arts and Social Sciences, National University of Singapore ● **Iason Athanasiadis**, a multimedia journalist, is the current holder of a Balkan Investigative Reporting Network Fellowship for Journalistic Excellence ● **Arif Ay** is a Turkish poet and famed essayist ● **James Brooks** is a science journalist ●**Abdelaziz El Amrani** is Associate Professor of Postcolonial Studies at Abdelmalek Essaadi University, Tetouan, Morocco ● **Anna Gunin** is a translator from Russian of literary fiction and memoir, films and fairy tales, plays and poetry and winner of an English PEN award for writing in translation ● **Jeremy Henzell-Thomas** is a Research Associate and former Visiting Fellow at the Centre of Islamic Studies, University of Cambridge ● **Robert Irwin** is author of *The Runes Have Been Cast*, a black comedy about 1960s Oxford ● **Adrianna Kalfopoulou** is a poet, essayist, and scholar based in Athens, Greece ● **Joshua S. Lupo** is editor and writer for the *Contending Modernities* Blog and the Classroom Coordinator for the Madrasa Discourses program at the University of Notre Dame in Indiana, US ● **Iftikhar H. Malik** is Professor Emeritus of History at the University of Bath ● **Ebrahim Moosa** is the Mirza Family Professor of Islamic Thought & Muslim Societies at the University of Notre Dame ● **Youshaa Patel** is Associate Professor of Islamic Studies at Lafayette College in Pennsylvania, US ● **Leela Prasad** is Professor of Ethics and Religious Studies at Duke University in the US ● **Masuma Rahim** is a clinical psychologist and contributor to *The Guardian* ● **Shanon Shah** is the Director of Faith for the Climate in the UK and was a multiple award-winning journalist, activist, playwright and singer-songwriter in Malaysia ● **Susannah Tarbush** is a freelance journalist specialising in Middle East cultural affairs, and runs the *Tanjara* blogspot ● **Sunera Thobani** is an Associate Professor at the Institute for Gender, Race, Sexuality and Social Justice at the University of British Columbia in Canada ● **Hassan Vawda** is undertaking a collaborative doctorate between Tate and Goldsmiths, looking at how religion is manifested in the art museum ● **Medina Tenour Whiteman** is author of the acclaimed *The Invisible Muslim: Journeys Through Whiteness and Islam* ● **Tawfiq Zayyad** was a Palestinian politician and doyen of 'poetry of protest'.

CRITICAL MUSLIM 44, AUTUMN 2022